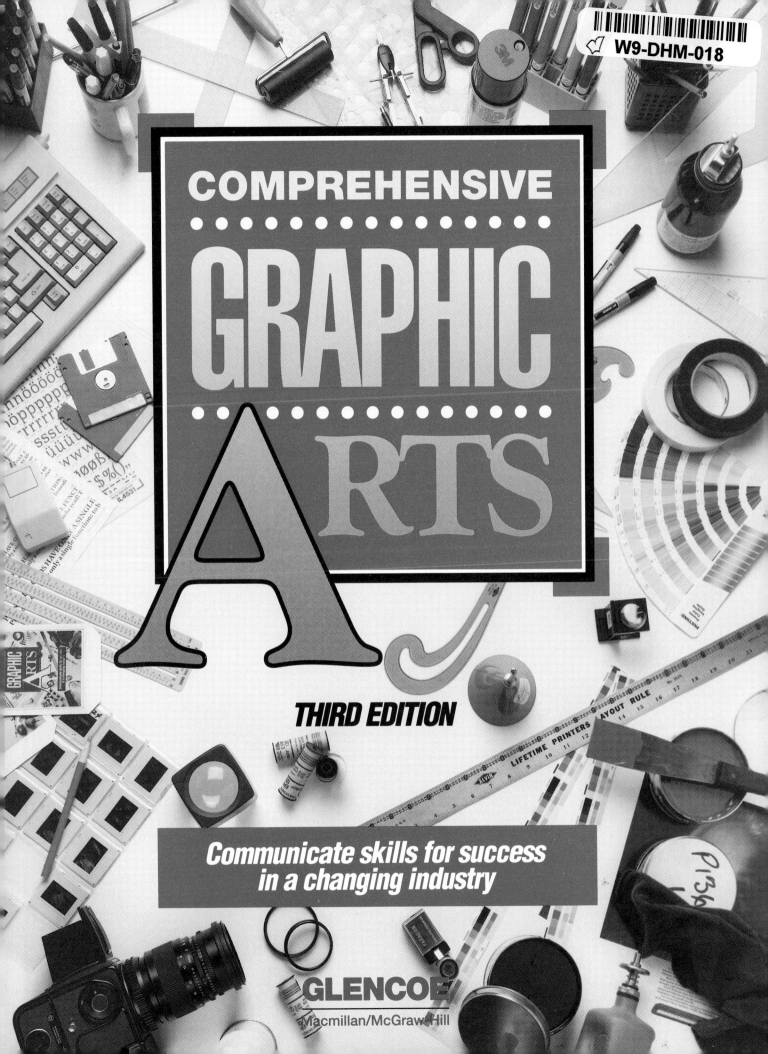

COMPREHENSIVE
GRAPHIC ARTS

THIRD EDITION

Communicate skills for success in a changing industry

GLENCOE
Macmillan/McGraw-Hill

SECTION 22 **DESKTOP COMPOSITION**

UNIT **182** WHAT IS DESKTOP COMPOSITION?

Desktop composition is an important part of the future of publishing and graphic arts. *Desktop composition* is the use of specialized computer software programs to create and integrate text and graphics in a page layout. Desktop composition also is called *electronic publishing* and *desktop publishing*. Briefly, computers using software programs designed for specific tasks allow the user to lay out pages of text and graphics on the screen. This is a new concept. Traditionally, computers used programs that were either text based or graphics based. With text-based programs, only one style of type could be viewed on the screen. With graphics-based programs, only graphics were shown. There was no high-resolution text.

Desktop composition is the marriage of text and graphics on the screen. It offers the flexibility of combining multiple typefaces and graphics on one page. It also allows many users to work together with their computers networked to share information and files quickly and easily.

In traditional publishing, each person involved in the project usually works alone at a specific task (Fig. 182-1). For example, the writers use typewriters or computers to input text. They then give their printed hard copy to the artist who will do the layout and design. The artist then sketches the layout. Type is specified. The copy is then sent for typesetting. The typesetter retypes the document, coding it for typesetting. To make the individual page paste-ups, the artwork is created and adhered to the board along with galleys of type from the typesetter. If the type

Fig. 182-1. In a traditional publishing environment there are constant revisions and editing changes to be made. The writer gives the copy to the artist, who works with the art director. The page is designed. The copy is then typeset and pasted to the layout. Each change in copy causes the cycle to begin again. This can be time consuming and costly.

does not fit the layout, the manuscript and type must be revised. This effort can be costly and time consuming.

In desktop composition, the writer works on a computer. The designer and artist also work on computers. Their information is passed from one to another electronically, with the designer controlling the layout and copyfitting. The designer can easily and quickly change type styles and sizes. Artwork can be resized to accommodate the copy. The completed document can then be printed on a laser printer or sent out for high-resolution

---

WHAT IS DESKTOP COMPOSITION? 557

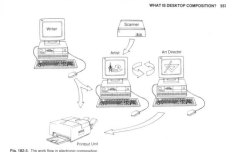

Fig. 182-3. The work flow in electronic composition.

Size is not as important for graphic applications because it is possible to zoom into work on the details of a drawing. For page makeup, it is important to see a full page to design a document. Some monitors are designed to show two full pages side by side.

Keyboard. The computer keyboard is a means of inputting information into the computer. It is much like the keyboard of a typewriter and serves as the primary input device for the computer.

Mouse. The mouse is an alternative device for inputting information into the computer. It has a rolling ball that sends X and Y coordinates to the monitor. It is attached to the computer by a wire. Digitizer pads and trackballs are also very popular. These operate on the same principle as the mouse.

Scanner. The scanner is another input device. A scanner is similar to a photocopy machine. However, the image is printed on the computer's monitor, instead of being printed on paper. Scanners can be used to import (transfer) images or text from hard copy (im-

ages on paper) to electronic signals as part of the computer software.

Printer. Almost any print-out device may be used with a computer, but laser printers are best for electronic publishing. Color printers may be used, but the colors usually do not match the screen colors on the monitor. Much progress has and will continue to be made in this area.

Software

Several software programs are essential in desktop composition. Computer software is available on diskettes. These diskettes, often called floppy disks, are available in 3.5 inch and 5.25 inch sizes (Fig. 182-4).

DOS (Disk Operating System). This software is the brain of the computer. It is designed to copy files, create directories, format disks, and keep track of where files are stored in the computer memory. The Apple Macintosh disk operating system has been easier to use than the IBM disk operating system because it is graphical, rather than text based.

---

424 PHOTOGRAPHY

f/22   f/16   f/11

Fig. 140-3. Metal leaves

flash has a lamp and a reflector (see Fig.). The lamp of the electronic flash can several thousand times. The flash bulb in a reflector socket and can be used on *Flash cubes* and *flash bars* have been de in recent years (Fig. 140-2). A flash c four bulbs and reflectors built into the u unit automatically turns a quarter-tu time an exposure is made. The flash eight or ten flash bulbs with built-in re Each time a picture is taken, the camer different bulb. The flash cube and flash thrown away after use. A camera must to use flash cubes or flash bars.

The amount of natural or constant light is measured by a light meter. Ma eras have a light meter built into the case. Flash attachments have a scale or the back of the flash unit to indicate exposures. The steps in deciding prop sures will be explained later in this un

Film exposure depends both on the am light entering the camera and the length that light is admitted into the came amount of light is controlled by the le ture and the time by the shutter. Fe results, you should know how to adjust b aperture and shutter speed.

IMAGE WILL BE OUT OF FOCUS BEYOND THIS POINT   PHOTOGRAPH V BETWEEN THES

Fig. 140-4. Only a certain range of the image i

---

162 PROCESS CAMERAS AND DARKROOM PROCEDURE

UNIT **56** EXPOSURE CALCULATIONS FOR A HALFTONE NEGATIVE

Halftones are reproductions made from continuous-tone copy. Continuous-tone copy has several shades of gray, from black to white. See Unit 43 for examples.

PRINTING CONTINUOUS-TONE COPY

Printing presses print only one shade of a color at a time. If there is black ink on the press, everything printed will be black. It is impossible to print gray and black with a single printing on a press that has been inked with black ink. The picture in Figure 56-1, however, appears to have black areas and several shades of gray.

This optical illusion is produced by breaking the copy into many small dots. Each dot is printed black; there are no gray dots. In Figure 56-2 there are small black dots with large white areas around them. There are also several small white dots with large black areas around them. When the picture is observed from a distance, the dots blend to form shades of gray. The areas around white dots appear to be darker than those white areas with black dots.

Fig. 56-1. A photograph printed as a halftone.

METHODS OF PRODUCING HALFTONE DOTS

Paste-up a course that fits your own classroom needs.

Special features of the student text make teaching easier for you.

- Short teaching units help students retain information.
- *Key Terms, Discussion Topics,* and *Activities* reinforce lessons.
- *Research Projects* and hands-on *Activities* support the text.
- Detailed illustrations and instructions help students comprehend complex procedures.

Student Workbook insures maximum exposure.

Study questions for each section of the text, safety review questions, and project assignments are all ready for you to use.

Instructor's Guide increases teaching effectiveness.

Objectives and *Teaching Outlines* for each unit keep you on course. *Teaching Tips* save hours of valuable preparation time.

Complete *Answer Keys* help you guide classroom activities and simplify your evaluation of students progress.

different size apertures.

aperture

aperture is the size of the lens opening. aperture is formed by a device called the iris. iris is formed by several metal leaves work together. When the aperture ring on era lens is turned, the opening in the f the leaves gets bigger or smaller (Fig. Simple cameras do not have irises but or two fixed openings. More complex have a range of aperture adjustments. ures are measured in *f-numbers* or *f-* ommon f-stops on a lens are f/1.2, f/1.4, 2, f/4, f/5.6, f/8, f/11, f/16, f/22. *Each f-stop in half as much or twice as much light stop next to it.* For example, f/5.6 lets much light into the camera as f/8 but only half as much light into the camera

smaller the f-number, the larger the opening. This can be seen in Figure next to f/2 is larger than the next to f/16. The smallest f-number opening) indicates the *speed of the lens.* s speed measures the largest amount of lens will let pass. If the smallest f-on a camera is f/2, the speed of the lens

IMAGE WILL BE OUT OF FOCUS FROM HERE TO THE CAMERA

h focus. This is known as the depth of field.

Many vocational high schools offer courses that deal directly with teaching the skills needed to work in commercial graphic arts plants. Students who complete these technical-vocational programs can begin work immediately after leaving school. Such career instruction requires teachers with knowledge and skills in many areas. For example, a teacher must be able to work with process cameras and darkroom film products.

Technical institutes and terminal technical programs in junior colleges provide further instruction in skills. Teachers for these types of programs must be highly knowledgeable in graphic arts production. Universities and colleges offering graphic arts management and technical curricula are in constant need of professors (Fig. 190-2). Industry needs people with special graphic arts skills who can teach employees the techniques needed to keep up with new techniques and machines. Because industry in our society changes constantly, necessary training often can only be given on-the-job in an industrial plant.

Teacher qualifications

No two teachers are alike, but those considering teaching as a career should have:
1. A personality acceptable to the people with whom they will work.
2. Above-average intelligence.
3. An interest in a specific subject.
4. An attitude that motivates and inspires students.

Fig. 190-2. A university professor discusses a technical graphic arts topic with some students.

5. Patience.
6. Ability to work long and hard with people until the educational objectives have been reached.
7. The ability to organize information.
8. The ability to demonstrate specific technical knowledge.

A bachelor's degree is the usual requirement for teaching in secondary schools, most technical-vocational high schools, and technical institute positions. However, in many

Fig. 190-1. A teacher shows young graphic arts students how to operate a lithography duplicator/press.

Fig. 190-3. Formal education prepares people for highly technical positions in the graphic arts industry.

DOW JONES & COMPANY

must feed through the machine efficiently and smoothly to give maximum reproduction quality.
22. Install the inking system rollers (Fig. 107-8). Make sure all rollers are perfectly clean. Follow the procedure as outlined in the duplicator/press manual.
23. Fill the ink fountain at least half full with a suitable ink for the image content and the kind of paper being used (Fig. 107-9).

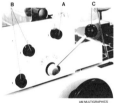

AM MULTIGRAPHICS

Fig. 107-11. Locations of important ink and dampening controls; A, water form roller knob; B, ink form roller knobs; and C, single-lever control.

AM MULTIGRAPHICS

Fig. 107-9. Using an ink gun to deposit an even bead of ink along the entire ink fountain. Identified parts are: A, ink fountain roller and B, ink ductor roller.

AM MULTIGRAPHICS

Fig. 107-12. Important dampening system parts: A, feed rate control knob; B, feed rate gauge; C, ductor lever; D, ductor roller; E, fountain roller; and F, fountain roller knob.

AM MULTIGRAPHICS

Fig. 107-10. Adjusting the ink flow to the rollers with the ink fountain adjusting screws. Identified parts are: A, ink fountain screws; B, ink feed rate control; and C, ink fountain roller crank.

24. With the ductor roller against the fountain roller turn the ink-fountain roller control knob counterclockwise; turn the ink-fountain adjusting screws in or out until a thin film of ink is spread evenly over the fountain roller (Fig. 107-10).
25. Place the ink-feed rate control (Fig. 107-10) on the third notch. Turn the two ink form roller knobs to the ink position (Fig 107-11). Also, turn the "night-latch" ink

UNIT 11 TEXT TYPE STYLE

Text typefaces (Fig. 11-1) are marked by heavy vertical and angular strokes. They are usually decorated with extra strokes and thin lines.

Text type is somewhat hard to read (Fig. 11-2) and is not often seen in modern publications. It is sometimes used to suggest great age. It may also suggest a religious or reverent mood, because it is based on a style of writing developed in monasteries.

This style of type is sometimes called Black-letter, because its heavy design makes a dark block on the page. It is also called Old English. This typeface should never be composed in all capitals because its capital letters are not designed to fit together. Combinations of text capitals are almost unreadable.

Wedding Text
Pack My Box With Five Do 123

Cloister Black
Pack My Box With F 123

Engravers Text

𝔗his kind of type would have been considered the most legible to any person who lived in the fifteenth and early sixteenth centuries anywhere in western Europe north of the Alps. In fact, it was only near the end of the sixteenth century that this letter disappeared from English printing, and yielded to the form called roman. Today, it survives only as a quaint type which we use discreetly to set a few words for a greeting card or a formal invitation. Nobody expects the reader to read continuous prose set in this type—are you still with us?—because it is considered to be illegible in the mass. Illegibility does not mean that it cannot be read, but

AND PAPER COMPANY

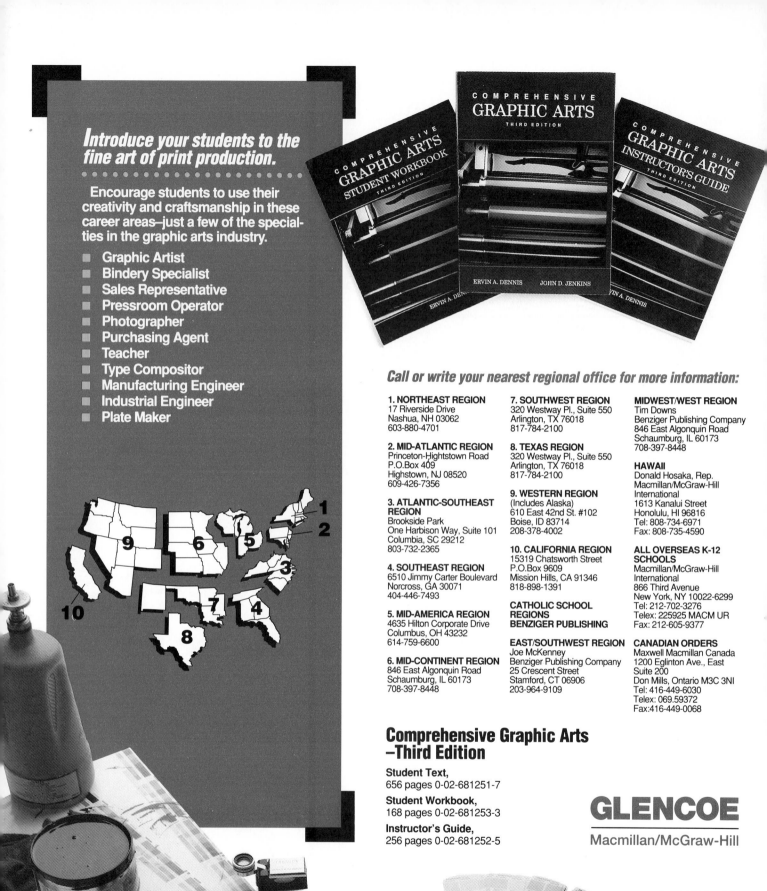

Comprehensive Graphic Arts

Instructor's Guide

THIRD EDITION

Ervin A. Dennis, Ed.D.
University of Northern Iowa

John D. Jenkins, Ed.D.
Eastern Kentucky University

GLENCOE
Macmillan/McGraw-Hill

Lake Forest, Illinois
Columbus, Ohio
Mission Hills, California
Peoria, Illinois

Send all inquiries to:
Glencoe Division, Macmillan/McGraw-Hill
Publishing Company
809 W. Detweiller Drive
Peoria, IL 61615

ISBN 0-02-681251-7 (Student Text)
ISBN 0-02-681252-5 (Instructor's Guide)
ISBN 0-02-681253-3 (Student Workbook)

1 2 3 4 5 6 7 8 9 10   95 94 93 92 91

TABLE OF CONTENTS

USING THE INSTRUCTOR'S GUIDE AND TEXTBOOK

I. The Instructor's Guide—*Comprehensive Graphic Arts*

A. Purpose

This *Instructor's Guide* has been prepared to assist you, the graphic arts/communications instructor, in teaching your classes. It has been prepared with the thought that you have less time than needed to prepare for a course and for individual class sessions during the school term. Hopefully, you will find the suggestions and data contained in this *Guide* to be helpful in your day-to-day teaching.

B. Organization

Organization of this *Instructor's Guide* is based on common sense versus a scientific approach. As you review the Table of Contents, you will note the practicality of the contents and the order in which it has been presented. It is not necessary for each major section to be reviewed here; but, it is suggested that you take the time to review this entire manual prior to beginning a course. There may be some key suggestions that could benefit you this year, next year, and in the years to come.

C. Suggested Method for Use

As noted in the previous paragraph, review the entire *Instructor's Guide* by first thoroughly looking through the Table of Contents and then through the remainder of the pages. Know what is here—just as you know or should know the contents of the course textbook.

As authors of this *Instructor's Guide* and the *Comprehensive Graphic Arts* textbook, we do not propose to suggest or believe that the many users of these two publications will or should teach the same. Such variances as personalities, abilities, interests, physical facilities, and students simply do not permit us all to teach alike. Use this *Guide* for your own personal benefit, and in turn your students will be recipients of improved education.

II. The Textbook—*Comprehensive Graphic Arts*

A. Purpose

This textbook has been prepared to help provide full appreciation and recognition of technical areas within the graphic arts industry. The book helps to acquaint readers with the many technological aspects of the various graphic arts processes, with the interrelationships among these areas, and with the other significant topics essential to successful performance and understanding of this important communications area.

B. Organization

The book is divided into twenty-three broad sections that have been planned to provide the reader with basic, but comprehensive, understanding of the processes of the graphic arts industry. Each section includes several units that are planned to provide the information required to have a fundamental knowledge of the section topic.

The first unit in each section is devoted to an introduction of that particular section, and the last unit in the section contains "Suggested Activities" which relate to the content of the technical-informative or procedural units in between. The number of units in each section varies, depending on the section topic. Some of the units are devoted to "manipulative" kinds of activities, while others primarily contain "related information" about graphic arts methods or the industry.

The comprehensiveness and profusely illustrated content with photographs and artists' illustrations from industry and school laboratory settings help to make the book an interesting publication to read. The use of a second color to emphasize important content and the use of four-color process photographs to make school and industrial settings look real, all help to make the organization of this textbook one of its most attractive features.

C.   Level of Book

The book is pertinent to high school courses, vocational-technical introductory courses, and college/university first- and second-level courses. It should be usable for business or industry groups desiring general-comprehensive information about graphic arts processes and the industry. Sales personnel—paper, machinery, systems, general suppliers—also can benefit from this book by obtaining a broad overview of the total graphic arts. It is emphasized, however, that anyone desiring in-depth study must seek other print and non-print publications.

III.   Suggested Course Content

One of the professional decisions that instructors must make is how to use the textbook with their classes. Few instructors use a textbook in the same way that another instructor would use it. It is expected that each instructor will adopt this textbook to meet the needs of the class and the conditions available in the laboratory.

The following chart suggests units that might be used for various lengths of courses. The textbook was planned originally for a one-year course; however, it is recognized that the ability level of the students in your program will determine the amount of textbook material you will be able to use. If the textbook is used with advanced high school students, it will be possible to use more of the textbook material than would be used for young, average, or below-average students in your classes.

Facilities also will determine the extent to which you will be able to use the textbook. For example, if you do not have the facilities and equipment to accomplish an activity such as screen process printing, you will be able to use only a small portion of Section 15.

All the courses are based on 1-hour classes that meet each day; therefore, the 9-week course would require 45 hours; the 18-week course, 90 hours; the 36-week course, 180 hours; and the 72-week class, 360 hours. The 72-week course will provide sufficient time for most students to complete the textbook and develop a fairly high degree of skill. In many instances, if the content of the 72-week course is narrow (focuses on only a few processes) and if the students are expected to develop a high degree of knowledge and proficiency, it may be necessary to utilize supplementary textbook material.

Your experience in the use of the textbook will help you determine how much of the content can be used with the students in your class. The following chart can serve as a checklist for planning your course.

SUGGESTED UNITS FOR VARIOUS COURSE LENGTHS

(Based on high school classes. Modify appropriately for advanced courses.)

Sections	Units	9-Week Course (45 hours)	18-Week Course (90 hours)	36-Week Course (180 hours)	72-Week Course (360 hours)
Section 1 Graphic Arts Industry	1	X	X	X	X
	2	X	X	X	X
	3	X	X	X	X
	4	X	X	X	X
	5	X	X	X	X
	6	X	X	X	X
Section 2 Type Styles	7	X	X	X	X
	8	X	X	X	X
	9	X	X	X	X
	10	X	X	X	X
	11	X	X	X	X
	12	X	X	X	X
	13	X	X	X	X
	14	X	X	X	X
	15	X	X	X	X
	16	X	X	X	X
	17	X	X	X	X
Section 3 Planning, Design, and Layout	18	X	X	X	X
	19	X	X	X	X
	20	X	X	X	X
	21			X	X
	22	X	X	X	X
	23	X	X	X	X
	24			X	X
	25			X	X
	26			X	X
Section 4 Type Composition Methods	27	X	X	X	X
	28		X	X	X
	29			X	X
	30	X	X	X	X
	31	X	X	X	X
	32	X	X	X	X
	33			X	X
	34		X	X	X
Section 5 Proofing Type Composition	35	X	X	X	X
	36		X	X	X
	37	X	X	X	X
	38	X	X	X	X
	39	X	X	X	X
	40		X	X	X

SUGGESTED UNITS FOR VARIOUS COURSE LENGTHS (cont'd)

(Based on high school classes. Modify appropriately for advanced courses.)

Sections	Units	9-Week Course (45 hours)	18-Week Course (90 hours)	36-Week Course (180 hours)	72-Week Course (360 hours)
Section 6 Copy Preparation for Process Photography	41		X	X	X
	42		X	X	X
	43		X	X	X
	44		X	X	X
	45		X	X	X
	46		X	X	X
	47			X	X
	48		X	X	X
	49		X	X	X
Section 7 Process Cameras and Darkroom Procedures	50		X	X	X
	51		X	X	X
	52		X	X	X
	53		X	X	X
	54		X	X	X
	55		X	X	X
	56			X	X
	57			X	X
	58			X	X
	59			X	X
	60				X
	61		X	X	X
	62		X	X	X
	63		X	X	X
Section 8 Letterpress Image Carriers	64		X	X	X
	65		X	X	X
	66				X
	67				X
	68				X
	69				X
	70				X
	71				X
	72		X	X	
	73		X	X	X
Section 9 Letterpress Imposition	74		X	X	X
	75		X	X	X
	76		X	X	X
	77		X	X	X
	78			X	X
	79		X	X	X

SUGGESTED UNITS FOR VARIOUS COURSE LENGTHS (cont'd)

(Based on high school classes. Modify appropriately for advanced courses.)

Sections	Units	9-Week Course (45 hours)	18-Week Course (90 hours)	36-Week Course (180 hours)	72-Week Course (360 hours)
Section 10 Letterpress Image Transfer	80		X	X	X
	81		X	X	X
	82		X	X	X
	83		X	X	X
	84		X	X	X
	85		X	X	X
	86				X
	87		X	X	X
	88	X	X	X	X
Section 11 Lithographic Imposition	89		X	X	X
	90		X	X	X
	91		X	X	X
	92		X	X	X
	93		X	X	X
	94			X	X
	95		X	X	X
Section 12 Lithographic Image Carriers	96		X	X	X
	97		X	X	X
	98		X	X	X
	99		X	X	X
	100	X	X	X	X
	101		X	X	X
	102		X	X	X
Section 13 Lithographic Image Transfer	103	X	X	X	X
	104	X	X	X	X
	105	X	X	X	X
	106		X	X	X
	107		X	X	X
	108		X	X	X
	109		X	X	X
	110			X	X
	111	X	X	X	X
	112			X	X
Section 14 Gravure Printing Process	113		X	X	X
	114			X	X
	115			X	X
	116				X
	117				X
	118			X	X
	119		X	X	X
	120		X	X	X

SUGGESTED UNITS FOR VARIOUS COURSE LENGTHS (cont'd)

(Based on high school classes. Modify appropriately for advanced courses.)

Sections	Units	9-Week Course (45 hours)	18-Week Course (90 hours)	36-Week Course (180 hours)	72-Week Course (360 hours)
Section 15 Screen Printing	121			X	X
	122			X	X
	123			X	X
	124			X	X
	125			X	X
	126			X	X
	127			X	X
	128			X	X
	129			X	X
	130			X	X
	131			X	X
	132			X	X
	133			X	X
	134			X	X
	135			X	X
	136			X	X
Section 16 Photography	137			X	X
	138			X	X
	139			X	X
	140			X	X
	141			X	X
	142			X	X
	143			X	X
	144			X	X
	145			X	X
Section 17 Duplicating and Special Printing Processes	146	X	X	X	X
	147	X			X
	148	X		X	X
	149		X	X	X
	150	X	X	X	X
Section 18 Finishing and Binding	151			X	X
	152				X
	153		X	X	X
	154		X	X	X
	155			X	X
	156	X		X	X
	157				X
	158				X
	159				X
	160				X

SUGGESTED UNITS FOR VARIOUS COURSE LENGTHS (cont'd)

(Based on high school classes. Modify appropriately for advanced courses.)

Sections	Units	9-Week Course (45 hours)	18-Week Course (90 hours)	36-Week Course (180 hours)	72-Week Course (360 hours)
Section 19 Pulp and Paper Manufacturing	161			X	X
	162			X	X
	163			X	X
	164			X	X
	165			X	X
	166			X	X
	167			X	X
Section 20 Printing Ink Manufacturing	168			X	X
	169			X	X
	170				X
	171				X
	172				X
	173			X	X
	174				X
Section 21 Legal Considerations for the Printer	175			X	X
	176			X	X
	177			X	X
	178			X	X
	179				X
	180			X	X
	181				X
Section 22 Desktop Composition	182		X	X	X
	183		X	X	X
	184		X	X	X
	185		X	X	X
Section 23 Graphic Arts Career Opportunities	186	X	X	X	X
	187	X	X	X	X
	188	X	X	X	X
	189	X	X	X	X
	190	X	X	X	X
	191	X	X	X	X
	192	X	X	X	X
	193			X	X
	194			X	X

SUGGESTED TEACHING STRATEGIES

THE PROGRAM

Instructors in every area and level of education have a basic presentation method all their own. These basic individualistic approaches begin with the initial teaching experience and continue to become more and more detailed and complicated as the instructors gain experience. There are, however, new teaching techniques and procedures all of us can learn whether in our first or forty-first year of helping students to learn. Hopefully, some of the thoughts and examples presented in this *Instructor's Guide* will give you a few more ideas to ponder and practice in your classrooms and laboratories of learning.

Course Outline and Objectives   It is important to prepare a course outline and several general outcomes, goals, or objectives. A course should never be taught unless an outline has been prepared. It is not easy to prepare outlines, especially when a course is taught for the first time. Some teachers prefer not to prepare an outline until the course has been taught once. Their rationale is that the outline probably will be wrong or cannot be followed, so why prepare it in the first place. Actually, it is more sound to prepare an outline; then revise it as necesary during and following the length of the course. See Appendix A for a sample course outline and objectives for an introductory graphic arts course at the college level.

Unit Outlines and Objectives   Unit outlines and objectives are considered subdivisions of the total course outline and objectives. Units of study can be from one day to several weeks in length, depending on how the teacher views the course and the various content areas. By dividing a course into study units, it helps to delineate the content into workable amounts of study. An entire course and its objectives easily can become overwhelming to the students, if they are not shown the smaller segments of the whole. The textbook section titles, their objectives, and general introductory information can serve as units of study for either basic or advanced courses in graphic arts.

Lesson Outlines and Objectives   Daily lesson plans should be developed and used. Their value cannot be overemphasized, even though the authors know the difficulty in preparing them. To assist you with this task, outlines including objectives, instructor preparation suggestions, study question answers, and suggested activities have been prepared for each content unit in *Comprehensive Graphic Arts*. The authors basically view each unit as one lesson; therefore, the prepared information should serve as excellent lesson outlines. See Appendix B for a sample lesson plan form.

Activity Selection   Students enroll in industrial technology education courses because they are interested in working with their minds and hands. They want to become involved in creating an idea that eventually will become a completed two- or three-dimensional product. As a teacher in an activity-oriented discipline, do not disappoint your students. Let them become involved!

It is, however, important to help students gain experiences that will give them an appreciation of the graphic arts industry. To do this, graphic arts instructors must use a variety of class activities. To help you select some appropriate student experiences, several laboratory and nonlaboratory activities have been suggested in each of the twenty-three "Learning Experiences" units in *Comprehensive Graphic Arts*. These units contain several multiple-type study questions and laboratory and nonlaboratory activities.

A *Student Workbook* is available with *Comprehensive Graphic Arts*. It contains a variety of laboratory and non-laboratory activities that can provide your students with the kinds of experiences necessary to gain an understanding and appreciation for the graphic arts industry.

Evaluation—Students, Course Content, and Teaching Methods   Without evaluation, little can be known about student learning, the value of the course content, and your own teaching methods. Plan to administer unit quizzes, midterm tests and comprehensive final tests. Students must be encouraged to read, observe, and learn specific information. Formal evaluations seem to be one of the best ways to achieve this outcome. You are encouraged to schedule several formal paper-and-pencil evaluations during a course. It is, however, important to prepare quiz and test questions that measure student learning with a respectable level of validity. It is beyond the scope of this *Instructor's Guide* to discuss test writing; but it is within the scope to suggest a management technique. It takes considerable time to write good test questions; therefore, begin writing a test or quiz well in advance of the scheduled administration date. Questions can be prepared on a periodic basis, used, revised, and used again. A 3-by-5 card file system is a good way to record, preserve, and organize tests and test questions. See Appendix C for a sample card (front and back) and a color-coding scheme.

Students need to know what will be expected of them during the course. Give them a course outline, along with a list of activities that they must complete or have the option to complete. Also, provide them with information concerning your evaluation method(s). A technique to accomplish these student and instructor needs is the "Learning Contract" (sometimes called a "Grade Contract"). By no stretch of the imagination is this document a legally binding agreement; however, it does provide some definite guidelines and specifications for both parties—student and teacher. See Appendix D for a sample contract that has been used successfully at the college level. It also should work well at the secondary level.

Print and Audio-Visual Teaching Learning Materials   Many printed and audio-visual auxiliary materials are available from a variety of sources that will assist you in your teaching and students in their learning. Instead of making a lengthy listing of unrelated AV materials, the authors have elected to recommend selected AV materials throughout the Instructor Preparation portions of each unit outline within this *Instructor's Guide*. The identified sources are listed alphabetically in Appendix E.

To assist you in recording and evaluating the AV materials plus others that will become available, a 3-by-5 card format is included in Appendix F. Use this card form to record pertinent information on all AV aids that you can locate. Upon previewing and using the AV aid, use the AV Aid Evaluation form to record your evaluation of the specific items (see Appendix G). This record can be used to help determine whether the aid should be used again next term.

Books are common reference tools and serve educational purposes well because of the convenient storage and retrieval system that bound pulications offer. If you have not done so already, establish an area in your laboratory that might be termed "the reference-research area." Place graphic arts books, plus others that you believe valuable, in this area and encourage the students to use them.

Trade journals are a valuable source of current technical information. You and your students should, without question, use these publications to keep yourselves up to date on the latest happenings, processes, and equipment within the graphic arts industry. A selected list of several national graphic arts trade journals is listed in Appendix H. Encourage your school librarian to subscribe to as many of these journals as possible. Also, do not forget to establish the journal reading habit.

Pamphlets and sundry other reading materials are available through manufacturers, distributors, and from various organizations. Obtain as many different titles as possible and place them in the reference-research area. Draw the students' attention to each new title as it becomes available. At times you may discover a pamphlet to be of excellent value and wish all the students to read it. In most situations, manufacturing companies and organizations can make these materials available in class quantities for little or not charge.

Display boards and showcases, if used in a positive way, can be assets to the learning process. Any good audiovisual education book will inform you of the value of these devices and also will present some pointers on how they should be prepared. Take the time to develop and maintain a display board or a showcase or both. Yes, they can be time-consuming, but well worth the time. Do not expect your students or colleagues to dash into your office or classroom to compliment you on how nice, attractive, and educational your newly designed display board or showcase, which you spent four to eight hours to prepare, might be, since it is likely that it will not happen. Your satisfaction will be obtained from observing the students and your colleagues as they stop and learn from your efforts. It is not necessary for you alone to prepare the display. Get your students involved!

ORGANIZATIONS AND ASSOCIATIONS

As an educator in the graphic arts technical area, you should seriously consider membership in one or more education- and industry-oriented organizations and associations. Professional bodies of people banded together for the basic purpose of furthering themselves in their personal knowledge and experiences serve their purpose rather well in most instances. Some people make the statement "Why should I join? It (organization) never does anything for me." We contend that these types of individuals need to open their minds to what a group really does attempt to do. These people must realize that personal involvement is demanded if benefits are expected. They must do more than pay the annual dues; they must become a part of the organization (committee work, conference-meeting attendance, occasional writer for the periodic newsletter or journal); thus involvement reaps benefits. If you are not now a member of one or more graphic arts organizations or associations, see Appendix I for a selected listing. Write for information. Then join, become involved, and begin to reap the benefits.

SAFETY

Safety can be overemphasized, according to some people, but it cannot be overpracticed. In industry the hours, days, and weeks of lost work due to accidents caused by unsafe conditions and practices are staggering. As an educator, you have an important responsibility to and for the young and old who come under your supervision in regard to safety. You must not ignore this responsibility; therefore, build safety instruction and attitude development into your course(s). Use your natural instincts, along with printed and AV information that is aviable. Seven safety units were included in selected sections of *Comprehensive Graphic Arts*. Use this material to good advantage. Also, write or telephone the National Safety Council for the latest information on OSHA (Occupational & Safety Health Act) and for their catalog of AV materials and posters. The address and telephone number are: National Safety Council, 444 North Michigan Avenue, Chicago, IL 60611. Telephone: (312) 527-4800, Extension 8706.

PRODUCTION PRINTING

Much has been written and many hours of discussion have been expended on this topic over the years. Some graphic arts educators believe production has no place in the graphic arts educational setting, while others believe strongly in including a considerable number of production experiences in their educational program. Obviously, these examples are at the extreme ends of a continuum line and offer direct opposing views. You may have already established a belief-position on this topic, but you are encouraged to consider this viewpoint.

Graphic arts programs can and should assume some production printing responsibilities. The amount depends upon the program level (junior high, high school, etc.) and the program objectives (exploration, vocational training, etc.). It is advisable for students to become involved in "live" assignments or jobs that require the student to answer to someone other than themselves and you, the instructor. Students should learn firsthand how to deal in a businesslike way with people, to meet work standards, and to meet time deadlines. Students can and should become involved in starting and finishing a job in an industry-like setting.

This discussion may sound as though production printing is recommended in all graphic arts classes. Production printing, however, can be and is beneficial in selected courses, but not in all courses. Basic courses at any level are not a good place to have actual production printing experiences. These courses should be designed to present fundamental facts and experiences about the total graphic arts industry. After basic understanding and experience have been gained, production printing experiences can be beneficial to the learning process. You are the judge, but whatever you do, base your decision on educational principles and not on economic principles of saving money for the school.

COMMERCIAL PLANT TOURS

This teaching technique has been used in the industrial technology education discipline for many years and continues to be a valuable method of providing industry-like experiences to students both young and old. You are encouraged to utilize commercial graphic arts shops and plants in your geographical area in your educational program. Personnel in these facilities generally are interested in contributing to the educational process by permitting tours through their plants or production facilities.

Other side benefits of these tours are the friends you make in the process of arranging the tour. These people also can help you in obtaining equipment, paper, supplies, trade journals, color separations, artwork, and printed examples at little or not cost. You also may be able to help them by recommending some of your students for part-time work in their plants. Good help is difficult to obtain and you may be able to provide the graphic arts business with a qualified employee who has learned well under your expert guidance.

SECTION 1
GRAPHIC ARTS INDUSTRY

Section Goal: To introduce the students to the vast and complex graphic arts industry.

Section Description: This section should be used as a foundation for studying the following 22 sections. Without being fortified with the information found in Section 1, students will be less able to understand, appreciate, and use the information found in any one or all of the other sections of this publication.

Units 1 through 4 are designed to lay the broad foundation that will allow students to grasp the meaning of the term *graphic arts*. The content of Unit 5 includes descriptions of the specific printing processes that are used to place images on the many receptors. Unit 5 is somewhat technical in nature, whereas the other units in this section include general information about the graphic arts industry.

Unit 6, entitled "Learning Experiences," is designed to help both you and the students by providing key terms and study questions pertaining to each of the previous units (1–5). Also listed are several activities that students can become involved in to help them to better understand the broad area of graphic arts.

Unit 1. Introduction to Graphic Arts

A. Objectives

Upon reading, defining the key terms, answering the study questions, and completing the one activity relating to this unit, students should be able to

1. Define the term *graphic arts*.
2. List the primary purpose of the graphic arts.
3. Suggest different ways in which graphic arts has influenced society.

B. Instructor preparation

Before teaching this unit, we suggest that you prepare by doing the following:

1. Thoroughly read and study Section 1—"Graphic Arts Industry."
2. Gather several graphic arts products for display to the students.
3. Think of ways that graphic arts has influenced your own personal life so you may use yourself as an example of utilizing the products of the graphic arts industry.
4. Obtain and plan to use DCA Educational Products transparencies *GA-1, What Is Graphic Arts?*; *GA-2, The Graphic Arts Industry Is…*; *GA-3, The Graphic Arts Industry Is…*; and *GA-4, The Graphic Arts Industry Is…*.
5. Consider obtaining and using the following videotape from the GAT/GAERF Videotape Project: Number 022, *Video Forum II*.

C. Suggested teaching outline

1. Introduction to graphic arts
2. Purpose of graphic arts
   a. Primary purpose
   b. Secondary purpose
3. Influence of graphic arts products
   a. Information explosion
   b. Cultural needs for graphic arts products
   c. Importance of graphic arts products upon the world scene

Unit 2. The Scope of Graphic Arts

A. Objectives

Upon reading, defining the key terms, answering the study questions, and completing the one activity relating to this unit, students should be able to

1. Identify several types of business enterprises that make up the total graphic arts industry.
2. Sketch a model representing the six common production phases of graphic arts.
3. Contrast the general commercial printer with the several kinds of specialty graphic arts businesses.

B. Instructor preparation

1. Review the United States government publication entitled *Occupational Outlook Handbook* under the section entitled "Printing and Publishing"; obtain the latest facts on the various divisions of the industry and also the size relationships of the many specific jobs within printing and publishing.
2. Prepare an overhead transparency showing the six production phases of the graphic arts, as illustrated in Fig. 2-3 of the textbook. See Appendix M. This transparency will permit you to describe the production phases of graphic arts during a class presentation.
3. Obtain advertisements from newspapers and trade journals in which general commercial printing firms are advertising for business, as well as specialty graphic arts firms such as type houses, creative artists, binders, etc. Use these ads to help describe the wide scope of the graphic arts.
4. Consider obtaining and using the following videotape from the GAT/GAERF Videotape Project: Number 010, *The Operation of a Medium-Size Daily Newspaper*.

C. Suggested teaching outline

1. Where does graphic arts exist?
2. Future of graphic arts
3. Business enterprise
   a. Commercial printing plants
   b. Newspapers
   c. Paper manufacturers
   d. Ink manufacturers
   e. Equipment and chemical manufacturers
4. Divisions of graphic arts
   a. Design-layout
   b. Copy preparation
   c. Photo-conversion
   d. Image carriers
   e. Image transfer
   f. Finishing and binding
5. Specialty graphic arts business establishments
   a. Creative graphic artist firms
   b. Type-composition houses
   c. Camera and darkroom business
   d. Platemakers
   e. Press facilities
   f. Trade binders

Unit 3. Cultural Contributions of Graphic Arts

A. Objectives

Upon reading, defining the key terms, answering the study questions, and completing the one activity relating to this unit, students should be able to

1. List several early significant events that led to the development of graphic arts technology.
2. Write a one-page paper concerning the historical significance of newspapers and people and machines in the early United States.

B. Instructor preparation

1. Review the highlights of graphic arts history than can be found in any good encyclopedia.
2. Review the life of Benjamin Franklin during the period in which he was involved in newspaper work.
3. Consider obtaining and using the videotape, *The World of Print*, from the International Film Bureau, Inc.
4. Construct a time line transparency that can be utilized to describe the significant events that have led to the moder graphic arts industry of today.

C. Suggested teaching outline

1. Early significant events
   a. First printing press
   b. Wood block printing
   c. Movable nonmetal type
   d. Movable metal type
2. Significant United States events
   a. First printing press
   b. First paper mill
3. The beginning of newspapers
   a. Printer journalist—James Franklin
   b. Benjamin Franklin and his newspaper work
4. People and machines
   a. Linotype—Otmar Mergenthaler
   b. Metal printing press
   c. Papermaking machine—Fourdrinier brothers
   d. Graphic communication via electronic means

Unit 4. Size of the Industry

A. Objectives

Upon reading, defining the key terms, answering the study questions, and completing the one activity relating to this unit, students should be able to

1. Discuss either orally or in writing why the graphic arts industry is considered a "growth" industry.
2. Identify specific points as to why the graphic arts industry is considered to be one of the ten largest manufacturing industries in the United States.
3. Describe the United States Government Printing Office either in writing or orally.

B. Instructor preparation

1. Thoroughly review the *Occupational Outlook Handbook* under printing and publishing to determine latest information on the size of the graphic arts industry.
2. Make a transparency showing the comparative size of the printing and publishing industry in the various aspects such as the payroll, value added, product value, and number of manufacturing establishments.

3. Review content found in any good encyclopedia concerning the United States Government Printing Office, the Superintendent of Documents, the Bureau of Engraving and Printing, and other related topics concerning the production of printed products by the United States Government. Plan to help your students distinguish between the United States Government Printing Ofice and the Bureau of Engraving and Printing.

C. **Suggested teaching outline**
1. Graphic arts—a changing industry
   a. Through products
   b. Through methods of production
   c. Through speed and quality of production
   d. Through people
2. Employment
   a. Stable
   b. Over one million employees
   c. Shortage of qualified management personnel and skilled production workers
   d. Wages and salaries
3. Industry growth
   a. Graphic arts industry highly competitive
   b. Specifid ranking of various aspects of graphic arts
4. United States Government Printing Office
   a. Largest single printing plant in the world
   b. Number of people employed—approximately 7,500
   c. Kinds of products printed by the United States Government Printing Office

Unit 5. Graphic Arts Printing Processes

A. **Objectives**

Upon reading, defining the key terms, answering the study questions, and completing the one activity relating to this unit, students should be able to
1. Name the six basic printing (image transfer) processes that are used to place images on the various receptors.
2. Differentiate among the six basic printing processes.
3. Name typical products that are manufactured with each of the six image-transfer processes.

B. **Instructor preparation**
1. Build a file of common products that are produced with each of the six image-transfer processes, and use these examples during your presentation to the class.
2. Obtain and use the DCA Educational Products trasnparency *GA-22, Image Transfer Methods.*
3. Obtain and use an appropriate audio-visual which describes the printing processes.
4. Obtain an actual example of a commercially prepared image carrier for the letterpress process, the lithography process, the gravure process, the screen process, and the photographic process. It may be difficult to obtain something for electrostatic, unless a screen used for "gap" printing can be obtained. It may be necessary to rely strictly on illustrations to depict the electrostatic techniques of image transfer.
5. Consider obtaining and using the following videotape from the GAT/GAERF Videotape Project: Number 013, *An Introduction to Graphic Communications Processes.*

C. **Suggested teaching outline**
1. Letterpress process
   a. Image-Transfer principle—raised

    b. Percent of printed products by letterpress
    c. Flexography—subdivision of letterpress
    d. Historical aspects—Chinese and Gutenberg
    e. Common products—newspapers, books, magazines, and tickets
2. Lithography
    a. Image-transfer principle—flat
    b. Common terms—litho or offset
    c. Offset principle—image transfer from plate to blanket to receptor
    d. Percent of printed products by lithography
    e. Historical aspects—Senefelder and the offset lithography press
    f. Common products—newspapers, books, magazines, and general commercial printing
3. Gravure
    a. Image-transfer principle—through
    b. Gravure—a variation of gravure
    c. Historical aspects—Kleitsch and first use by *The New York Times*
    d. Percent of printed products by gravure
    e. Common products—paper money, calendars, magazines, Sunday newspaper supplements, and packaging material
4. Screen
    a. Image-transfer principle—through
    b. Other names
    c. Major advantage of screen printing—can be used to produce images on nearly any solid surface, material, or shape
    d. Percent of printed products by screen
    e. Historical aspects—Chinese, Egyptian and Japanese. First use in the United States
    f. Common products—sports pennants, posters, bumper stickers, food containers, and others
5. Photographic
    a. Basic image-transfer principle
    b. Primary use of photographic printing—transparency and photographic prints
    c. Historical highlights—first attempt in 1802; first flexible film in 1884
6. Electrostatic
    a. Basic principle—like electrical charges repel and unlike charges attract
    b. Status of electrostatic imaging—progressing rapidly
    c. Historical aspects—first patent issued in 1940
    d. Primary use—office copying machines

SECTION 2
TYPE STYLES

Section Goal: To develop background appreciation for the modern alphabet and the many typefaces that are in use today.

Section Description: This section is quite unique in that type and type styles or typefaces are the core of most printed products. Certainly, without the alphabet and, in turn, without typefaces, there would be little need for a graphic arts industry.

The first four Units (7–10) include foundation information for a basic understanding of the evolution of the alphabet and the development and characteristics of typefaces. Typefaces can be categorized into several groupings, but for purposes of this textbook six groupings have been chosen as reviewed and illustrated in Units 11–16.

Unit 17, entitled "Learning Experiences" is designed to help both the instructor and student learner. The key terms, study questions, and activities provide a structure for both teaching and learning. Use them with the appropriate textbook content Units 7 through 16.

Unit 7. Introduction to Typefaces

A. Objectives

Upon reading, defining the key terms, answering the study questions, and completing the activity relating to this unit, students should be able to

1. Appraise the value of typefaces.
2. Name and describe the five important factors to consider when choosing a typeface.
3. Discuss why there is need for classifying typefaces.

B. Instructor Preparation

1. Thoroughly read and study Section 2 entitled "Type Styles." Be very familiar with each unit in Section 2.
2. Develop a series of slides and/or transparencies as examples of how some typefaces "talk."
3. Develop a series of slides and/or transparencies illustrating the five important factors to consider when choosing a typeface: (1) legibility; (2) readability; (3) appropriateness; (4) reproducibility; and (5) practicality. An overhead transparency master is available in Appendix M titled, *Choosing A Typeface.*
4. Consider obtaining and using the following videotape from the GAT/GAERF Videotape Project: Number 017. *Type Faces For Graphic Communications: Introduction and Selection.*
5. Consider obtaining and using the slide/audio series titled *Typefaces*, from the Graphic Arts Technical Foundation.

C. Suggested teaching outline

1. Typefaces and communication
2. Psychology of a typeface
   a. Some typefaces talk
   b. Some typefaces shout
   c. Some typefaces look old
   d. Some typefaces look new
   e. Some typefaces display a bold feeling
   f. Some typefaces help display gaiety

3. Kinds of letters
    a. Lowercase
    b. Uppercase
4. Choosing a typeface
    a. Legibility
    b. Readability
    c. Appropriateness
    d. Reproducibility
    e. Practicality
5. Typeface classifications
    a. Several classification systems are available.
    b. Six classifications used in this section include specific examples and are presented for the students in Units 12–16.

Unit 8. Evolution of the Alphabet

A. Objectives

Upon reading, defining the key terms, answering the study questions, and completing the one activity relating to this unit, students should be able to

1. Describe early (before the alphabet) visual methods of communication.
2. Explain why the Egyptian hieroglyphics cannot be considered an alphabet.
3. Summarize either in writing or orally, the highlights of the development of the real alphabet.
4. Explain how the word "alphabet" came into being.

B. Instructor preparation

1. Several reference books are available in most libraries concerning the development of the alphabet. These books are written at different levels of ability and interest and you may desire to locate several of these books for use not only by yourself but also by your students.
2. Encyclopedias carry a considerable amount of information on the alphabet, and most encyclopedias include the history of each letter in written and graphic form as the first event in each of the 26 letter categories.
3. Obtain and use the 16mm film entitled "The Alphabet—The Mark of Man."
4. Obtain and use DCA Educational Products transparencies *GA-5, Early Graphic Communication; GA-6, Egyptian Hieroglyphics;* and *GA-7, Comparison of Three Alphabets.*

C. Suggested teaching outline

1. Early visual communication
    a. Twigs, tree trunk marks, and rock piles
    b. Picture drawing
    c. Pictograms
    d. Ideograms
    e. Phonograms
2. Egyptian hieroglyphics
    a. The system
    b. Why not an alphabet
3. The real alphabet
    a. Credited to the Phoenicians
    b. Greek contributions
    c. Roman contributions
    d. The name—alphabet origination

Unit 9. Development of a Typeface

A. Objectives

Upon reading, defining the key terms, answering the study questions, and completing the one activity relating to this unit, students should be able to

1. Note the importance of a well-designed typeface
2. Explain the basic process involved in developing a new typeface.

B. Instructor preparation

1. Thoroughly study several different type designs and plan to indicate why some type designs are more adaptable to one printing process than others.
2. Little preparation is necessary for this unit, since it is suggested that students be encouraged to read and study this content as a related information unit. Once read, this material can be discussed briefly in a class situation.

C. Suggested teaching outline

1. Typeface design
   a. Typeface purpose must be established.
   b. Typefaces must meet legibility and readability requirements.
   c. Continuity of the 26 letters
2. Creating a face
   a. Key letters—n, o, H, and O
   b. Key word—Championed
   c. Using computers to design
   d. Type designers work area
   e. Unitizing the characters
3. Type production methods
   a. Designing foundry type
   b. Use of the pantograph
   c. Typecasting machine
4. Typography
   a. Designing the printed page
   b. Work of a typographer

Unit 10. Characteristics of Typefaces

A. Objectives

Upon reading, defining the key terms, answering the study questions, and completing the one activity relating to this unit, students should be able to

1. Distinguish among the several parts of a typeface.
2. Summarize in writing, or orally, some of the major distinguishing characteristics of typefaces.
3. Distinguish between the terms "font," "series," and "family" used in relationship to type.

B. Instructor preparation

1. Obtain DCA Educational transparencies *GA-15, Type Face Measurement and Parts; GA-46, A Type Font; GA-47, A Type Series;* and *GA-48, A Type Family.*
2. Obtain actual examples of type fonts such as a complete foundry font, a photographic film font, a photographic headline-size type font, and/or a font disc used in a sophisticated composition machine.
3. Obtain one or more samples of type catalogues that can be shown to the students.
4. Plan to show the students actual fonts, series, and families of type that you have available in the school laboratory.

5. On the next field trip to a commercial printer, remember to ask the tour guide to specifically point out the many typefaces that are in use within their commercial plant.

C. **Suggested teaching outline**
1. Typeface parts
   a. Thick strokes
   b. Thin strokes
   c. Serifs
   d. Ascender
   e. Counter
   f. Bowl
   g. Descender
2. Distinguishing features
   a. Serifs
   b. Typeface weight
3. A type font
   a. Definition
   b. Subdivisions of type fonts
   c. Examples of type fonts within the school laboratory
4. A type series
   a. Definition
   b. Size ranges common to type series
   c. Series available in the school laboratory
5. A type family
   a. Definition
   b. Families of type available in the school laboratory
6. Italic typefaces

Unit 11. Text Type Style
Unit 12. Roman Type Style
Unit 13. Sans Serif Type Style
Unit 14. Square Serif Type Style
Unit 15. Script Type Style
Unit 16. Novelty Type Style

We suggest that the six basic type styles or classifications be studied together as one large unit. Therefore, the following materials has been prepared with that thought in mind.

A. **Objectives**

Upon reading, defining the key terms, answering the study questions, and completing the one activity relating to these units, students should be able to

1. Arrange with over 75 percent accuracy specific typefaces into the six established typeface classifications.
2. Choose typefaces according to uses that are noted for each of the six typeface classifications.
3. Generalize the historical highlights of each of the six typeface classifications.

B. **Instructor preparation**
1. Obtain DCA Educational Products transparency *GA-49, Type Face Classifications.*
2. Prepare your own set of overhead transparencies by locating several printed samples of each classification. Make one transparency of each of the six classifications.

3. Have the fonts of type in your own school laboratory classified according to the six classifications. For an auxiliary activity you may desire to have students become more familiar with the typefaces in the school laboratory by asking them to classify selected typefaces according to the six classifications found in *Comprehensive Graphic Arts.*

4. Prepare a display board showing samples of each of the six classifications. Also, note specific uses and historical highlights of each classification.

C. **Suggested teaching outline**

1. Text type
   a. Distinguishing characteristics
   b. Uses
   c. Historical highlights

2. Roman type
   a. Distinguishing characteristics
   b. Subdivision of Roman type
      (1) Old style
      (2) Modern
      (3) Transitional
   c. Italic faces
   d. Uses
   e. Historical highlights

3. Sans serif type
   a. Distinguishing characteristics
   b. Uses
   c. Historical highlights

4. Square serif type
   a. Distinguishing characteristics
   b. Uses
   c. Historical highlights

5. Script type
   a. Distinguishing characteristics
      (1) Joining letters
      (2) Nonjoining letters
   b. Uses
   c. Historical highlights

6. Novelty type
   a. Distinguishing characteristics
   b. Uses
   c. Historical highlights

SECTION 3
PLANNING, DESIGN, AND LAYOUT

Section Goal: To introduce information on planning, designing, and layout and to encourage student involvement in this important preliminary production phase of the graphic arts.

Section Description: This section is related to other sections in the book that are involved in copy preparation, photo-conversion, image carriers, image transfer, and finishing and binding. Without proper planning, designing, and layout, manufactured products will not meet the needs and standards of the customers and consumers of graphic products.

Content for Units 18–25 is grouped together because it centers around information that must be known and dealt with prior to the beginning of the actual manufacturing process. Some people might point out that the point- and metric-measurement systems should not be included in this section; but, it is emphasized that measurement is necessary if proper planning and layout are to be accomplished.

We wish to emphasize the fact that the content in Section 3 should be integrated into the total course during the study and actual practice of the various production phases of graphic arts. Nothing can reduce the enthusiasm for a laboratory course in which intriguing and complicated equipment is involved than to stay in the classsroom day after day studying content such as that found in Secion 3.

The content within Section 3 was grouped here for textbook organizational purposes, therefore, is not necessarily designed for a course outline. Unit 26, entitled "Learning Experiences" is designed to help both the instructor and student learner. The key terms, study questions, and activities provide a structure for both teaching and learning. Use them with the appropriate textbook content in Units 18 through 25.

Unit 18. The Value of Planning, Design, and Layout

A. Objectives

Upon reading, defining the key terms, answering the study questions, and completing the activity relating to this unit, students should be able to:

1. Recite the normal sequence in the preparation of a complete set of layouts.
2. Discuss the value of good planning.
3. Assemble tools and supplies that are appropriate to use during the preparation of two-dimensional layouts.

B. Instructor preparation

1. Read and study very thoroughly the content of Section 3 entitled "Planning, Design, and Layout."
2. Obtain DCA Educational Products transparencies *GA-41*, *Two Dimensional Layout*; and *GA-42*, *Layout Sequence*.
3. Prepare a complete set of layouts (prelayout planning sheet, thumbnail sketches, rough layout, comprehensive layout, and finished layout). Use these to emphasize the general procedures to follow in preparing a product for manufacture. From a commercial printing plant obtain a complete set of layouts which you can use for a "live" example. It is noted here that commercial plants not often go through this lengthy procedure of planning, at least on paper, prior to the production of the printed product. The reason for this is that commercial printers probably have had several experiences or jobs that are very much the same; therefore, most of their planning is done via the mental process only, instead of the complete graphic process. A second reason why a complete set of layouts is not always made is that the printed job is somewhat routine and does not necessarily demand considerable design work. Printed jobs that are wide open for creative thinking normally receive considerable attention through the production of a complete set of layouts, as noted in this unit and discussed further in Section 3.
4. Consider obtaining and using the following videotape from the GAT/GAERF Videotape Project: Number 006, *Layout and Design*.

C. Suggested teaching outline

1. Layout defined
2. Value of good planning
3. Prelayout planning
4. Layout sequence
   a. Thumbnail sketches
   b. Rough layout
   c. Comprehensive layout
5. Needed tools and supplies
6. Design and layout considerations

Unit 19. The Point and Metric Measurement Systems

A. Objectives

Upon reading, defining the key terms, answering the study questions, and working with the two measurement systems in the laboratory, the student should be able to

1. Use the point system to measure type size, line length, and line spacing.
2. Review the historical highlights of the point system.
3. Accurately use a line gauge for both pica and inch measure.
4. Describe and use the metric measurement system where appropriate.

B. Instructor preparation

1. Obtain DCA Educational Products transparency *GA-12, The Point System*; and *GA-47, A Type Series*.
2. Obtain samples of the various styles of line gauges used in the graphic arts. Possibly, it may be wise to have several styles of line gauges available in the laboratory so students can become familiar with them; therefore, they are not surprised if they should see something different when out on the job.
3. Obtain the metric system charts that are available from the United States Government Printing Office. Help your students understand and use this measurement system. Show students the dual dimensioning—inch and metric—used in the textbook. Keep in mind that the point system will continue to be the standard for type size measurement and other facets of the type composition area; therefore, it probably will be essential to continue to study both the point and the metric systems of measurement.

C. Suggested teaching outline

1. The point system
   a. Comparison to the inch system
   b. Points and picas
   c. The line gauge
2. Historical highlights
   a. 1737—Simon-Pierre Fournier developed a measurement system
   b. 1879—European type founders system
   c. 1886—U.S. type founders association
   d. Differences between the United States and European systems
3. Common type sizes
   a. Measurement of a typeface
   b. Letters and the four guidelines
   c. Measurement of foundry type
   d. Common sizes—6- through 72-point type
   e. Larger sizes available

4. The metric system
   a. The relationship to "Ten"
   b. Present use: United States, Canada, other countries
   c. Present use: graphic arts industry

Unit 20. Graphic Design Principles

A. Objectives

Upon reading, defining the key terms, answering the study questions, and completing the activity relating to this unit, the students should be able to

1. Describe the importance of properly utilizing two-dimensional space.
2. Recognize several common page proportions and to enlarge or reduce a given proportion via the diagonal line method.
3. Illustrate the two basic kinds of balance—formal and informal, and also be able to arrange graphic elements according to the optical center of a two-dimensional space.
4. Show by sketching several different ways of emphasizing words through the basic principle of contrast.
5. Utilize the principles of unity and rhythm in the preparation of a two-dimensional layout.

B. Instructor preparation

1. Obtain several printed examples that illustrate the design principles, as presented in this unit. Plan to use these examples in a formal presentation and/or to place these examples on a display board with proper identification as to which principle(s) is emphasized.
2. Obtain several printed examples; that have been prepared according to various page proportions. Again, you may plan to use these in a presentation and/or to display them on a classroom board.
3. Obtain and use DCA Educational Products transparencies *GA-35, Two Dimensional Design*; and *GA-36, Page Proportion*; *GA-37, Balance*; *GA-38, Contrast*; *GA-39, Rhythm*; *GA-40, Unity*; and *GA-9, Enlargements and Reductions: Diagonal Line*.
4. Prepare an overhead transparency of a rectangular two-dimensional blank space. See Appendix M for the transparency master copy. After emphasizing the importance of design principles, place this transparency on the overhead projector and ask the students to describe what they see. After it has been identified and described, help them understand the importance of properly using two-dimensional space.

C. Suggested teaching outline

1. Design principles—their relationship through layout preparation
2. Space—what, value, how to use
3. Common design principles
   a. Page proportion
   b. Balance
      (1) Formal
      (2) Informal
      (3) Optical center
   c. Contrast
   d. Unity
   e. Rhythm

Unit 21. Color Principles

A. Objectives

Upon reading, defining the key terms, answering the study questions, and completing the activity relating to this unit, the student should be able to

1. Distinguish among the several pigment colors known as primary, secondary, and intermediate.
2. Design multi-color graphic products utilizing the following four-color harmonies—monochromatic, analogous, complementary, and triadic.
3. Apply the "psychology of color" and some of the modern uses of color in designing a two-dimensional, multi-color product.

B. Instructor preparation

1. Several reference books are available in most libraries concerning color and its use. These book are written at different levels of ability and interest, and you as an instructor may desire to locate several of these books for use not only by yourself but also by your students.
2. Encyclopedias carry considerable information on color. We suggest that you review this content to obtain an overall understanding of colors—both primary pigment color and primary light colors.
3. Plan to help your students distinguish between primary light colors and primary pigment colors through the use of DCA Educational Products transparencies *GA-66, The Visible Light Spectrum; GA-67, The Additive Process;* and *GA-68, The Subtractive Process.* Transparency *GA-67* illustrates the mixing of the light colors, whereas transparency *GA-68* illustrates the mixing of pigment colors.
4. Prepare transparencies of the various color combinations that are shown in Unit 21 and in the reference books that you may have.
5. Build a file of printed products that specifically illustrates the common color harmonies, the psychology of color, and some modern uses of color. Plan to show these various examples during a class presentation of this unit.

C. Suggested teaching outline

1. Color—"Where is it?"
2. The color wheel
   a. Primary colors
   b. Secondary colors
   c. Intermediate colors
3. Black and white
4. Color harmony
   a. Monochromatic
   b. Analagous
   c. Complementary
   d. Triadic
5. Primary pigment colors
   a. Yellow
   b. Blue (Cyan)
   c. Red (Magenta)
6. Primary light colors
   a. Green
   b. Red
   c. Blue
7. Psychology of color
8. Modern use of color

Unit 22. Thumbnail Sketches

A. Objectives

Upon reading, defining the key terms, answering the study questions, and completing the activity relating to this unit, the students should be able to

1. List the three primary purposes of thumbnail sketches.
2. Prepare a set of thumbnail sketches based upon some given content.

B. Instructor preparation

1. Prepare a set of four thumbnail sketches on a current school topic. Use these thumbnail sketches in your class preparation on how to make "layouts." We suggest that $\frac{1}{8}$- or $\frac{1}{4}$-inch light blue grid paper be used on which to sketch the thumbnail sketches. Grid paper provides easy alignment and size relationships.
2. Obtain and use DCA Educational Products transparency *GA-43*, *Thumbnail Sketches*.
3. If possible, visit a commercial art studio and/or a commercial printer who might be large enough to prepare and use sketches and layouts to their fullest extent. Ask for samples of thumbnail sketches they have prepared. Use these samples in class to help the students understand the full value of preparing thumbnail sketches in the whole production process.
4. Consider obtaining and using the slide/audio series titled *Planning Printing*, from the Graphic Arts Technical Foundation.

C. Suggested teaching outline

1. Thumbnail sketches
   a. What are they?
   b. Purposes
2. Method of preparation
3. Examples
   a. Student made
   b. Instructor made
   c. Commercially made

Unit 23. The Rough Layout

A. Objectives

Upon reading, defining the key terms, answering the study question, and completing the activity relating to this unit, students should be able to

1. Name the three purposes of a rough layout.
2. Prepare a rough layout based upon a selection or combination of thumbnail sketches according to an acceptable standard.

B. Instructor preparation

1. Prepare one or more rough layouts based upon some given thumbnail sketches. As with the thumbnail sketches, use these sample rough layouts in your class presentation, and/or place them on your classroom display entitled "How to Prepare a Set of Layouts."
2. Obtain some commercial rough layouts, as suggested with thumbnail sketches in Unit 22.
3. Obtain and use DCA Educational Products transparency *GA-440*, *Rough Layouts*.

C. Suggested teaching outline

1. The rough layout
   a. What is it?
   b. Purposes
2. Method of Preparation

3. Examples
   a. Student made
   b. Instructor made
   c. Commercially made

Unit 24. The Comprehensive Layout

A. Objectives

Upon reading, defining the key terms, answering the study questions, and completing the activity relating to this unit, students should be able to

1. Write the major purposes of the comprehensive layout.
2. Produce a comprehensive layout based upon a prepared rough layout, according to acceptable standards as established by the instructor.
3. Utilize and apply the basic design principles of page proportion, balance, contrast, and unity, as illustrated and presented in Unit 20.

B. Instructor preparation

1. Prepare one or more complete comprehensive layouts based upon a prepared rough layout. Use this comprehensive layout as an example in your class presentation and/or for placement upon the display board "How to Make a Set of Layouts."
2. Obtain DCA Educational Products transparency *GA-45, Comprehensive Layout.*
3. As suggested in the thumbnail sketches and rough layout units, obtain some examples of completed comprehensive layouts from a commercial facility. Use these as examples in your class presentation, as well as a display on your classroom display board.
4. Build a folder of top quality comprehensive layouts that have been prepared by your former students for use in present and future classes.

C. Suggested teaching outline

1. The comprehensive layout
   a. What is it?
   b. The primary purposes
2. Steps of preparation
3. The overlay sheet
   a. Why made?
   b. How made?
   c. Content
4. The mechanical layout
   a. What is it?
   b. How made?
5. Design principles reviewed
   a. Page proportion
   b. Balance
   c. Contrast
   d. Unity

Unit 25. Page and Signature Layout

A. Objectives

Upon reading, defining the key terms, answering the study questions, and completing the activity relating to this unit, students should be able to

1. Establish page margins for a single page and for two facing pages in the book.

2. Prepare a dummy layout for a booklet of eight or more pages.

3. Copyfit a given amount of copy using a specific type-kind, size, and style.

B. Instructor preparation

1. Prepare one or more dummy layouts of a booklet that was or will be prepared for a club within your school. By doing this, it makes the dummy layout more realistic, thereby helping to give the students a better understanding of its value.

2. Use this dummy layout in your class presentation, and/or place it on the classroom display board that is involved in layout preparation.

3. As mentioned in previous units, visit a commercial facility and obtain examples of their layout materials. The dummy layout examples also should be available from these commercial firms.

4. Talk to management personnel of a typesetting company and find out how they handle their copyfitting needs.

C. Suggested teaching outline

1. Margins
   a. For single pages
   b. For double pages

2. Signature
   a. What is it?
   b. How made?
   c. Common signature sizes

3. The dummy layout
   a. Purpose
   b. How prepared?

4. Copyfitting
   a. Three different methods
   b. Procedure—character count method

SECTION 4
TYPE COMPOSITION METHODS

Section Goal: To introduce the broad area of type and image composition within the total graphic arts area by providing related information and practical experiences.

In graphic arts, imagesetting is to printed product as a foundation is to a completed building. The only difference in this analogy is the fact that results of the compositor are in full view for all to see, whereas the contractor's work is mainly covered and out of sight.

Section Description: The important thing in this section is to emphasize to your students the importance of producing as high a quality of type and image composition as possible because, obviously, this is the core of communications via graphic means. The seven units in this section, plus the learning experiences unit, are designed to provide students with broad information as well as specific how-to-do-it information on the various methods of type and image composition.

This specific area of graphic arts has and is changing very rapidly. You as an instructor are encouraged to read the trade journals each month for the expressed purpose of keeping up-to-date in the total graphic arts and, also, specifically, within the imagesetting area. This is the only way you and your students are going to know what is happening at any given time.

Unit 34, entitled "Learning Experiences" is designed to help both you and the student learner. The key terms, study questions, and activities provide a structure for both teaching and learning. Use them with the appropriate textbook content which includes Units 27 through 33.

Unit 27. Introduction to Type and Image Composition

A. Objectives

Upon reading, defining the key terms, answering the study questions, and completing the activity relating to this unit, students should be able to

1. Clarify the meaning of the words "Type Composition," "Imagesetting," and "Typesetting."
2. Summarize the historical highlights of the graphic arts area known as type and image composition.
3. Recognize the major value of word processing within the typesetting area.

B. Instructor preparation

1. Thoroughly read and study Section 4—Type and Image Composition Methods. This will give you an overall understanding of the content of this section and will assist you in interpreting specific content for your students.
2. Establish a file folder entitled "Type and Image Composition Methods," and begin saving commercially produced examples in which it is possible to identify the imagesetting method used to produce the specific product. Label these examples and use them for display during a class presentation and/or for a classroom display board.
3. Consider obtaining and using the video tape titled *Typesetting*, from Sunshine Enterprises, Spokane, WA.
4. Obtain and use DCA Educational Products transparencies *GA-50, Hot Composition Methods* and *GA-51, Cold Composition Methods*.
5. Consider obtaining and using the following videotape from the GAT/GAERF Videotape Project: Number 011, *Image Generation/An Introduction to Typesetting*.

C. Suggested teaching outline

1. Definition of type composition typesetting, and imagesetting
2. Methods of type composition
   a. Hot composition
   b. Cold composition
3. Quality and speed in typesetting and imagesetting

4. Historical notes
    a. Foundry type composition
    b. Mechanical composition—the Linotype
    c. Photographic composition
    d. Imagesetting
5. Word and information processing
    a. Word processing—What is it?
    b. Word processing interface with typesetting
    c. Page description languages
    d. Facsimile transmission and reception

Unit 28. Foundry Type Composition

A. Objectives

Upon reading, defining the key terms, study questions, and completing the one activity relating to this unit, students should be able to

1. Define terms, such as the California job case, composing stick, galley, and other terms associated directly with foundry type composition.
2. Identify and use the seven basic sizes of word spacing materials found in the California job case.
3. Recognize and use line spacing materials such as leads and slugs.
4. Compose and properly justify three to six lines of foundry type.
5. Dump, tie, and distribute a 3- to 6-line type form.

B. Instructor preparation

1. Limited time should be spent on this unit. Obviously, foundry type is *not* being used within the graphic arts industry except in rare situations. Having the students "hand stick" some type provides an opportunity for them to learn about and experience some important history. At one time in our historical past, the use of foundry type was "high tech."
2. Check all equipment, tools, and supplies thoroughly prior to the classroom demonstration. Be certain all equipment and tools are in proper working order, the type cases are in the proper order within the bank, and a sufficient supply of galleys are free and clean for student use. As much as possible, have the type cases neatly organized, including the seven basic word spacing materials.
3. Duplicate Visual Master-4, Appendix M, "Layout of California Job Case," and distribute it to the students for their use during the process of composition. This will save having the students memorize the lay of the case and also will help to reduce the mixing of the letters as the type is distributed back into the case. It is highly recommended that you as an instructor do not force the students to memorize the lay of the California job case, since there is little educational value in having the students complete this task. Probably, it would do more harm to student interest in graphic arts than any other activity that you ask them to complete.
4. Obtain and use DCA Educational Products transparencies *GA-11, California Job Case* and *GA-14, Foundry Type Spacing*.

C. Suggested teaching outline

1. Foundry type composition
    a. Its use yesterday
    b. Its use today
2. California job case
3. Spacing materials
    a. Word spacing materials
    b. Line spacing materials
4. Composing stick and galley

5. Demonstration
    a. Composing type
    b. Dumping and typing type
    c. Distributing type
       Please note: You may desire to jump ahead and have the students not only read Unit 36, Proofing Relief Type, but demonstrating this procedure prior to presenting the distribution of type. You also may desire to jump to Unit 39, Correcting Type Composition, and discuss how foundry type composition is corrected if errors are found in the proofing stage.

Unit 29. Hot-Metal Type Composition

A. Objectives

Upon reading, defining the key terms, answering the study questions, and completing the one activity relating to this unit, students should be able to

1. Recognize hot-metal composition equipment.
2. Classify the three different categories of hot-metal composition.

B. Instructor preparation

1. As with foundry type composition, there is little use being made of hot-metal type composition within the graphic arts industry. There are, though, some commercial printers still operating hot-metal equipment. They find it useful for such things as short-run envelope printing, imprinting on pre-printed booklets or flyers. In some cases slugs are also being used for making rubber stamps. This unit material must be put into the proper perspective, but it is important. Emphasize the nearly one-century long dominance of hot metal typesetting.
2. Obtain several examples of hot-metal slugs and individual characters. Also, obtain a Linotype or Intertype matrix, a coded tape, and a Ludlow matrix. Use these items to stimulate interest during a class presentation; or they can be used in a bulletin board display.
3. Obtain and use DCA Educational Products transparencies *GA-50, Hot Composition Methods;* and *GA-52, A Line Casting Machine.*

C. Suggested teaching outline

1. Hot-metal type composition
    a. Past use
    b. Present use
2. Line casting
    a. Linotype
    b. Intertype
    c. Ludlow
3. Single character casting—Monotype
4. Line space casting—Elrod
5. Categories of hot-metal composition
    a. Foundry type
    b. Slug or line casting
    c. Single-character casting

Unit 30. Impact, Thermal, and Laser Imaging Systems

A. Objectives

Upon reading, defining the key terms, answering the study questions, and completing the one activity related to this unit, students should be able to

1. Recognize impact, thermal, and laser imaging systems and the machines that are used to produce these kinds of original images.

2. Explain the advantages and disadvantages of impact, thermal, and laser imaging methods.

3. Prepare some original imageset copy by one or all of these imaging systems—impact, thermal, and laser.

B. Instructor preparation

1. Obtain examples of impact, thermal, and laser imageset copy. Also, if possible, obtain printed copies of products known to have been imageset by each of these methods. Use these examples in your class presentations, or use them for display board presentation.

2. Obtain company advertising literature for each system—impact, thermal, and laser. Encourage students to review this material for a more thorough understanding of these important imagesetting methods.

C. Suggested teaching outline

1. Impact, thermal, and laser imaging systems
   a. Past use
   b. Present use
   c. Future use
2. Equipment for each system
   a. Regular typewriter
   b. Computer printers
   c. Interchangeable typeface typewriters
3. Justifying left and right margins
   a. Flush left and flush right
   b. Ragged right or left
4. Lettering machines

Unit 31. Dry-Transfer and Hand-Mechanical Type Composition

A. Objectives

Upon reading, defining the key terms, answering the study questions, and then completing the one activity relating to this unit, students should be able to

1. Recognize and use dry-transfer type composition.
2. Recognize and use hand-mechanical type composition.

B. Instructor preparation

1. Obtain several sheets of dry-transfer composition materials and have them available in the laboratory for student use.

2. Obtain catalogues from several dry-transfer composition manufacturers and have them available in the lab for students to review so they may become more acquainted with the different materials and kinds of type that are available with the dry-transfer method.

3. Obtain printed examples of products that have been composed via the dry-transfer and hand-mechanical type composition methods.

C. Suggested teaching outline

1. Dry-transfer and hand-mechanical type composition
   a. Past use
   b. Present use
2. Demonstration—Dry-transfer type composition
3. Demonstration—Hand-mechanical type composition

Unit 32. Photographic Type Composition

A. Objectives

Upon reading, defining the key terms, answering the study questions, and completing the one activity relating to this unit, students should be able to

1. Recognize and know the use of photographic composition.
2. Recognize and describe each of the four generations of photographic typesetting.
3. Distinguish between display and text photographic composition.
4. Operate a common brand of display photographic composition machine.
5. Process exposed phototypesetting paper.

B. Instructor preparation

1. Prepare the photographic composition device(s) which are available in your graphic arts laboratory so that students may begin using them immediately following the class or individual presentations.
2. Obtain and use DCA Educational Products transparencies *GA-53, A Photographic Composing Machine;* and *GA-54, An Electronic Composing Machine.*
3. Obtain examples of type composition from several brands and styles of photographic composition machines, both display and text. Use these examples in your class presentation and/or your classroom display board.

C. Suggested teaching outline

1. Photographic typesetting
   a. The principle
   b. Historical development
2. Four generations
   a. Mechanical
   b. Electromechanical
   c. Electronic
   d. Laser Imaging
3. Categories of phototypesetters
   a. Display
   b. Body
4. Using phototypesetters
   a. Basic parts
   b. Demonstration
5. Processing photocomposition
   a. Stabilization
   b. Regular photographic
6. Typographic Communication

Unit 33. Electronic Imagesetting

A. Objectives

Upon reading, defining the key terms, and answering the study questions, students should be able to

1. Recognize and describe third generation typesetting equipment.
2. Recognize and describe fourth generation typesetting equipment.
3. Describe an electronic publishing system.

B. Instructor preparation

1. Read another source, book or trade journal, to gain additional information about electronic image generation.

2. Visit a commercial graphic arts company that has a third or fourth generation typesetting system. Learn as much as possible about the equipment so you can better explain electronic image generation to your students.

3. Obtain commercial audio-visual materials which might be helpful in describing the concepts associated with electronic image generation.

4. Obtain typeset examples from both third and fourth generation typesetting equipment. Use these examples to compare regular photographic typesetting products.

C. Suggested teaching outline

1. Electronic image generation and computers

2. Third generation equipment
   a. Using the CRT (Cathode Ray Tube)
   b. Image lines formed by a roster scan
   c. Digitizing of images
   d. Typesetting speed very fast

3. Fourth generation equipment
   a. Using the laser to create images
   b. Type characters, artwork, halftones created
   c. Type sizes available—2 to 999 point
   d. Electronic publishing

SECTION 5
PROOFING TYPE COMPOSITION

Section Goal: To introduce students to the equipment and processes involved in proofing and proofreading type and image composition.

Section Description: This section is designed to emphasize proofing and proofreading, as well as the methods involved in doing both of these operations. Much of the time, students do not appreciate the importance of proofreading the image composition thoroughly prior to printing the copies, and to their dismay reproduce mistakes many times over.

Unit 35 has been designed to emphasize the importance of proofing and proofreading. Information about proofing relief type for both reading and reproduction proofs is provided in Unit 36. With Unit 37, equipment and procedures involved in proofing photographic and digital type are covered. Proofreading procedures are briefly presented in Unit 38 and step-by-step information on how to correct various methods of type and image composition are given in Unit 39. Each of these units is rather short. Therefore, you may desire to discuss and present more than one unit at each class session.

Study questions and suggested activities are provided in Unit 40 which is the Learning Experiences unit. Use these key terms, study questions, and activities to best serve your students in your own particular situation.

Unit 35. Introduction to Proofing

A. Objectives

Upon reading, defining the key terms, answering the study questions, and completing the one activity relating to this unit, students should be able to

1. Summarize the importance of quality proofing and proofreading in relationship to the final printed product.
2. Briefly review the historical development of the art of proofreading.

B. Instructor preparation

1. Talk with a local commercial printer and/or newspaper editor and determine the proofing and proofreading operations being performed in their firms. You may desire to obtain this information from several commercial firms with the thought of passing on your findings to the students. In this way, you would be able to present a practical illustration of proofing and proofreading in your own locality.
2. Consider obtaining and using the slide/audio series titled *Proofreading*, from the Graphic Arts Technical Foundation.

C. Suggested teaching outline

1. Proofing procedures
   a. The reading proof
   b. The reproduction proof
2. Proofreading
   a. Its importance
   b. Where and when done
   c. Historical development

Unit 36. Proofing Relief Type

A. Objectives

Upon reading, defining the key terms, answering the study questions, and completing the one activity relating to this unit, students should be able to

1. Recognize and briefly describe letterpress proof presses that are used for reading proofs, reproduction proofs, and four-color proofs.
2. Perform the tasks associated with making reading proofs from relief images.

B. Instructor preparation

1. Obtain several examples of reading proofs and reproduction proofs that have been pulled on letterpress proof presses. Commercial firms will be pleased to give you some assistance.
2. Prepare the proof presses that are available in your laboratory for the students to use immediately following your class presentation and demonstration.

C. Suggested teaching outline

1. Letterpress proof presses
   a. Hand operated
   b. Power operated
   c. Used for reading proofs
   d. Used for reproduction proofs
   e. Used for four-color proofs
2. Making reading proofs
   a. Preparing the proof press
   b. Inking the typeform
   c. Positioning the paper
   d. Pulling the proof
   e. Cleaning the typeform
   f. Cleaning the proof press

Unit 37. Proofing Photographic and Digital Type Composition

A. Objectives

Upon reading, defining the key terms, answering the study questions, and completing the two activities relating to this unit, students should be able to

1. Recognize and briefly describe copy input and continuous proofing procedures.
2. Use spell-check software to proof their keyboarded input.
3. Describe the limitations associated with spell-check software.
4. Perform the tasks associated with proofing and editing photographic and digital type composition.

B. Instructor preparation

1. Obtain reading proofs of photographic and digital type composition from commercial imagesetting companies to show to your students.
2. Build a file of brochures describing the latest equipment for proofing photographic and digital type composition. This should also include information on hard-copy proofing printers.
3. Make arrangements in your school to allow students to use an electrostatic copier to proof their photographic or digital imagesetting. This may be the department office or your top administrator's office. This may be encouragement for your administrator to purchase an electrostatic copier for your graphic arts laboratory.

C. Suggested teaching outline

1. Copy input and continuous proofing
   a. Inputting type and images
   b. WYSIWYG features
   c. Spell-check software

2. Proofing and editing procedure
   a. Set original images
   b. Make electrostatic copies
   c. Proofread the content
   d. Correct errors
   e. Send corrected proofs to the customer
3. Hard copy proofs
   a. Concept—why needed?
   b. Economic value
   c. Time-saving value

Unit 38. Proofreading Procedures

A. Objectives

Upon reading, defining the key terms, answering the study questions, and completing the two activities relating to this unit, students should be able to

1. Explain the responsibilities of the copyholder and the proofreader.
2. Review the basic qualifications of proofreaders and copyholders.
3. Utilize several of the common proofreading marks, without the example sheet.

B. Instructor preparation

1. Become familiar with and use several of the common proofreading marks during the process of evaluating student papers, thereby introducing the students to this technique.
2. Select six to twelve common proofreading marks which you desire your students to learn and use. Prepare overhead transparencies showing the meaning of the mark, with an example of each of these selected proofreading marks. Use these transparencies in your classroom presentation; hold the students responsible for learning these selected marks. See Appendix M, Visual Masters 5 and 6, for copies of proofreader's marks and examples of uses.

C. Suggested teaching outline

1. Proofreading—its major purpose
2. The proofreader
   a. Their responsibilities
   b. Their qualifications
3. The copyholder
   a. Their responsibilities
   b. Their qualifications
4. Proofreader's marks
   a. Purpose
   b. Selected examples

Unit 39. Correcting Type Composition

A. Objectives

Upon reading, defining the key terms, answering the study questions and completing the activity relating to this unit, the student should be able to

1. Perform the task of correcting the following kinds of type composition: foundry type, hot metal, impact, dry-transfer, hand-mechanical and photographic.
2. Recognize the importance of carefully preparing the original type composition.

B. Instructor preparation

This unit is primarily a "doing" unit; therefore, for demonstration purposes, it will be necessary for you to obtain the various examples of type composition and the associated supplies and tools necessary for demonstrating the proper correcting procedures for each of the illustrated methods of typesetting.

C. Suggested teaching outline

1. Time and cost involved in correcting type composition
2. Demonstration—Correcting foundry type composition
3. Demonstration—Correcting hot metal type composition
4. Demonstration—Correcting impact type composition
5. Demonstration—Correcting dry-transfer type composition
6. Demonstration—Correcting hand-mechanical type composition
7. Demonstration—Correcting photographic type composition

SECTION 6
COPY PREPARATION FOR PROCESS PHOTOGRPAHY

Section Goal: To provide the students with the knowledge and skills to prepare and use copy for the purpose of process photography.

Section Description: In most cases, students will not become accomplished copy preparation artists; but, they will be called upon to handle copy in several different ways. In some cases, they will be required to prepare simple copy that does not require a great deal of artistic talent. They will be given a sketch and be expected to paste-up copy, as described in the sketch. At other times they will be given copy with a description of what is to be done with the copy. They will have to be able to determine how to treat the copy photographically. It is imperative that students are able to understand how copy will react to photographic treatment so that they can explain the situation to the customer.

Beyond working with the customer, the student must know how to mark the copy so that the photographer will know precisely what to do with the copy. This is especially true when the copy is not in one unit, when enlargements or reductions must be made, or when special photographic treatments must be made. This section was prepared to help students gain enough experiences to help those students who will handle only copy, as well as for students who actually will prepare copy.

Unit 41. Introduction to Copy Preparation

A. Objectives

Upon completion of this unit, students should be able to

1. Either in oral or in written form give a description of copy to be used for photographic reproduction.
2. Describe the two major elements of a piece of copy (type matter and illustrations).

B. Instructor preparation

1. Gather several pieces of commercially prepared copy to use as examples with students.
2. It is suggested that students be encouraged to distinguish among line and continuous-tone elements in several pieces of copy.
3. Consider obtaining and using the following videotape from the GAT/GAERF Videotape Project: Number 004, *Basic Image Assembly (Paste-Up)*.
4. Consider obtaining and using the videotape titled *Pasteup*, from Sunshine Enterprises, Spokane, WA.

C. Suggested teaching outline

1. Define copy
   a. Color
      (1) Black and white
      (2) Red and white
   b. Exact duplicate of what is to be reproduced
      (1) Proportionate
      (2) Elements in exact location
   c. Elements
      (1) Line
      (2) Continuous-tone

2. Transforming customers' sketches to copy
   a. Questioning the customer
      (1) Paper
      (2) Ink
      (3) Purpose of the product
   b. Printing process to be used

Unit 42. Equipment and Materials for Copy Preparation

A. Objectives

As a result of completing the unit and receiving the demonstration related to the unit, students should be able to

1. Identify the typical equipment required by an artist to produce a variety of kinds of copy.
2. Select the appropriate material and equipment to produce a specific kind of effect.

B. Instructor preparation

1. Collect various kinds of background material to demonstrate how:
   a. Various kinds of effects can be obtained
   b. Color differences among background material
   c. Layout sheets
2. Select drawing instruments that will be available to students in the laboratory, such as:
   a. Boards
   b. T-squares and triangles
   c. Instruments
   d. Curves
   e. Pencils (blue and sketching)
   f. Inking pens
   g. Brushes
3. Obtain materials and equipment required to fasten elements to copy
   a. Tape
   b. Cement
   c. Waxing machine
4. Identify other items used in copy preparation
   a. Paints
   b. Charcoal or chalk
   c. Masking film
   d. Knives

C. Suggested teaching outline

It is suggested that the instructor present a series of short demonstrations to help the students see the purpose and results obtained from using the various materials and equipment identified in this unit. Individual situations will determine whether the instructor will want students to practice with the materials and equipment at the time of the demonstration or later. If possible, the instructor should let at least one or two students use the material or equipment—this will help to stimulate interest and hold student attention.

1. Background for copy
   a. Color
   b. Weights
   c. Surfaces
   d. Layout sheets

2. Drawing equipment
   a. Board or drawing surfaces
   b. T-square and triangles—drawing machines
   c. Instruments
   d. Rules and scales
   e. Curves
   f. Pencils
      (1) Blue
      (2) Sketching
   g. Inking pens
   h. Paint brushes
   i. Airbrush
3. Attaching elements
   a. Double-surface tape
   b. Waxing machine
   c. Rubber cement

Unit 43. Kinds of Copy

A. Objectives

Activities and experiences related to this unit should lead students to be able to distinguish clearly between line copy and continuous-tone copy.

B. Instructor preparation

Preparation for helping students learn to distinguish between line and continuous-tone copy (or element) is similar to Unit 44. The instructor should have numerous examples of both line and halftone copy. Line copy examples are much easier to obtain, since printed items can be used; but, continuous-time copy must be original, if students are to be able to distinguish between line and continuous-tone. There is a tendency to use only photographs as continuous-tone copy; but every attempt should be made to secure other examples like pencil drawings, charcoal sketches, and watercolors.

1. Obtain examples of line copy. Use original copy when available.
   a. Type matter
   b. Industrial drawings
   c. Scratch board
   d. Block prints
   e. Reversals
   f. Screen tints
2. Secure examples of continuous-tone copy
   a. Photographs
   b. Pencil and charcoal drawings or sketches
   c. Airbrush renderings
   d. Wash or watercolor drawings
3. Combination copy which includes both continuous-tone and line copy.
4. Consider obtaining and using the slide/audio series titled *Prepress Production*, from the Graphic Arts Technical Foundation.

C. Suggested teaching outline

The teaching outline is implied by reading the unit, but the teaching technique is more critical. While students' exposure to various kinds of copy is essential, they must have the opportunity to make individual decisions from among several pieces of copy. In some cases, students can be given copy with both line and continuous-tone elements on the copy. Students could be asked to identify the kind of copy represented by each element.

1. Line copy
   a. Type matter
   b. Inked drawings
   c. Scratch board
   d. Block print
   e. Screen tints
2. Reversal
   a. Artist prepared
   b. Photographically accomplished
3. Combination of line and halftone

Unit 44. Copy Considerations

A. Objectives

From reading this unit and engaging in appropriate related activities, students will be able to

1. Describe the results of enlarging and reducing copy.
2. Identify and use appropriate techniques for protecting copy.
3. Systematically and accurately check copy prior to photography.

B. Instructor preparation

1. Obtain printed examples of a single piece of copy that has been reduced and enlarged to show problems of distortion and clarity.
2. Prepare diagram to show the effects of enlargement and reductions (see Fig. 44-2 in the textbook).
3. Secure copy that has protection or a cover in place.
4. Obtain a piece of copy without a cover attached, so that attaching a cover can be demonstrated.
5. Prepare copy with errors for students to identify. Include such problems as misaligned lines, spelling errors, and crooked lines. It would be desirable if the student could compare the copy with the customer sketch.

C. Suggested teaching outline

As with the previous unit, student learning should occur as a result of exposure to examples. When possible, student experiences should include situations in which students can engage in activity or decision making.

1. Size of copy
   a. Results of enlargement
   b. Results of reduction
2. Protecting copy
   a. Purpose
      (1) Damage
      (2) Soiled
   b. Overlay sheet
      (1) Method of attaching
      (2) Protection
      (3) Holes
   c. Handling
      (1) Copy
      (2) Photographs
      (3) Technique

3. Checking the final copy
   a. Procedure
   b. Proofread
   c. Image damage
   d. Completeness
   e. Straight elements
   f. Parallel lines
   g. Accurate placement of elements

Unit 45. Cropping, Scaling, and Register Marks

A. Objectives

Students, after reading and completing the activities related to this unit, will be able to

1. Determine the areas of photographs to be cropped.
2. Make crop marks, using two different techniques.
3. Accurately scale copy, using the "proportioned rule method," "mathematical formula technique," and the "diagonal line technique."
4. Precisely specify reductions and enlargements, utilizing proper notation methods.
5. Recognize the register mark on copy.

B. Instructor preparation

1. Obtain several photographs on which students can practice cropping. The photographs should include a wide variety of subjects so that students will have to make decisions about the best location for cropping. The instructor might want to use the overlay technique to crop the photographs before the students crop them. Students can compare their decisions with the instructor decisions.
2. Secure a sifficient number of grease pencils and quantity of overlay material for the student to use in cropping the photographs.
3. Collect a proportional scale to use as an example for the students. It would be helpful if there were enough rules for every two or three students.
4. Have several pieces of copy with various kinds of notes to the cameraman. These can be used by students to practice scaling copy. When possible, have students use real examples rather than abstract problems.
5. Obtain and use DCA Education Products transparencies *GA-9, Enlargements and Reductions: Diagonal Line*; and *GA-10, Enlargements and Reductions: Proportional Scale*.
6. Secure several examples of register marks tht students can use to place on copy. The instructor also should have copy on which the students can place the register marks. This can be accomplished by printing both colors of a two-color job with black ink and without register marks.

C. Suggested teaching outline

1. Cropping
   a. Selecting the appropriate area
   b. Marking crop marks on the copy
   c. Cropping a photograph by the overlay technique
   d. Marking the appropriate size
2. Scaling copy
   a. Proportioned rule technique
   b. Mathematical formula technique
   c. Diagonal line technique

3. Specifying reduction and enlargement
   a. Actual size
   b. Percentage
4. Register marks
   a. Purpose
   b. Kinds of marks
   c. Placement of the marks

Unit 46. Making the Paste-Up

A. Objectives

As a result of the information included in Unit 46 and from the student experiences used to reinforce the unit, students will be able to effectively prepare paste-ups for photographic reproduction, including:

1. Selecting correct size and kind of material for the base.
2. Treatment of illustration not attached directly to the paste-up.
3. Satisfactorily attaching elements to the paste-up.

B. Instructor preparation

1. Secure the elements that will be used to demonstrate the paste-up technique. These would include:
   a. Several kinds of base material
   b. Paste-up elements including type material and illustrations. At least one illustration should be inappropriate for use on the paste-up, because of its size of the value of the illustration.
2. Obtain the equipment and materials needed to make the paste-up, and demonstrate treatment of illustrations that will not fit on the paste-up.
   a. Light table
   b. Drawing instruments (T-squares, triangles, scales, etc.)
   c. Knives to cut elements to size
   d. Blue pencils
   e. Double-surface tape
   f. Rubber cement
   g. Waxing machine, if possible
   h. Material for cover sheet
   i. Inking pens
   j. Material, either black or red, to demonstrate the block method illustration treatment
3. Have an example of a paste-up, negative of the paste-up, and print of the pate-up to help the student recognize the kind of reproduction that can be obtained from a paste-up.
4. Consider obtaining and using the slide/audio series titled *Paste-Up Techniques*, from the Graphic Arts Technical Foundation.

C. Suggested teaching outline

1. Purpose of making a paste-up
   a. Economy
   b. Special effects
2. Determine the size of the base
   a. Determine the final desired printed size
   b. Establish the reduction enlargement
   c. Cut the base to size

3. Secure the elements
   a. Kinds of elements
      (1) Type matter
      (2) Illustrations
   b. Consider enlargement or reduction
   c. Scale items not attached to the copy
4. Treatment of photographs on copy
   a. Block method
   b. Outline method
   c. Prescreened halftone method
5. Attaching the elements
   a. Waxing
   b. Taping
   c. Cementing

Unit 47. Copy Division for Multi-Color Reproduction

A. Objectives

By completing the reading material and related activities, students will be able to

1. Distinguish between process-color and mechanical-color printing.
2. Describe the processes required to produce color separations.
3. Explain the differences between reflection and transmission copy.
4. Illustrate various methods of producing mechanical-color copy, so that accurate registration can be obtained.

B. Instructor preparation

1. Obtain several examples of printed materials that have used the color techniques. These should include process-color items of several qualities (fine books to quick-and-dirty newspaper items) and mechanical-color illustrations. While there are some examples of mechanical-color illustrations in the textbooks, interest and expanded understanding of other situations will be increased if other samples are collected.
2. Identify examples of photographs and other illustrations that could be used for either transmission or reflection copy. If you consult some printing companies, they may have a complete set of materials (copy, separations, and print) that they would permit you to use for illustrating process-color work.
3. A set of colors, yellow, magenta, and cyan should be available for students to examine (see Unit 60). Color patches also are printed on the edge of sheets, and these can be obtained from almost any printer who does process-color work.
4. Obtain and use DCA Education Products transparency *GA-65, Color Separations*.

C. Suggested teacher outline

The textbook introduces process-color first and mechanical copy last. Some instructors may prefer to approach the topic in the reverse order. It is sometimes easier for students to approach mechanical-color before working with process-color, because of the more complicated detail. However, since this unit deals only with copy preparation, the more complicated aspects of process-color will occur later, when students treat the copy photographically.

1. Define multi-color printing
   a. More-than-one-color ink
   b. Process-color
      (1) Photographs
      (2) Transparencies
      (3) Drawings
   c. Mechanical—prepared by the artist

2. Explain process-color (DCA Educational Products transparency *GA-65*)
   a. Photographs through filters
      (1) Reflection
      (2) Transmission
   b. Explain, by illustration, that three or four negatives are produced from the copy-called separations
   c. Each separation is printed with different color
      (1) Yellow
      (2) Magenta
      (3) Cyan
      (4) Black

3. Mechanical-color copy instructors may want to approach this portion of the unit differently. This will depend on the depth of understanding and skill expected of students. That is, some instructors will want students to be familiar enough with mechanical-color copy, so they can deal with copy photographically. Others will want the student actually to be able to prepare copy. It is assumed that in either case the instructor will become familiar enough and skilled enough, with the methods explained in the text, to demonstrate how each is accomplished. This "does not" mean that the instructor must do the actual artwork; but he/she should illustrate the steps necessary to accomplish the printed product. The outline below will relate to the operations the instructor must do to make sure the various methods are printed correctly. Instructors may want to explain other methods not included in the text.
   a. Masking
      (1) Produce or have available one negative of a piece of copy
      (2) Place the negative on a golden rod
      (3) Block off the items to be printed with the second color
      (4) Make a plate of the first color printer (You may want to have this already done)
      (5) Remove the masking material
      (6) Mask off the items included in the first printer
      (7) Make a plate of the second printer
      (8) It would be extremely helpful if you have available a printed copy of the plate—print of color #1, print of color #2, and print of colors #1 and #2.
   b. Overlays—one color must overlap another.
      (1) Primary illustration on heavy illustration board
      (2) Second color on tracing paper
      (3) Two pieces must match perfectly when they are in contact
      (4) Registration accomplished by register marks
      (5) All elements are either black and white or red and white
   c. Key line—The instructor should have two negatives of a key-line illustration prepared before the demonstration.
      (1) Purpose of a key-line for colors that must butt with other colors.
      (2) Follow the procedure shown in Unit 47.

Unit 48. Notes and Instructions to the Printer

A. Objectives

After completing this unit, students will

1. Be able to explain the importance of accurate notes for copy.
2. Know the kind of information to be included with copy.
3. Know and be able to use appropriate techniques for making notes on copy.

B. Instructor preparation

This unit is an information unit, but it is important that students be involved actively rather than passively. One way to do this is to print some sample pieces of copy on which students can actually make some notes.

1. Sample pieces of copy for students
2. Examples of "job tickets," such as the one shown in Fig 48-3, could be duplicated for students to complete.

C. Suggested teacher outline

1. Importance of accurate notes and instructions to the printer
    a. Describes what is to be done and how
    b. Common source of errors
    c. Waste of time to keep gathering information
2. Personal data
    a. Name of customer
    b. Address and telephone number of customer
    c. Person to consult for additional questions
    d. Delivery address
3. Technical data (examples)
    a. Size
    b. Special photographic treatment
    c. Location of copy items (when stored separately)
    d. Kind of paper
    e. Color(s) of ink
    f. Finishing operator
4. Methods of making notes and instructions
    a. Directly on copy
    b. Notes attached to copy
    c. Notes on envelope in which copy is placed.

SECTION 7
PROCESS CAMERAS AND DARKROOM PROCEDURES

Section Goal: To permit students to become familiar with darkroom equipment, materials, and procedures and to be able to perform common darkroom activities.

Section Description: This section was organized to include topics which students must know to function adequately in the darkroom with process photography activities. Emphasis has been placed on black-and-white photography, with only a very brief introduction to process-color reproduction. It is expected that students will be able to become proficient in the areas of producing line negatives, halftones, contacts and diffusion transfer positives. Students also should become knowledgeable about the aspects of efficient darkroom management procedures.

Process photograph was viewed by the authors to be a graphic arts activity that would apply to several printing processes. That is, the knowledge gained from this section should apply to lithography, letterpress, screen process, etc. The instructor should help, by using examples, the students see this broad application of process photography.

Unit 50. Introduction to Process Cameras and Darkroom Procedures

A. Objectives

After completing this unit, students will be able to

1. Identify the various parts of a process camera.
2. Describe the purpose of a process camera.

B. Instructor preparation

1. Obtain DCA Education Products transparencies *GA-17, A Horizontal Process Camera; GA-18, Enlarging and Reducing with a Process Camera; GA-57, A Vertical Process Camera;* and *GA-58, Process Camera Focal Length.*
2. Prepare your camera so that you can show the students the various parts and how each part operates.
3. Consider obtaining and using the following two videotapes from the GAT/GAERF Videotape Project: Number 007, *An Introduction to Camera Work (Line Photography)*, and Number 020, *Advanced Camera Work.*
4. Consider obtaining and using the videotape titled *Basic Camera*, from Sunshine Enterprises, Spokane, WA.

C. Suggested teaching outline

1. Purpose of process cameras
   a. Photograph flat copy
   b. Make precise enlargements and reductions
2. Parts of a camera
   a. Lens
      (1) Expensive
      (2) Sensitive
   b. Lens parts
      (1) Barrel
      (2) Diaphragm
         (a) Produces aperture opening
         (b) F-stops—collar

(3) Elements

(4) Manual diaphragm control

(5) Cover—emphasize need to keep covered

c. Shutter

(1) Electrical

(2) No shutter light controlled by timer

d. Bellows

(1) Light-tight closure between front case and camera back

(2) Compresses and stretches

(3) Easily damaged

(4) Need to be inspected periodically

e. Camera back—located in darkroom

(1) Holds film accurate distance from lens

(2) Vacuum back most popular

(3) Frequently a door

(4) Ground-glass focusing plate

f. Copyboard

(1) Attached to rail or track

(2) Holds the copy

(3) Copy pressed against inside of glass

(4) Most copyboards rotate for loading

(5) Moves back and forth on the rail

g. Lights

(1) Incandescent

(2) Quartz

(3) Pulsed xenon

(4) Adjustable with copyboard

(5) Lights the copy

Unit 51. Classifications of Process Cameras

A. Objectives

As a result of completing this unit, students will be able to

1. Distinguish between horizontal and vertical cameras.

2. Explain the appropriate use of both the horizontal and vertical process cameras.

3. List advantages and disadvantages of both the horizontal and vertical process cameras.

B. Instructor preparation

1. Obtain DCA Education Products transparencies *GA-17, A Horizontal Process Camera* and *GA-57, A Vertical Process Camera*.

2. Prepare the process camera for a demonstration to the students.

3. The instructor may want to combine Units 50 and 51 into one lesson because they are closely related.

4. Consider obtaining and using the slide/audio series titled *Introduction to the Process Camera*, from the Graphic Arts Technical Foundation.

C. Suggested teaching outline

1. Gallery and darkroom cameras

a. Gallery cameras

(1) Located entirely in lighted room

(2) Film placed in film-holder in the darkroom

        (3) Difficult to use because of film loading

        (4) Advantage is that it does not utilize darkroom space

    b. Darkroom cameras

        (1) Located entirely in darkroom

            (a) Exposures cannot be made while developing film

            (b) Uses darkroom space

            (c) Sometimes placed in adjacent room

            (d) Can more effectively control external light

        (2) Camera back only in darkroom

            (a) Can develop film and expose at the same time

            (b) Requires less darkroom space

            (c) Camera operator must leave darkroom to change copy

  2. Horizontal and vertical cameras

    a. Horizontal cameras

        (1) Operate in horizontal position (line of exposure)

        (2) How darkroom and light room parts differ

            (a) Camera back in darkroom

            (b) Front case, lens-board, and copy-board in light room

        (3) Can be placed entirely in the darkroom

        (4) Requires more space than vertical, but less darkroom

    b. Vertical camera

        (1) Line of exposure is vertical

        (2) Used in darkroom

        (3) Can use film loader in light room

        (4) Has more size limitations than horizontal

        (5) Requires more darkroom floor space than horizontal camera

        (6) Requires less total floor space than a horizontal camera

Unit 52. Films and Chemicals for Process Photography

A. Objectives

After completing the activities for this unit, students will be able to

1. Describe, orally and pictorially, the different parts of a piece of film.
2. Distinguish between panchromatic, orthochromatic, and silverless film.
3. Explain the correct procedures for handling and storing film.
4. Identify the common chemicals and explain their purpose.

B. Instructor preparation

This unit is planned merely to acquaint students with film and chemicals and their storage location. Many instructors will use a tour for the purpose of teaching chemicals and find that it will have to be repeated for most students after they actually begin to work in the darkroom.

1. Become familiar with the terminology associated with film, chemicals, and the handling of chemicals.
2. Collect samples of film, both exposed and unexposed, to show students.
3. Be sure your film and chemicals are stored in the proper way for illustrating to students.
4. Obtain and use DCA Education Products transparency *GA-16, High Contrast Photographic Film.*

C. Suggested teaching outline

1. Structure of film

    a. Base

        (1) Supports light-sensitive emulsion

       (2) Transparent or translucent
       (3) Acetate, polyester, glass, paper
       (4) Dimensional stability
       (5) Thickness
           (a) Thin—0.0035 in.
           (b) Regular—0.005 in.
           (c) Thick—0.007 in.

  b. Silver emulsion film
     (1) Light-sensitive
     (2) Silver halides
     (3) Turn black when exposed to light and developed

  c. Overcoat
     (1) Thin layer of clear gelatin
     (2) Prevent scratching

  d. Antihalation backing
     (1) A dye applied to base slide
     (2) Prevents light from reflecting back to the emulsion
     (3) Absorbs the light that presses through the emulsion
     (4) Removed from the film during development

3. Anticurl

2. Kinds of film

  a. Blue sensitive film
     (1) Sensitive to blue light
     (2) Used to copy black and white photographs
     (3) Used to duplicate halftone negatives

  b. Panchromatic film
     (1) Sensitive to all colors
     (2) Used for copy with multiple colors
     (3) Develops in total darkness

  c. Orthochromatic
     (1) Sensitive to blue, green, yellow
     (2) Insensitive to red
     (3) Used for photographing black and white or red and white
     (4) Can be developed in red light
     (5) Light—blue guidelines can be used without erasing

  d. Silverless film
     (1) Diazo emulsion
     (2) Processed in ammonia
     (3) Handled in subdued light
     (4) Used for making duplicate negatives and positives

  e. Rapid access film
     (1) Made for fast processing
     (2) Best for line photography

  f. Contacting film
     (1) Used to make contact reproductions
     (2) Not influenced as much by processing

  g. Duplicating film
     (1) Used to make exact copies of negatives or positives

3. Handling film
   a. Extremely delicate and sensitive
   b. Temperature and humidity
      (1) Best storage temperature is 68° to 75°F
      (2) Best humidity 40% to 50%
      (3) Some unused film stored in refrigerator
   c. Pressure
      (1) Causes fogging
      (2) Scratches
      (3) Store on edges
   d. Handling
      (1) Handle by edges to avoid fingerprints
      (2) Have hands dry
      (3) Be sure surfaces are clean
      (4) Always put film down with base side down
      (5) Don't slide film
      (6) Keep Package Closed
4. Chemicals
   a. Chemical produce visual latent image
   b. Developer
      (1) Changes latent image (exposed silver salts) to black metallic silver
      (2) Alkaline or basic solution
      (3) Most developers have parts A & B
      (4) Mixed immediately before development
      (5) Short life of developer after mixing
   c. Rinse bath
      (1) Sometimes called "stop bath"
      (2) Weak acetic acid or clear water
      (3) Removes developer solution before mixing
   d. Fixing solution
      (1) Also called "fixer" or "hypo"
      (2) Removes undeveloped silver salt
      (3) Fixer must be washed from the film

Unit 53. Darkrooms

A. Objectives

As a result of the reading materials, activities, and questions, students will be able to

1. Name common darkroom equipment.
2. Describe several darkroom arrangements.
3. Identify the essential aspects of darkroom cleanliness.

B. Instructor preparation

This unit is planned to be an informational unit and does not imply much student activity. Most instructors will want students to become totally familiar with the equipment located in their respective laboratories; but, other pieces of equipment and darkroom plans should be discussed to extend student understanding of the darkroom beyond the local facilities or situation.

1. Prepare darkroom equipment for demonstration and tour.
2. Study aspects of the unit and be prepared to discuss equipment not available in the darkroom and to help students understand other darkroom plans and organization.

3. The instructor might want to plan examples, such as light leaks, dried chemicals, etc. This will help students understand the necessity of cleanliness in the darkroom. Negatives with pin holes also will illustrate the result of a dirty darkroom.

C. Suggested teaching outline

1. Darkroom equipment
   a. Sinks
      (1) Source of water
      (2) Location of chemicals
      (3) Steel or fiberglass
      (4) Some have temperature control
      (5) Some have other features like:
         (a) Inspection lights
         (b) Storage
         (c) Refrigeration
   b. Water mixers
      (1) Mixed hot and cold
      (2) Control water with constant temperature $\pm\frac{1}{2}°$ or $\pm\frac{1}{4}°$
   c. Processing trays
      (1) Hold chemicals
      (2) Trays should be larger than film
      (3) Not too large—extra chemicals
      (4) Made from plastic, fiberglass, stainless steel.
   d. Thermometers
      (1) Delicate
      (2) Different sizes and accuracy
   e. Safelights
      (1) Red with orthochromatic film
      (2) Locate where most activity
      (3) Best to use special safelight rather than red bulbs
   f. Graduates, beakers, pails, funnels
      (1) Used for mixing, measuring, and pouring chemicals
      (2) Available in various sizes
      (3) Made of plastic, stainless steel, rubber, etc.
   g. Storage containers
      (1) Hold chemicals
      (2) Should be dark—prevent light from access to chemicals
      (3) Need at least one for each kind of chemical
      (4) Containers must be marked clearly
   h. Timers
      (1) Several operations require timer
      (2) Should have luminous dial
      (3) Buzzer and automatic reset
   i. Contact printers
      (1) Make same size contact reproductives
      (2) Large enough for largest reproduction
      (3) Quality ranges from pressure contact to vacuum pressure
   j. Light source
      (1) Contact printing
      (2) Halftone flashing

        (3) Point source
    k. Inspection lights
        (1) Examine negatives
        (2) Equipped with red and white light
        (3) Some sinks have inspection lights
2. Darkroom arrangements
    a. Essential features
        (1) Light-tight
        (2) Large enough for freedom of work
        (3) Ability to enter and leave without disturbing activities
        (4) Sink's temperature controls of hot and cold running water
        (5) Supply of fresh, clean air—air conditioner helpful
        (6) Sufficient electrical outlets
        (7) Complete storage
        (8) White-light and safelights
    b. Making the darkroom light-tight
        (1) Darkrooms must be DARK
        (2) Must check for light leaks
        (3) Should be regular schedule for checking
    c. Darkroom plans
        (1) Work flow
            (a) Distance between operations
            (b) Make as compact as possible without crowding
        (2) Storage and work space
            (a) Must be kept clean
            (b) Large enough for equipment and materials
        (3) Electrical outlets
            (a) About every 5 feet
            (b) Enough circuits to prevent overloading
        (4) Darkroom doors
            (a) Must prevent light from entering the darkroom
            (b) Light trap
                1. Two or more passages
                2. Uses a lot of space
            (c) Double doors
                1. Go through one door while other door is closed
                2. Does not use as much space as light traps
            (d) Revolving doors
                1. Two cylinders
                2. One revolves inside the other with one opening
                3. Second door has two or more openings
3. Multiple darkrooms
    a. Three activities accomplished in darkroom
        (1) Total darkness
        (2) Processing red-safe materials
        (3) Exposing materials with white light
    b. By having multiple darkrooms, several operations can be in process
    c. These darkrooms usually adjacent for movement among them

4. Darkroom cleanliness
   a. Major problem
   b. Can enter from outside
   c. Chemical from within
   d. Requires constant attention
   e. Regular cleaning schedule
   f. Fill light leaks—also dirt leaks
   g. Develop proper attitude

Unit 54. Safety in the Darkroom

A. Objectives

Students will understand and practice safe procedures while working in the darkroom.

B. Instructor preparation

This unit can be integrated with Unit 53 or spread throughout the course. In fact, it is an aspect that needs constant reinforcement. Preparation for the unit includes reviewing safety procedures to be emphasized at the appropriate times during the darkroom tours and demonstrations.

C. Suggested teaching outline

1. Darkness
   a. Become familiar with equipment, materials, and darkroom arrangement
   b. Let eyes become adjusted to darkness
2. Chemicals
   a. Irritates some persons' skins and hands
   b. Avoid handling in darkness
   c. Always wash thoroughly after use
3. Moisture
   a. Falls
   b. Electrical shock
4. Chemical storage
   a. Easily reached
   b. Safe containers
5. Electrical equipment
   a. Grounded
   b. Place away from moisture

Unit 55. Exposing and Processing a Line Negative

A. Objectives

Students as a result of completing the activities related to this unit will be able to

1. Prepare the darkroom for making a line negative.
2. Establish camera standards for making line negatives.
3. Expose and develop a line negative.

B. Instructor preparation

This unit shuld help students learn to make line negatives. Depending on the goals and length of your course, students should be introduced to the procedure required to establish darkroom standards for making line negatives. Some instructors may prefer to begin activities by using existing standards and introduce standarization procedures after students have engaged in activities. If this is done, the instructor should select the appropriate portions of the unit for students to study.

1. Review procedures for establishing conditions for making line negatives.
2. Be sure there are adequate materials available for the demonstration(s).
3. Check the camera, timer light, etc., to be sure they are in proper working order.
4. Obtain DCA Education Products transparencies *GA-19, Developing High Contrast Film*; *GA-56, Photographic Film and Light*; *GA-59, Reproduction of Line Copy*; and *GA-60, Exposure and Development Comparisons of Line Copy*.
5. Consider obtaining and using the slide/audio series titled *Photographic Film Processing-Tray Method*, from the Graphic Arts Technical Foundation.

The information covered in this unit is complex and lengthy enough that there is justification for using multiple class periods for presenting and demonstrating. It might be helpful to plan demonstrations so that ones which can be done in white light are accomplished in larger groups and those required in the darkroom can be done in smaller groups. The instructor should plan activites for remaining students when working with small groups in the darkroom (this is a time when problems could occur).

Organize and plan specific activities for students to accomplish while demonstrations are in progress. These should be productive activities, such as copy preparation, or group tasks that require a product to be accomplished.

C. **Suggested teaching outline**
  1. Prepare the darkroom
     a. Surfaces
        (1) Work surfaces
        (2) Copyboard
        (3) Lens
        (4) Camera backs
        (5) Clean entire camera
     b. Prepare sinks and chemicals
     c. Tray arrangement
        (1) Film processing flow
        (2) Don't move over another tray
        (3) Sequence
           (a) Developer
           (b) Stop bath
           (c) Fixer
           (d) Wash
     d. Prepare develop
        (1) Part A in tray
        (2) Part B in beaker
        (3) Mix immediately before developing
        (4) Discard after use or about 1 hour
     e. Stop bath
        (1) Could be clean water
        (2) Some use acetic acid solution—8 ounces of 28% acetic acid to 1 gallon of water
        (3) Commercially prepared indicator stop bath
     f. Fixer
        (1) Place in tray one-half to two-thirds full
        (2) Reuse fixer
        (3) Discard only when exhausted—does not clear milky areas in about 1½ minutes
     g. Temperature
        (1) Maintained by constant flow of water
        (2) Water should be at the desired temperature—68°F

2. Adjust the camera
   a. Basic camera adjustments
      (1) Time
      (2) Lens
      (3) Enlargement
   b. Identify basic exposure time
      (1) Variables
         (a) Kind of film
         (b) Developer mixture
         (c) Temperature
         (d) Time
         (e) Copy conditions
         (f) Camera lens
         (g) Lighting
         (h) Enlargement
      (2) Attempt to control variables
      (3) Procedure (see textbook Unit 55—"Adjust the Camera" for detailed procedure)
3. Place copy on copyboard
   a. Place copy in center of copyboard (image area of the copy)
   b. Place copy upside down in the copyboard
4. Locate the film
   a. Be sure lights are turned off
   b. Film must be where image is projected—use the center of the vacuum back
   c. Emulsion side should be toward lens—base side against vacuum back
   d. Show how to determine emulsion side
      (1) Usually the lightest color
      (2) Sometimes the dull side
      (3) Panchromatic film will have notches
5. Develop film
   a. Make latent image visible
   b. Process sequence
      (1) Developer
      (2) Stop bath
      (3) Fixer
      (4) Wash
   c. Development methods
      (1) Time-temperature
         (a) Develop for specific length of time
         (b) Must have constant temperature
         (c) Difficult, because of short developer life
      (2) Visual inspection
         (a) Film observed during development
         (b) Requires experience
         (c) Easy to make errors
      (3) Gray scale
         (a) Most accurate
         (b) Observe gray scale during development
         (c) Accounts for variations in time, temperature, developer strength, and copy quality and detail.

(d) Gray scale placed on copy during exposure

(e) When film is developed, the fourth step will be black—with a gray image in the fifth step.

(f) Adjustments made for the kind and quality of copy

(4) Development procedure—see the specific procedure shown in the portion of Unit 55 called "Develop the Film."

Unit 56. Exposure Calculations for a Halftone Negative

A. Objectives

As a result of studying this unit, completing activities, and answering the questions at the end of the units, students will be able to

1. Define and describe what is meant by halftone.
2. Identify copy that should be printed as halftone.
3. Compute halftone negative exposures.
4. Calibrate the *Kodak Halftone Negative Computer*.
5. Use the *Kodak Halftone Negative Computer* to compute exposure times for continuous-tone copy.

B. Instructor preparation

This unit may be one of the most difficult to teach and will probably require repeated review throughout the course. Students should be given several opportunities to utilize the *Kodak Halftone Negative Computer*. The production of halftone negatives is a much more precise and complicated procedure than line photography, and the instructor should work to help students develop an attitude about working with precision and accuracy. Many instructors prefer to introduce halftone photography only after students become quite proficient in working with line photography. One technique used by instructors is to have several groups complete the standardization process and then compare the results of the groups.

1. Obtain *Kodak Halftone Negative Computer*. If possible, try to have a computer for every two or three students.
2. Obtain and use DCA Education Products transparencies *GA-61, Halftone Negative Dot Percentages; GA-62, Halftone Screens; GA-63, Continuous Tone Copy;* and *GA-64, Using the Contact Screen.*
3. Have several examples of continuous-tone copy available.
4. Be sure a contact screen is available.
5. Check equipment and materials.
   a. Chemicals
   b. Timers
   c. Camera
   d. Lights—camera and flashing lamps
   e. Thermometers
6. Prepare water temperature ahead of time.
7. Consider obtaining and using the slide/audio series titled *Introduction to the Halftone Process*, from the Graphic Arts Technical Foundation.

C. Suggested teaching outline

1. Printing continuous-tone copy
   a. Print black or nothing
   b. Optical illusion by using dots
      (1) Small dots produce gray
      (2) Larger dots yield darker image

2. Methods
   a. Glass screen
      (1) Oldest method
      (2) Two pieces of glass with lines
      (3) Obsolete method
      (4) Used for extremely fine quality
      (5) Expensive
   b. Contact screens
      (1) Most widely used method
      (2) Screen in contact with film
      (3) Vignetted dots
      (4) Inexpensive
   c. "Autoscreen" film
      (1) Dot formation built into film
      (2) Does not require a screen for exposure
      (3) Not as flexible
      (4) Shorter exposure time
      (5) Does not require a vacuum back
3. Nature of continuous-tone copy
   a. Lightest areas called "highlights"
   b. Darkest areas called "shadows"
   c. Gray tones called "middle tones"
   d. Printing process is not able to produce total range
   e. To be able to produce detail in both the shadow and highlight areas, the tonal range is "compressed"
4. Computing halftone negative exposures
   a. Kodak Halftone Negative Computer used to obtain correct exposure
   b. Exposure Computer parts
      (1) Reflection Density Guide—calibrated gray scale
      (2) Exposure Computer
   c. Exposure Computer calibrated by test negatives of the Reflection Density Guide to conditions of the equipment and materials
   d. Conditions that must remain constant in the test exposure and all other exposures are:
      (1) Camera lens
      (2) Screen
      (3) Lighting
      (4) Temperature
      (5) Development time
      (6) Agitation
   e. When any of these change, the computer must be calibrated again.
5. Calibrating the computer

   Follow the outline given in Unit 56—the topic called "Calibrating the Computer." While the instructor should demonstrate this process, he/she also should have the students accomplish the process. It will help them understand the purpose and use the Kodak Halftone Negative Computer.
6. Using the computer

   Use the procedure outlined in the textbook in Unit 56 called "Using the Computer." Students can do this using several examples of continuous-tone copy. They can compare their results after computations have been made. Students should be permitted to make a halftone negative to test the accuracy of the computer standardization (this can be done in small groups to save time).

Unit 57. Exposing and Processing a Halftone Negative

A. Objectives

Upon completing the unit activities and answering the questions, students will be able to

1. Determine exposure times for making halftone negatives from a variety of continuous-tone examples.
2. Make a halftone negative to faithfully reproduce the continuous-tone copy.

B. Instructor preparation

This unit is a follow-up of Unit 56 and is planned to help students apply the knowledge gained from Unit 56. In certain cases, some instructors may want to use this unit prior to Unit 56. This would permit students to make halftone negatives and become encouraged prior to engaging in the complicated details of calibrating the computer.

1. Secure a correctly calibrated Kodak Halftone Negative Computer. The standardization data should be attached to the computer.
2. Review the procedure for making a halftone negative.
3. Obtain continuous-tone copy to be used by students.
4. Consider obtaining and using the slide/audio series titled *Making Halftones with the Contact Screen* from the Graphic Arts Technical Foundation.

C. Suggested teaching outline

1. Determine exposure time
   a. Can be determined in lighted room
   b. Write down the calculations as shown in Unit 56 examples
   c. Compare copy to Reflection Density Guide (57-1)
      (1) Identify highlight areas
      (2) Find shadow areas
   d. Determine the kind of contact screen
      (1) Magenta
      (2) Gray
   e. Obtain a calibrated Kodak Halftone Negative Computer
   f. Follow the procedure in the textbook to determine exposures
      (1) Main
      (2) Flash
2. Prepare the darkroom
   a. Duplicate conditions used to standardize the computer
   b. Arrange trays as for line negative
   c. Prepare the developer
   d. Be sure temperature is accurate
   e. Keep thermometer in developer tray
3. Prepare the camera
   a. Check for dirt
   b. Check light angles
   c. Place copy and sensitivity guide in copyboard
4. Prepare flashing lamp
   a. Duplicate calibrating conditions
   b. Be sure correct filter is used (00 filter)
   c. Check the timer
   d. Check distance from lamp
   e. Check angle with camera back

5. Make the main exposure
   a. Place film on camera back (use red light)
   b. Emulsion side toward lens
   c. Place contact screen over the film
   d. Smooth the screen over the film
   e. Screen must be larger than the film
   f. Move the back into place
   g. Make the exposure for the calculated time
6. Make the flash exposure
   a. Open the camera back
   b. Do not disturb the screen
   c. Make the appropriate flash exposure with flashing lamp
7. Develop the negative
   a. Development is critical point
   b. Remove the contact screen
   c. Place screen in safe place
   d. Place in developer solution
      (1) Same time as for standardization of computer
      (2) Agitate same as for standard
      (3) Use the same time
      (4) Be sure temperature is accurate
   e. Place in stop bath
      (1) Use acetic acid solution
      (2) Will stop developing action more rapidly
   f. Fix the negative
   g. Wash the negative
   h. Dry the negative
8. Duotones
   a. Made from a single photograph
   b. Printed in two colors (black and a color)
   c. Adds interest to printing
   d. Make two halftone negatives of one photograph
      (1) Screen angles should be 45° and 75°
      (2) Will avoid moiré pattern

Unit 58. Contact Printing

A. Objectives

Upon completing the unit activities and answering the appropriate questions, students should be able to

1. Identify common kinds of contact printing methods and applications.
2. Name typical kinds of equipment and materials used in contact printing.
3. Make contact negatives and/or positives using the equipment and materials available in the laboratory.

B. Instructor preparation

This unit has been planned to help students understand processes used to do contact printing. Because of the numerous kinds of materials and equipment available in most school laboratories, instructors will have to adapt the instructional procedures to fit the specific situation.

The authors feel that it is important that students have a conceptual understanding of contact printing and recognize some of the common applications. It is understood that most laboratories will not have a wide enough variety of materials and equipment to demonstrate all of the kinds of contact printing described in the textbook. However, most laboratories will have enough equipment and materials to make a contact positive from a negative. It is suggested that the instructor demonstrate contact printing by making a contact positive using conventional orthochromatic film.

1. To reinforce your lecture-demonstration, it is suggested that you find printed examples of where contact printing has been applied to produce printed products. Some examples might be a reversal with a solid background, a reversal with a tint or halftone background, and some outline type.

2. A sequence of materials including original copy, a negative, a film positive, and the final printed product where the film positive was used will be helpful in causing students to visualize the process.

C. **Suggested teaching outline**
1. Produce a same size photographic reproduction
    a. Direct reproductions
    b. Indirect reproductions
2. Equipment
    a. Vacuum printing frame
    b. Point source light
3. Materials
    a. Contact film
    b. Duplicating film
    c. Orthochromatic film
    d. Contact paper
4. Making contact prints—follow procedure given in textbook
    a. Right-reading image
    b. Reversal (wrong-reading)
5. Demonstrate how to make a film positive
6. Duplicates
    a. Use for multiple copies
    b. Used to make chokes and spreads
7. Chokes and spreads
    a. Used to make outline letters
    b. Used for close registration of multi-color images

Unit 59. Diffusion Transfer Process

A. **Objectives**

Upon completing the unit activities and answering the appropriate questions, students will be able to
1. Describe the basic principles of the diffusion transfer process.
2. Identify several applications of the diffusion transfer process.
3. Use the diffusion transfer process to make line positive prints, line film prints, and halftone prints.

B. **Instructor preparation**

This unit is planned to introduce students to the diffusion transfer process. It consists primarily of topics for helping students recognize applications of the diffusion transfer process and demonstrating how to make various diffusion transfer prints.

One of the most effective ways to illustrate the application of the diffusion transfer process is to have several examples of where it can best be used. Some kinds of examples that are useful are:

1. An enlargement and reduction of a copy element such as a logo or type that has been reproduced to fit a mechanical.
2. A paper print that has been made from a copy element of a different color than the remainder of the mechanical.
3. A reproduction of soiled copy.
4. A film positive of some copy—you may also want to show how the film positive could be used.
5. A halftone positive—it is quite useful to show a print of the halftone positive.

C. Suggested teaching outline

1. Purpose is to make a positive from positive copy
   a. Paper print
   b. Film print
   c. Plate
      (1) Paper
      (2) Metal
   d. Line prints
   e. Halftone prints
2. Material
   a. Negative material
   b. Receiver material
      (1) Paper
      (2) Film
      (3) Plates
3. Equipment
   a. Process camera
   b. Contact printing frame
   c. Diffusion transfer processor
4. Make diffusion transfer print
   a. Expose negative material
   b. Sandwich negative material with receiver material—exposed side to coated side of receiver
   c. Feed into processor
   d. Wait for chemical action
   e. Separate negative from receiver

Unit 60. Process-Color Reproduction

A. Objectives

As a result of studying the unit, answering questions from Unit 63, and completing related activities, students will be able to

1. State the basic principle underlying color separation photography.
2. Describe the fundamental procedures used to produce a process-color print.

B. Instructor preparation

Unit 60 was planned to be an introductory unit to the concepts of process-color reproduction. It was not planned to contain enough information to permit students to engage in the production of color separations. If the instructor wants students to become involved with color separation activities, it is suggested that he or she consult several excellent volumes on the topic and visit printers in the geographic area who do color separation work.

1. Obtain and use DCA Education Products transparencies *GA-65, Color Separation; GA-66, The*

Visible Light Spectrum; GA-67, The Additive Process; GA-68, The Subtractive Process; GA-69, Principle of Process Color Separation; GA-70, Color Separation Filters; GA-71, Screen Angles…for Process Color; and *GA-72, Color Reflection and Transmission Copy.*

2. Obtain a set of color separations. These can be secured from most printers, and several paper companies provide them on loan.

3. Have available a set of separation filters to show and discuss.

4. Overlay proofing material would help illustrate color separation principles.

5. Consider obtaining and using the videotape titled *Colour,* available from the International Film Bureau, Inc.

C. Suggested teaching outline

1. Introduction
2. Optical illusion
   a. Actually three or four colors are printed
      (1) Yellow
      (2) Cyan
      (3) Magenta
      (4) Black
   b. Combination produces other colors
      (1) Yellow and cyan—green
      (2) Yellow and magenta—orange
      (3) Cyan and magenta—violet
      (4) Yellow, cyan, and magenta—black (brown)
   c. Black is often added for increased detail
3. Color
   a. Eye sensitive to various wave lengths
      (1) White has all wave lengths
      (2) Three primary colors
         (a) Blue
         (b) Red
         (c) Green
   b. Light reflected
      (1) Can reflect all light
      (2) Only certain rays
      (3) Absorb all light
   c. All light reflected—white
   d. All light absorbed—black
   e. Certain waves reflected—a color
4. Color separations
   a. Copy
      (1) Prints—Reflection
      (2) Transparencies—Transmission
   b. Equipment
      (1) Process camera
      (2) Contact printer
      (3) Enlarger
      (4) Scanner

c. Methods
    (1) Direct—screened when separated
    (2) Indirect—screened after separation
    (3) Scanned—electronic separation
d. Light must be true white—Pulsed Xenon
e. Subtractive color separation
    (1) Use filters
        (a) Same as primary colors
        (b) Red
        (c) Blue
        (d) Green
    (2) Filters work like colored window panes
        (a) Red Filter
            1. Red rays pass through
            2. Blue and green do not
        (b) Resulting negatives called printers
            1. Cyan printer—red filter
            2. Magenta printer—green filter
            3. Yellow printer—blue filter
    (3) If copy has white areas, all negatives will have same black areas
    (4) If copy has black areas, all negatives will have same clear areas
    (5) Ink contamination
        (a) Produces brown instread of black
        (b) Need a black printer
            1. Gives detail
            2. Increases contrast
        (c) Black printer
            1. Three-filter method
            2. Exposure varies, depending on main color

5. Color correction
  a. Correct for ink variance
  b. Methods
    (1) Photographically
    (2) Manually
    (3) Photographically and manually
    (4) Electronically
  c. Manual correction
    (1) "Dot etching" done to separations
    (2) "Re-etching" done to plates
  d. Photographic corrections
    (1) Called masking
    (2) Masking system available—Kodak Tri-Mask System

6. Screens for process color
  a. Must be halftone
  b. Contact screen used
  c. Must be gray screen
  d. Different screen angles
    (1) Three colors
        (a) Cyan—45°

   (b) Magenta—75°

   (c) Yellow—105°

  (2) Four colors

   (a) Black—45°

   (b) Magenta—75°

   (c) Yellow—90°

   (d) Cyan—105°

7. Film for color separations

 a. Panchromatic

  (1) Sensitive to all colors

  (2) Develop in total darkness

 b. Time-temperature development method

Unit 61. Difficulties and Answers in Working With Negatives

A. Objectives

Students, after completing the unit, will be able to

1. Identify defects in process negatives.

2. Determine causes of defects; prescribe remedies.

B. Instructor preparation

The purpose of this unit is to emphasize the importance of preparing quality negatives. Instructors may want to use the unit as the basis for a lesson; or others may want to use the unit for reference purposes. Regardless of the way the instructor uses the unit, periodic attention should be given to improving and maintaining high-quality negatives.

1. Collect negatives with difficulties or imperfections. If possible, obtain the resulting prints from poor negatives, which will help illustrate the importance of high-quality negatives.

2. Review the causes of negative difficulties, so that students can develop a systematic procedure of negative analysis.

3. Obtain and use DCA Education Products transparency *GA-60, Exposure and Development Comparisons of Line Copy.*

C. Suggested teaching outline

1. Systematic examination essential

 a. Done on illuminator

 b. Will detect darkroom or procedural difficulties

 c. Sources of negative difficulties

  (1) Exposure procedures

  (2) Development procedures

2. Exposure procedures

 a. Underexposure

  (1) Black areas not too dense

  (2) Image areas are thicker

  (3) Difficult to distinguish between

   (a) Underexposed

   (b) Underdeveloped

  (4) Causes

   (a) Faulty lighting

   (b) Improper lens adjustment

   (c) Inaccurate test exposure

b. Overexposure
  (1) Negative very dense
  (2) Loss of detail
  (3) Fine lines close together
  (4) Causes
    (a) Faulty lighting
    (b) Improper lens adjustment
    (c) Inaccurate test exposure
c. Importance of lighting
  (1) Placement of lights
  (2) Variance in brightness

3. Development procedure
  a. Underdevelopment
    (1) Similar to underexposed
    (2) Image area thicker
    (3) Excessive pinholes
    (4) Causes
      (a) Developer too cool
      (b) Insufficient development time
      (c) Inaccurately formulated developer
      (d) Exhausted developer
  b. Overdevelopment
    (1) Similar to overexposed negative
    (2) Loss of detail in the image area
    (3) Causes
      (a) Developer too warm
      (b) Too much development time
      (c) Poor stop bath procedure
      (d) Excessive agitation
      (e) Inaccurately formulated developer
  c. Fogging
    (1) Light coat of silver in clear areas
    (2) Resembles overdevelopment and overexposure
    (3) Result of
      (a) Light striking film
      (b) Poor development procedures
    (4) Causes
      (a) Dirty lens
      (b) Improper safelights
      (c) Darkroom light leaks
      (d) Exhausted fixer
      (e) Insufficient fixing

4. Darkroom cleanliness
  a. Greatest cause of pinholes
  b. Dust and dirt accumulate
  c. Darkrooms need regular cleaning
  d. Main sources of dirt
    (1) Outside dirt
    (2) Dried chemicals

e. Regularly clean
   (1) Copyboard
   (2) Vacuum back
   (3) Developing trays
f. Particular problem when air is dry
g. Copy should be clean

Unit 62. Standardizing Darkroom Procedures

A. Objectives

Upon completing the reading, answering the Unit 63 questions, and engaging in darkroom activities, students will be able to

1. State reasons for extablishing standardized procedures in the darkroom.
2. Enumerate specific procedures to be standardized.
3. Demonstrate their understanding by performing accurate and systematic procedures in the darkroom.

B. Instructor preparation

Throughout the other units in this section there have been many references to precise procedural techniques and standardized routine. This unit has been included to give added emphasis to this important dimension of darkroom procedure. However, this unit is not enough to ensure that students perform in the laboratory. The instructor must continually reemphasize and provide an example of preciseness, to be sure that the attitude is internalized by the students.

It is suggested that this unit be used as a review unit shortly after students have initiated activities in the darkroom. Many intructors prefer to put procedures for standardizing darkroom activities into written form, rather than assume that students will remember the procedures. It is suggested that such aspects as material preparation, darkroom preparation, clean-up, etc., be put in written form and distributed to students, as well as posted in a location close to the darkroom. If this is done, the instructor can reasonably expect students to assume responsibility. Other procedures, such as exposure standardization and processing procedure, can be treated in a similar way but probably will change periodically.

C. Suggested teaching outline

1. Calculating exposure times
   a. Follow accurate procedures
   b. Verify procedures
      (1) Additional tests
      (2) Comparison with tests by others
   c. Keep accurate records
      (1) Procedures
      (2) Data
2. Preparing materials
   a. Bulk preparation
   b. Job preparation
   c. Follow manufacturer's instructions
3. Preparing darkroom
   a. Develop routine
   b. Don't rush procedure
   c. Be precise
      (1) Temperature
      (2) Mixtures
   d. Be clean

4. Making exposures
   a. Be clean
   b. Follow standards accurately
   c. Check accuracy
5. Processing materials
   a. Many variables
      (1) Time
      (2) Temperature
      (3) Quality of developer solutions
      (4) Cleanliness
      (5) Agitation
   b. Develop efficient routine
   c. Mechanical devices
      (1) Mechanical tray rockers
      (2) Film processors
6. Cleaning up
   a. Restoring the darkroom and camera
   b. Establishing clean-up procedures
      (1) Continual—during darkroom operation
      (2) Daily—at the end of each day (or beginning)
      (3) Weekly—Extensive clean-up

SECTION 8
LETTERPRESS IMAGE CARRIERS

Section Goal: To introduce the students to the various kinds, uses, and methods of producing letterpress image carriers.

Section Description: This section gives the students a comprehensive background of the letterpress image carriers area. It not only reviews industrial uses of the various image carriers but also gives "how to do it" information on producing several image carriers which possibly can be produced in the school laboratory, depending on the equipment available.

It is known, of course, that the letterpress process is not being used as much today as in previous years; but, it is still being used sufficiently to justify the inclusion of this content in *Comprehensive Graphic Arts*. Your students should have the opportunity to become aware of these different kinds of image carriers, so they not only can utilize and make some of them in the graphic arts laboratory but also will be able to better understand and talk about this specific area with commercial graphic arts personnel. Actually, there may be some part-time work available with one or more of the local commercial printers, especially in the area of rubber stamp making for one or more of your students.

Unit 73, Learning Experiences, like previous learning experience units, is designed to provide the students with several opportunities to reinforce their learning through defining key terms, answering study questions and becoming involved in various "doing" activities. Use these learning experiences both to the students' and to your own advantage.

Unit 64. Introduction to Letterpress Image Carriers

A. Objectives

Upon reading, defining the key terms, answering the study questions, and completing the one activity relating to this unit, students should be able to

1. Name the two major divisions of letterpress image carriers.
2. Identify the image carriers that are categorized as first-generation and those image carriers that are categorized as second-generation.
3. Sketch the three basic shapes of relief image carriers.
4. Review orally and in writing the historical highlights of relief image carriers.

B. Instructor preparation

1. Obtain examples of each of the eight image carriers illustrated in this unit.
2. Prepare and use a transparency showing the standard shapes of letterpress image carriers.
3. Talk with representatives of local and area graphic arts firms, and determine the extent of use that letterpress image carriers have at the present time.

C. Suggested teaching outline

1. Basic kinds of relief image carriers
   a. First-generation originals
      (1) Photoengravings
      (2) Photopolymer plates
      (3) Electronic engravings
   b. Second-generation duplicates
      (1) Stereotypes
      (2) Electrotypes
      (3) Rubber-flexographic

2. Materials used for relief image carriers
   a. Metallic
      (1) Copper
      (2) Zinc
      (3) Magnesium
      (4) Lead
      (5) Tin
      (6) Antimony
   b. Nonmetallic materials
      (1) Plastic
      (2) Rubber
3. Relief image carrier shapes
   a. Flat
   b. Curved
   c. Wraparound
4. Historical highlights
   a. First newspaper illustration—1493
   b. Photoengraving—1880

Unit 65. Safety With Letterpress Carriers

This unit has been prepared and placed in this position within this section with one primary thought in mind. That thought is to assist you and your students with personal safety. The introductory paragraphs provide a small amount of background information, with the remaining content being concerned with safety practices. Be sure your students study this unit very thoroughly prior to working on laboratory assignments relating to letterpress image carriers.

Unit 66. Photoengravings

A. Objectives

Upon reading, defining the key terms, answering the study questions, and completing the one activity relating to this unit, students should be able to

1. Summarize the importance and historical developments of the photoengravings.
2. Discuss the procedure of producing a photoengraving.

B. Instructor preparation

1. Obtain several examples of photoengravings, both halftones and line engravings. If possible, obtain engravings made of zinc and magnesium. Use these in your class discussion or for display purposes.
2. If etching equipment is available in your laboratory, you may desire to obtain the necessary materials to demonstrate the procedure for preparing a photoengraving.

C. Suggested teaching outline

1. Photoengravings
   a. Description
   b. Use
   c. Historical highlights
2. Producing a photoengraving

Unit 67. Rigid Photopolymer Relief Plates

A. Objectives

Upon reading, defining the key terms, answering the study questions, and completing the one activity relating to this unit, students should be able to

1. Describe a photopolymer plate and tell how and where it is used.
2. Explain the basic processing procedures involved in preparing a photopolymer plate.

B. **Instructor preparation**

1. Obtain several examples of these image carriers. These should be available directly from manufacturers and from graphic arts commercial companies in your geographical area.
2. If you are fortunate to have laboratory equipment by which rigid photopolymer relief plates can be prepared, you may desire to demonstrate this process to your students. Therefore, it will be necessary to prepare the necessary equipment and materials for such an activity.

C. **Suggested teaching outline**

1. Rigid photopolymer relief plates
   a. Light sensitive plastic material
   b. Two basic layers—photopolymer and metal
   c. Several thicknesses available
   d. Used on platen, cylinder and rotary presses
   e. Used to print many different products
2. Producing photopolymer plates
   a. Cut to size and pre-curved
   b. Sensitization of the photopolymer
   c. Exposing the plate
   d. Washout procedure
   e. Finishing the plate
   f. Inspecting for quality

Unit 68. Flexible Photopolymer Relief Plates

A. **Objectives**

Upon reading, defining the key terms, answering the study questions, and completing the one activity relating to this unit, the student should be able to

1. Tell the basic processing procedures needed to produce a flexible photopolymer relief plate.
2. Describe letterset plates and explain where and how these plates are used.

B. **Instructor preparation**

1. Obtain several examples of these image carriers. These should be available directly from manufacturers and from graphic arts commercial companies in your geographical area.
2. If you are fortunate to have laboratory equipment by which flexible photopolymer relief plates can be prepared, you may desire to demonstrate this process to your students. Therefore, it will be necessary to prepare the necessary equipment and materials for such an activity.

C. **Suggested teaching outline**

1. Flexible photopolymer relief plates
   a. Similar to rigid photopolymer plates
   b. Several support base materials used
   c. Plates can be made rapidly
   d. Methods of attaching plates to cylinders
   e. Plates attached to printing belts
2. Letterset plates
   a. Printing concept
   b. Use on lithographic presses
   c. Press cylinder requirements

Unit 69. Stereotypes and Electrotypes

A. Objectives

Upon reading, defining the key terms, answering the study questions, and completing the one activity relating to this unit, students should be able to

1. Recognize and know the use of stereotypes in former years.
2. Illustrate the basic steps involved in producing a stereotype.
3. Recognize and electrotype relief image carrier.
4. Explain either verbally or in writing the basic process involved in producing an electrotype.

B. Instructor preparation

1. Obtain examples of both flat and curved stereotype castings. Also, obtain examples of the matrices that accompany or match the stereotype castings. Use these for class examples or display purposes. These examples normally can be obtained from a newspaper or commercial plant that still utilizes letterpress printing.
2. Obtain several samples of electrotypes, both flat plate and curved. Use these in your class presentation or as a classroom display.
3. Talk with a colleague in the science department and determine whether the two you could cooperatively set up a demonstration of the electrotype process. If the cooperative adventure could be accomplished, it quite likely might be the beginning of several cooperative activities with your fellow school colleagues.

C. Suggested teaching outline

1. Stereotypes
   a. Historical highlights
   b. Their use
   c. Their classification within the group of relief image carriers.
2. Making a stereotype
   a. Original type or engraving
   b. The matrix or engraving
   c. Pouring the metal
   d. Finishing procedures
3. Electrotypes
   a. Their description
   b. Their use
4. Making an electrotype

Unit 70. Flexographic Printing Plates

A. Objectives

Upon reading, defining the key terms, answering the study questions, and completing the one activity relating to this unit, students should be able to

1. Discuss the flexographic printing method with regard to the printing process, significant dates, and type of printing plate used.
2. Describe in a brief manner the three types of flexographic plates/rollers in common use.

B. Instructor preparation

1. Obtain examples of each of the three common flexographic printing plates. Contact the manufacturing companies or see commercial or publication printers in your geographical area to obtain these examples.
2. Prepare a display which shows each plate, its advantages, and some typical products that are printed with each type.

3. Consider obtaining and using the following videotape from the GAT/GAERF Videotape Project: Number 021, *Flexographic Platemaking*.

C. **Suggested teaching outline**
   1. Flexography printing plates
      a. The printing method
      b. Significant dates—1952 & 1974
      c. Used to print quality products
   2. Photopolymer flexographic plates
      a. Why created
      b. How made
   3. Rubber flexographic plates
      a. Why used for flexography
      b. Making rubber plates
      c. Rubber design rollers
   4. Laser engraved flexographic cylinders and rollers
      a. Electronic scanners and laser used to produce
      b. The basic equipment to make the rollers
      c. How a laser engraved roller is made

Unit 71. Rubber Stamp Making

A. **Objectives**

Upon reading, defining the key terms, answering the study questions, and completing the one activity relating to this unit, students should be able to
   1. Recognize and know the basic uses for rubber stamps.
   2. Produce a complete rubber stamp.
   3. Summarize the commercial process involved in producing a rubber stamp.

B. **Instructor preparation**
   1. Obtain several samples of rubber stamps. Use these in your class presentations and in classroom displays.
   2. Prepare your rubber stamp machine, and inventory your rubber stamp supplies in preparation for a demonstration and use by students in making rubber stamp.

C. **Suggested teaching outline**
   1. Rubber Stamps
      a. Description
      b. Use
   2. Demonstration—molding rubber stamps
      a. Preparation procedures
      b. Vulcanizing the rubber die
      c. Mounting the die
   3. Molding commercial rubber image carriers

Unit 72. Creating Linoleum Blocks

A. **Objectives**

Upon reading, defining the key terms, answering the study questions, and completing the one activity relating to this unit, students should be able to
   1. Clarify the present-day use of linoleum blocks and the historical significance of block cutting and printing.
   2. Identify and draw the four common designs that are appropriate for linoleum block illustrations.
   3. Design, cut, and prepare a linoleum block for use on a platen or cylinder letterpress machine.

B. Instructor preparation

1. Obtain several examples of good-quality linoleum blocks that have been created and prepared by students. Use these blocks to stimulate interest with your students.

2. Obtain several sources of illustrations that are appropriate for linoleum blocks, and place them in your design and layout center. The students then can make good use of them in completing the activity related to this unit.

3. Obtain and use DCA Educational Products transparency *GA-8, Types of Line Illustrations*.

4. Inventory and ready the necessary equipment and supplies that students will need in the completion of the related linoleum block activity.

C. Suggested teaching outline

1. Block printing
   a. Wood blocks
   b. Linoleum blocks
   c. Historical highlights

2. Illustrations for linoleum block
   a. Positive design
   b. Negative design
   c. Line—positive design
   d. Line—negative design

3. Demonstration
   a. Designing
   b. Cutting
   c. Making the block type high
   d. Proofing the block
   e. Printing the block

SECTION 9
LETTERPRESS IMPOSITION

Section Goal: To permit the students to have experiences that will cause them to learn the terminology, tools, equipment, and procedures necessary to understand and perform letterpress lockup and imposition.

Section Description: Units for Section 9 have been organized to provide students with basic information relating to letterpress lockup and imposition. An attempt has been made to present the units in a sequence of increasing difficulty. Students should be introduced to the units in the order of their presentation. Successful understanding of Units 75–78 requires that students understand the previous units.

In most cases, instructors will want to include activities relating to all units. In some short-term introductory courses (6–12 weeks), instructors might want to reduce direct student involvement with Unit 78; but, the instructor should recognize that there are concepts involved in Unit 78 that will transfer to subsequent units.

Unit 74. Introduction to Letterpress Lockup and Imposition

A. Objectives

Upon completing Unit 74, students will be able to:

1. Describe the purpose of letterpress lockup.
2. Identify the origin of the term "stone" as used in lockup and imposition.

B. Instructor preparation

As the unit title suggests, this unit should set the stage for understanding subsequent units. The instructor should have the following items available, if he is going to deal with the unit as a major lesson.

1. Typeform with loose type
2. Empty chase
3. Furniture
4. Quoins
5. A chase or chases with a typeform properly located in the chase. One chase might have multiple forms locked up.
6. Platen press set up so that the chase can be placed into the press and make prints.

It would be wise for the instructor to review the unit and related units from other sources prior to introducing the lockup procedures. If the instructor has not locked up a typeform for some period of time, he/she should practice the procedure until an adequate degree of confidence is attained.

Some instructors might want to combine this unit with subsequent units dealing with letterpress lockup. When this unit is combined with other units for instructional purposes, it is important that the instructor not neglect the readiness intent of this unit. Sufficient attention should always be devoted to preparing students for new content.

C. Suggested teaching outline

1. Loose typeform difficult to handle
    a. Difficult to move
    b. Impossible to hold in a printing press
2. Lockup permits typeform to be used
    a. In printing press
    b. To make plates
3. Accomplished by compressing typeform elements
4. Lockup historically called stone work
    a. Originally lockup was accomplished on a flat stone
    b. Stones made from metal today

5. Must be familiar with the job and printing press
   a. Must select proper chase
   b. Must locate typeform(s) for accurate placement on paper
   c. Has to place typeform elements in correct location to other elements.
6. Lockup follows composition
   a. Essential that typeform elements are accurate
   b. Lockup must be precise for effective presswork

Unit 75. Tools and Equipment

A. Objectives

Upon reading Unit 75 and answering the appropriate questions from Unit 79, the student will be able to

1. Recognize and orally name the primary tools and equipment used to make letterpress lockups.
2. Describe the use of each tool or piece of equipment.

Note: The above objectives are stated with the understanding that it will be difficult for students to attain them until they have had the opportunity to manipulate the tools and equipment. Should the instructor expect mastery of the objectives before the students have used the tools and equipment, students might be discouraged because of the abstract meaning of the tools and equipment.

B. Instructor preparation

After the student has had the opportunity to read Unit 75, it is recommended that the instructor review the tools and equipment with the students. When possible, the instructor should not only show the students the tools and equipment, but he/she should illustrate how each is actually used. As with Unit 74, some instructors might want to combine the information in this unit with subsequent units, at least for demonstration purposes.

The instructor should have the following tools and equipment collected and arranged in a way that will permit the instructor to efficiently utilize them.

1. Imposing stone. While the imposing stone obviously will be available, the instructor might want to check to see that it is clean and the storage areas are well organized. One of the best ways to get students to care for tools and equipment is to have them in good working condition and stored in an orderly manner.
2. Chases. Have as many examples available as possible. Some instructors might want to have a typeform locked up in one of the chases.
3. Furniture and reglets. Show as many kinds and sizes as possible. Be sure that students learn how to determine size so they can be returned to the proper locations.
4. Quoins. Wedge-shaped, cam-type, high-speed quoins, and quoin keys should be available.
5. Planer block.

C. Suggested teaching outline

The following outline assumes that the instructor will follow the reading in the unit with a demonstration designed to initially expose students to the tools and equipment. Many instructors might want to expose students to the tools and equipment for letterpress lockup when demonstrate the procedure for making a lockup. There might be some value in repeating student exposure to the equipment by a demonstration now and at the lockup demonstration.

1. Tools and equipment unique to lockup
   a. Names important to communicate in laboratory
   b. Need to know name and equipment to be efficient
   c. Will let students communicate with people outside the school
2. Tools and equipment to review with students
   a. Imposing stone
      (1) Top

              (a) Precisely machined—protect

              (b) Rabbeted edge—move type to galley

          (2) Storage areas

              (a) Drawer for quoins, keys, string, etc.

              (b) Compartment for planer block and cleaner fluids

              (c) Galley storage

              (d) Furniture storage—relate the numbers to sizes

              (e) Chase racks

          (3) Protection of imposing stone

              (a) Prevent rust

              (b) Prevent dents

          (4) Keep storage areas organized

              (a) Furniture

              (b) Galleys

              (c) Chase

          (5) Protect type stored in imposing stone

              (a) Chases

              (b) Galleys

   b. Chases

       (1) Kinds

           (a) Standard

           (b) Skeleton

           (c) Spider

           (d) Show one with lockup

       (2) Show storage location

       (3) Emphasize protection of locked up chases

   c. Furniture and reglets

       (1) Kinds

           (a) Wood

           (b) Metal

       (2) Sizes

           (a) Lengths

           (b) Widths

       (3) Storage

       (4) Emphasize need for accurate storage

   d. Quoins and keys

       (1) Kinds

           (a) Wedge-shaped

           (b) Cam-type

           (c) High-speed

       (2) Keys

       (3) Show storage location

   e. Planer block

       (1) Show location

       (2) Emphasize protection

Unit 76. Kinds of Lockups

A. Objectives

Upon completing Unit 76, students will be able to

1. Recognize and name the two primary methods of locking up typeforms.
2. Determine the most appropriate lockup technique to use.

B. Instructor preparation

It would appear that Units 76 and 77 might be treated together since Unit 76 describes methods that can be used for making lockups and Unit 77 deals with the actual procedure for making lockups.

Beyond using chalkboard diagrams to illustrate the two methods, it is suggested that instructors demonstrate both methods of enclosing a typeform when the demonstration for a total lockup is given to the students.

1. Obtain and use DCA Education Products transparency *GA-20, Letterpress Lock-Up.*
2. Prepare two or more actual lockups for showing to the students.
3. Draw possible lockup situations on the chalkboard and plan to discuss solutions.

C. Suggested teaching outline

The instructor should use the outline prepared for Unit 77.

Unit 77. Lockup Procedure

A. Objectives

Students will be able to lock up typeforms, using both the chaser and furniture-within-furniture lockup techniques. (Instructors might want to add a time factor to this objective that is consistent with the developmental level of the students in the class.)

Note: The above objective assumes students will be able to do several suboperations such as moving typeforms from a galley to the imposing stone, planing the typeform, and checking for loose lines.

B. Instructor preparation

The logical expansion activity for this unit, and possibly previous units, is a demonstration that exposes students to the proper procedures for making lockups, using both lockup methods. The instructor should practice the procedure until they are thoroughly familiar with the procedures. Demonstrations such as this should duplicate, as nearly as possible, the situations that students will encounter. It is important that all tools, equipment, and materials are available and organized. Below is a list of items that should be located before beginning the demonstration. Organization of materials is extremely important.

1. Typeform that has dimensions that do not equal standard pica lengths for use with the chaser method.
2. Typeform that has dimensions of equal pica lengths for use with the furniture-within-furniture method.
3. Furniture—both wood and metal, if possible.
4. Quoins—as many kinds as possible.
5. Quoin key for each kind of quoin.
6. Planer block and mallet.
7. String for typing the typeform.

C. Suggested teaching outline

This outline is presented as a guide to help the instructor with the presentation of a demonstration dealing with the letterpress lockup. It is assumed that both the chase method and furniture-within-furniture method will be introduced to students.

1. Practice the chase and furniture-within-furniture techniques—placement of the first four pieces of furniture.
2. Collect the materials suggested above.
3. Diagram the two methods on the chalkboard (optional)
   a. Emphasize the location of the top of the typeform with respect to the top or side of the chase
   b. Illustrate the placement of the first four pieces of furniture.

4. Assemble students around the imposing stone
    a. Be sure all students can see
    b. Might be necessary to present the demonstration in small groups.
5. Clean the imposing stone—prevent dirt from getting under the type characters
6. Select the galley with chaser typeform
    a. Careful handling to prevent damage to the type
    b. Emphasize caution to reduce chances of pi occurring
7. Move typeform so that head (top) is:
    a. At your left hand, if the typeform is to be printed parallel to the short edge of the paper
    b. Nearest to you, if the typeform is to be printed parallel to the longer edge of the sheet of paper
8. Place the appropriate chase around the typeform
    a. One long edge should be near you
    b. That edge will be placed at the bottom of the press
9. Move the typeform to the best location within the chase
    a. Place it as near the center as possible
    b. The size of the paper and the location of the print on the paper might determine the typeform location within the chase
10. Select the appropriate pieces of furniture for the chase method
    a. Two pieces should be slightly larger than the ends of the typeform
    b. Two pieces should be slightly longer than the sides of the typeform
    c. These pieces of furniture should be as wide as possible
11. Fill in the space between the typeform and the chase
    a. Place furniture between the typeform and the bottom of the chase and between the typeform and the left-hand side of the chase
        (1) Establish a constant distance between the type and the edges that correspond to the gauge pin locations on the press
        (2) Pieces of furniture should get longer between the typeform and the edges of the chase
    b. Place quoins next to the reglets—number of quoins depends on the length of typeform
    c. Carefully remove the string from around the typeform
    d. Fill the remaining space with furniture—should get longer
12. Tighten the quoins
    a. Alternately tighten the quoins until all are tight
    b. Excessive pressure could break the chase
13. Check the typeform for loose lines
    a. Lift one edge of the chase and place on a quoin key—be careful—lines could fall from the typeform
    b. Tap all lines with fingers to identify loose lines
    c. If all lines are right, remove the quoin key and let the lockup move downward onto the imposing stone surface
14. Plan the typeform
    a. If the lines are tight, place the lockup flat on the imposing stone
    b. Loosen the quoins until they are snug
    c. Place the planer block on the typeform
    d. Tap the top of the planer lightly with a quoin key or mallet
    e. Tighten the quoins carefully

15. Place the chase on the rack

    Note: Some instructors might want to have a press setup, so that the typeform actually can be printed.

16. Follow the same procedure to demonstrate the furniture-within-furniture method, with the exception of the placement of the first four pieces of furniture.

17. The lockup should be disassembled in the reverse order of making the lockup to illustrate orderly cleanup procedures and how easy it is to disassemble a lockup

Unit 78. Multiple-Page Lockup and Imposition

A. Objectives

Upon reading and completing the related activities for Unit 78, the students should be able to

1. Recognize situations in which it is more efficient to lock up multiple pages.
2. Lock up multiple pages and use the correct terminology to describe the lockup.
3. Identify the parts of a signature by the correct name and show how signatures are combined to form a book.
4. Determine a stone layout from a page layout and provide for margins, trimming, and creep.
5. Prepare sheetwise, work-and-turn, and work-and-tumble impositions.

General Discussion

This unit introduces students to more efficient and sophisticated production applications of the lockup procedures. It is sometimes difficult to illustrate the techniques explained in the unit, since the need to use them, in most instructional graphic arts laboratories, is not great. While the instructor can demonstrate the techniques to students, and the students can practice them, it might be difficult to provide meaningful reinforcement experiences for students, because of press capacities and the typical kinds of jobs usually done in graphic arts classes. A field trip to a printing plant or newspaper, where imposition techniques are used, might help establish more credibility for the study of imposition techniques. It is suggested that the instructor demonstrate only one technique at a time, followed by activities that reinforce the demonstration. As with all demonstrations, the demonstrator should practice the demonstration prior to presenting it to students. Following are suggested demonstrations and activities for helping students learn about multiple-page lockup and imposition. The outline of this unit varies from that of the remaining units, so that each portion of the unit can be treated independently from the other portions.

Duplicate Forms

A. Information

This is the simplest form of the multiple-page impositions. Emphasis should be placed on helping students to recognize when the techniques would be more appropriate and efficient to use than printing a single form. Prior to demonstrating how to prepare a multiple-form lockup, the instructor might want to conduct a discussion regarding the considerations to be made, using duplicate forms and composition time as printing time and press size.

B. Instructor preparation

The following items should be collected prior to giving a demonstration and should be located on or close to the imposing stone where the demonstration will be given.

1. Two duplicate typeforms—plates or blocks would work too
2. Chase
3. Furniture and reglets
4. Quoins and key
5. Planer block
6. Line gauge
7. Paper on which forms will be printed

C. **Suggested teaching outline**

The instructor should be sure that the student can perform the demonstration accurately. If necessary, practice the demonstration prior to presenting it to the students.

1. Initial placement of the typeform
   a. Place the heads at the bottom or left-hand side of the chase
   b. Determine distance between typeforms
      (1) Compute the margins on each side of a typeform.
      (2) Space between the forms should equal the space on both sides of one typeform.
   c. Add the proper amount of space between forms with furniture or reglets
      Note: When possible, encourage students to suggest ways to compute distances between forms. This can be done by asking them leading questions and will involve them more actively in the demonstrations.
2. Use furniture and reglets to shape the two typeforms into one rectangular shape. The two forms can now be treated as one large typeform.
3. Complete the lockup, using the chase or furniture-within-furniture technique.
4. This demonstration might have more meaning if the instructor actually prints some copies on the press.

Imposition of Signatures

Several aspects are to be learned before students understand how to complete signature impositions. It might be helpful for students to see examples of items that could be printed in the form of signatures. Examples ranging from a four-page athletic schedule to a complex book could be shown. These items will be useful to describe terminology relating to a signature. Students can prepare a signature by folding a blank sheet of paper. When the signature is folded properly, the various parts can be identified on the signature. The instructor can help students locate the image areas on the pages to provide for accurate margins, allowance for trimming, and provision for creep. The "dummy" signature (page layout) also will provide the guide for making a stone layout (placement of typeforms).

Sheetwise Method

A. **Information**

This method is the most common method used to print signatures, and it is the most accurate method. When possible, it would be wise to encourage students to use the sheetwise method.

B. **Instructor preparation**

Below is a list of items that should be available before demonstrating the procedure for preparing sheetwise lockups.

1. Page layout
2. Stone layout
3. Typeforms. It would be wise to have enough forms for at least eight pages. Plates and blocks can be used.
4. Two chases
5. Quoins and keys
6. Furniture and reglets
7. Planer blocks
8. Line gauge
9. Paper on which forms can be printed

C. **Suggested teaching outline**

Signature imposition can be confusing to people who are experienced, as well as to beginners. Care should be taken to be sure the procedure are clear in the mind of the instructor before making the demonstration.

1. Examine the stone layout and determine the forms to be placed in each chase. It might be helpful to compare the page layout with the stone layout.

2. Select the typeforms for the first side of the signature
    a. Locate the typeforms in the appropriate locations
    b. Place the correct amount of space between the typeforms
3. Prepare the forms to form a single rectangular unit
4. Complete the lockup, using either the chase or furniture-within-furniture method.
5. Locate the typeforms for the second page, as for the first page

Work-and-Turn and Work-and-Tumble Methods

A. Information

These two methods are used to print signatures from a single lockup. The methods are similar in that all pages are printed on both sides of the paper. It is not as accurate as the sheetwise method, because the register edges change.

B. Instructor preparation

The items required for this demonstration are the same as were needed to perform the demonstration for the sheetwise method, except only one chase is required.

C. Suggested procedure

It might be helpful for the instructor to have a page available to illustrate the two methods prior to the demonstration. The procedure used to demonstrate these two methods is essentially the same as the procedure used to demonstrate the sheetwise method. Teachers should use the stone layout as a guide. This will emphasize the need to prepare a stone layout.

SECTION 10
LETTERPRESS IMAGE TRANSFER

Section Goal: To provide information relative to the process of letterpress image transfer and to the techniques associated with achieving satisfactory printed images.

It is well known that letterpress image transfer is used to print only a small percentage of the total industry output. Nevertheless, this process still has an important place within some areas of the industry. This is especially true with flexography; which is a letterpress process. Relief images are used to transfer images to many kinds of substrate. Flexography is a growing segment within the graphic arts industry, and students need to know about it.

Few platen presses, either hand or power, are still used in schools. This is unfortunate because platen presses can still be used to teach some important aspects of graphic arts. Short-runs of envelopes, cards, and imprinting can economically be printed using platen presses. Finishing jobs involving die cutting, scoring, embossing, and foil stamping also are prime examples of platen press work.

Section Description: Nine units are centered around the specific area of transferring ink from one surface to another surface through the relief or letterpress method. Unit 80 has been designed to introduce this area, whereas Unit 81, entitled "Flexography Printing," gives a brief overview of this important method of reproduction that categorically falls within the letterpress image-transfer method Unit 84 covers a unique book production system. Unit 83 emphasizes some safety points that must be adhered to if safe operation of the platen and cylinder presses is expected. Units 84, 85, and part of Unit 87 are directly concerned with the preparation, operation and cleanup of the power platen press.

If a power platen press is not available in your laboratory, the same operating procedures will be appropriate for the operation of a hand-operated platen press, as shown in Fig. 80-3. The power platen was used for illustrative purposes, because it was thought that it would be easier to have the students move from power instructions to hand instructions, than in the opposite direction.

Unit 86 and the second half of Unit 87 are directly concerned with the preparation and operation of the vertical cylinder press. This press is not often found in the typical school graphic arts laboratory, although vocational-oriented schools both at the high school and the post high school levels do contain presses of this variety; therefore, it was believed that information relative to this press should be included within this publication. However, if you do not have a cylinder press in your graphic arts laboratory, you obviously would not ask your students to spend much time on this unit, other than possibly to scan it for purposes of becoming somewhat familiar with its operation.

As in previous units, the Learning Experiences—Unit 88 is designed to assist you and your students in revealing the content in this section. Use the key terms, study questions and activities that you deem most appropriate for your own situation.

Unit 80. Introduction to Letterpress Image Transfer

A. Objectives

Upon reading, defining the key terms, answering the study questions, and completing the one activity relating to this unit, students should be able to

1. Sketch the operating principle of each of the three styles of letterpress machines—platen, cylinder, and rotary.
2. Recognize and distinguish among the various letterpress presses according to the three basic styles—platen, cylinder, and rotary.
3. Summarize the development of early letterpress presses.

B. Instructor preparation

1. Obtain company advertising materials on the various letterpress presses illustrated in this unit; also, study others that are available. Allow your students to review these brochures, so they may better understand and recognize the various machines that are available and used within the graphic arts industry.

2. Obtain and use these several DCA Educational Products transparencies: *GA-23, Basic Press Designs; GA-73, Hand-Operated Platen Press; GA-74, Power Platen Press; GA-75, Automatic Platen Press; GA-76, Horizontal Cylinder Press; GA-77, Vertical Cylinder Press;* and *GA-78, Rotary Letterpress Printing Unit.*

C. Suggested teaching outline

1. The platen press
   a. Operating principle
   b. Some common presses
   c. Typical products
   d. Operating speeds
2. The cylinder press
   a. The operating principle
   b. Some common presses
   c. Typical products
   d. Operating speeds
3. The rotary press
   a. Operating principle
   b. Some common presses
   c. Typical products
   d. Operating speeds
4. Early presses
   a. Gutenberg's press
   b. 18th Century American Colonial presses

Unit 81. Flexographic Printing

A. Objectives

Upon reading, defining the key terms, answering the study questions, and completing the one activity relating to this unit, students should be able to

1. Explain the principle of image transfer utilizing the method known as flexography.
2. Recite the uses of the flexography image transfer method.
3. Clarify the need to use proper inks when printing with flexography.

B. Instructor preparation

1. Obtain brochures describing the various flexography presses. Utilize these brochures in your class presentation and allow students to review them, so they may become able to recognize one of these presses.
2. Obtain examples of products that have been produced by the flexography method. Use these products to illustrate the need for utilizing proper ink both from the standpoint of adhering to the material that was printed and also, if this were a food package, that the ink actually does not come in contact with or harm the food product.
3. Obtain and use DCA Educational Products transparencies *GA-85, Flexographic Press Schematic; GA-86, Flexographic Image Transfer Unit;* and *GA-87, Flexographic Press Designs*
4. Consider obtaining and using the slide series titled, *The Flexographic Printing Process,* from the Graphic Arts Technical Foundation.

C. Suggested teaching outline

1. Flexography image transfer
   a. Image-transfer principle
   b. Uses of flexography
   c. Historical highlights

2. Image carriers and ink
   a. Rubber and photopolymer image carriers
   b. Ink and Pure Food and Drug laws
3. Image-transfer devices
   a. Stack design
   b. Central impression cylinder design
   c. Inline design
4. Advantages of flexography

Unit 82. Book Production System

A. Objectives

Upon reading, defining the key terms, answering the study questions, and completing the one activity relating to this unit, students should be able to

1. Explain the book production concept of this total system.
2. Tell how the visual images are controlled and printed on the web of paper.
3. Describe the finishing and binding portion of the book production system.

B. Instructor preparation

1. Obtain literature directly from the company that manufactures the "Cameron Book Production System," Somerset Technologies, Inc., P.O. Box 791, New Brunswick, NJ 08903. This literature will be helpful to both you and your students.
2. Locate a publishing company within your geographical area that has this book production system. Make the needed personnel contacts so it might be possible to take your students on a tour and see this system in operation.
3. Obtain two or three books that have been printed on this system. Plan to show the students how the quality and style compares to a book printed via regular letterpress or by lithography.

C. Suggested teaching outline

1. "Cameron Book Production System"
   a. A patented system
   b. High speeds obtained
   c. The total concept
2. Production steps
   a. The flexible image carrier
   b. Proofing the printing belt
   c. The printing cycle
   d. Printing quality
   e. Finishing and binding

Unit 83. Safety with Letterpress Presses

This unit has been prepared and placed within this section with one primary thought in mind. That thought is to assist you and your students with personal safety. The introductory paragraphs provide a small amount of background information, with the remaining content being concerned with safety practices. Be sure your students study this unit very thoroughly prior to working on laboratory assignments relating to platen and cylinder presses.

Unit 84. Platen Press Preparation

A. Objectives

Upon reading, defining the key terms, answering the study questions, and completing the one activity related to this unit, students should be able to

1. Identify the parts and uses of a power platen press
2. Apply the learned information in preparing the platen press for the printing operation.

B. Instructor preparation

1. Obtain and use either DCA Educational Products transparencies *GA-73, Hand-Operated Platen Press* or *GA-74, Power Platen Press*. Use either one of both of these transparencies to introduce the parts and uses of the machine that is available in your laboratory. It is suggested that you do not force your students to memorize the names of the various parts; but encourage them to become familiar with the parts and their uses prior to utilizing the press, thereby making them safer and more qualified operators of the particular machine.
2. Check over the press or presses that your students will be using to see that they are operating properly and safely. Also inventory the various supplies and materials that must be used in conjunction with the platen press, such as platen packing paper, ink, gauge pins, and other essential items.

C. Suggested teaching outline

1. Platen press parts and uses
   a. Platen
   b. Ink fountain
   c. Ink disk
   d. Platen guard
   e. Feed board
   f. Delivery board
   g. Impression lever
   h. Counter
2. Demonstration—platen press preparation
   a. Platen packing
   b. Inking
   c. Placing the chase in the press
   d. Paper positioning
   e. Gauge pin placement
   f. Gripper placement

Unit 85. Platen Press Operation

A. Objectives

Upon reading, defining the key terms, answering the study questions, and completing the one activity relating to this unit, students should be able to

1. Perform the process of platen press makeready
2. Operate the power platen press to achieve the desired number of printed copies.

B. Instructor preparation

1. Inventory your laboratory supplies to see whether a sufficient quantity of tissue for makeready purposes and makeready paste are available. Also, be certain that there is a sufficient quantity of paper for student projects. Another specific item needed in this unit will be a makeready knife.
2. Prior to the demonstration on this phase of platen press operation, be certain that all operations have been completed, as outlined in Unit 84, for the platen press preparation. In this way, the demonstration will proceed much more rapidly and will be more meaningful for the students.

C. Suggested teaching outline

1. Makeready
   a. Definition
   b. Purpose

2. Demonstration—Press makeready
   a. Trial impression
   b. Determination of heavy or light areas
   c. Reduction or build-up of light areas
   d. Placement of makeready sheet
   e. Repositioning of pressboard
3. Demonstration—Press operation
   a. Clear the working area
   b. Locate paper on feedboard
   c. Turn on press power
   d. Feed paper
   e. Deliver paper

Unit 86. Cylinder Press Operation

A. Objectives

Upon reading, defining the key terms, answering the study questions, and completing the one activity relating to this unit, students should be able to

1. Recognize a vertical cylinder letterpress press.
2. Identify the parts and their uses on a vertical cylinder press.
3. Accomplish the preparation steps on a vertical cylinder press.
4. Solve the necessary makeready problems for a given specific typeform.
5. Operate the cylinder press to achieve the desired number of printed copies.

B. Instructor preparation

1. Inventory the laboratory supplies to be sure there is a sufficient quantity of packing papers and makeready paste. Also check to see that all necessary tools are in their proper locations and are readied for use.
2. Check the cylinder press to make sure it is in proper working order. If you have not operated the press recently, it would be beneficial to print a short-run job to make sure the machine is working properly and to refresh your operating skills.
3. Obtain and use DCA Educational Products transparency *GA-77, Vertical Cylinder Press.*

C. Suggested teaching outline

1. The vertical cylinder press
   a. Its basic design
   b. Type and image carriers used
2. Press parts and uses
   a. Typeform and chase bed
   b. Feeder unit
   c. Impression roller
   d. Ink rollers
   e. Ink fountains
   f. Operating lever
   g. Motor control panel
   h. Left cylinder end guard
   i. Delivery unit

3. Demonstration—Cylinder press operation
   a. Cylinder press preparation
   b. Packing the impression cylinder
   c. Cylinder makeready
   d. Operation and making necessary adjustments

Unit 87. Platen and Cylinder Press Cleanup

A. Objectives

Upon reading, answering the study questions, and completing the one activity related to this unit, students should be able to

1. Thoroughly clean a platen press.
2. Wash up a cylinder press.
3. Lubricate a platen press and/or a cylinder press.

B. Instructor preparation

1. Inventory the necessary cleanup materials, such as solvents and rags. Be certain all solvents are in safety containers and that a metal safety container is available to place soiled rags in once they have been soaked with solvent.
2. Have the necessary lubrication materials and press lubrication charts available, so the students can complete the activity relating to this unit.

C. Suggested teaching outline

1. Demonstration—Platen press cleanup
   a. Removing and washing the typeform
   b. Washing the ink disk
   c. Washing the ink rollers
   d. Wiping down the press
2. Demonstration—Cylinder press cleanup
   a. Removing and cleaning the typeform
   b. Removing the excess ink from the ink fountain
   c. Cleaning the fountain
   d. Cleaning the rollers
   e. Removing ink from the ink plate
   f. Wiping down the press
3. Press lubrication
   a. Kinds of oil and grease used
   b. Oil and grease press charts
   c. Lubrication procedures

SECTION 11
LITHOGRAPHIC IMPOSITION

Section Goal: To provide information for students to learn how to construct a flat for the purpose of making a photolithographic image carrier (plate).

Section Description: An essential step in the photolithographic printing process is the construction of a flat from which a photolithographic plate will be produced. This section was organized to help students understand the fundamental procedures of stripping a flat. It is expected that students will learn about the tools and materials unique to the stripping procedure. In addition, students will be expected to prepare flats using accurate, systematic, and efficient techniques. Examples used in this textbook have been limited to duplication-type situations; however, the fundamental principles are similar for other printing equipment. The instructor should expand the students' experiences by providing examples of other stripping situations in live production situations.

The section has been divided into units which represent somewhat discrete stripping operations. The authors are not suggesting that each unit be handled separately. In fact, as an instructor demonstrates to a class, he/she will probably want to combine several units into one demonstration. For example, Units 89, 90, 91, 92, and 93 will probably be covered in one demonstration. Depending on the time limitation of the class, Unit 94, Flats Used for Multiple Stripping, may be treated as a separate demonstration.

It is clearly recognized that the stripping procedures vary widely among printers. Only two procedures have been illustrated in the textbook. They are shown because they are simple and efficient, as compared with other methods. Some instructors may want to use another procedure with their students.

Unit 89. Introduction to Lithographic Imposition

A. Objectives

Students, as a result of Unit 89 experiences, will be able to

1. Describe the purpose of stripping a flat.
2. Learn terminology unique to stripping.
3. Either orally or pictorially show how a flat is used.

B. Instructor preparation

It is suggested that this unit be used to demonstrate the purpose of a flat, with little emphasis on specific procedure. This will help the students understand what the product is and how it is used. The details of how a flat is assembled will be included in later units of instruction.

1. Instructor should have the following items available:
   a. Masking sheet
   b. Negative
   c. Tape
   d. Flat, with resulting plate
2. Prepare platemaking equipment for demonstrating use of the flat. There is some value in actually making a plate at this time.
3. Consider obtaining and using the following videotape from the GAT/GAERF Videotape Project: Number 005, *Basic Film Assembly (Stripping)*.
4. Consider obtaining and using the videotape titled *Basic Stripping*, from Sunshine Enterprises, Spokane, WA.

C. Suggested teaching outline

1. Terminology and flat elements
   a. Imposition

b. Stripping

c. Flat

d. Masking sheet

2. Platemaking procedure (illustrates use of flat)

a. Masking sheet over sensitive plate

b. Light through negative

c. Masking sheet blocks light

Unit 90. Tools and Materials for Stripping

A. Objectives

Students, after engaging in activities related to Unit 90, will be able to

1. Identify, by correct name, the tools and materials used by a stripper.

2. Use the tools and materials to assemble a satisfactory flat.

B. Instructor preparation

Information in Unit 90 is likely to constitute only a few minutes of a larger demonstration on the stripping procedure.

1. Collect the following tools and materials:

   a. T-squares and triangles

   b. Rules

   c. Magnifying glass

   d. Knives

   e. Scissors

   f. Brushes

   g. Masking sheets

   h. Opaque

   i. Tape

   j. Negatives

2. Clean and organize light table

C. Suggested teaching outline

1. Stripping equipment

   a. Light table or line-up table

      (1) Base

      (2) Glass top (safety)

      (3) Cleanliness

   b. T-squares and triangles

      (1) Layout on masking sheet

      (2) Guide for cutting (only if stainless steel) negatives

   c. Rule

      (1) Measuring

      (2) Sometimes as straightedge (if stainless steel)

   d. Magnifiers

      (1) Check accuracy

      (2) Identify imperfections

   e. Knives

      (1) Cutting negatives

      (2) Cutting in masking sheet windows

      (3) Must be very sharp

  f. Scissors

  g. Brushes for opaquing

 2. Materials

  a. Masking sheet

   (1) Size of the plate

   (2) Paper or plastic

   (3) Some have guidelines

   (4) Serve as block-out

  b. Opaque solution

   (1) Cover pinholes

   (2) Block-out unwanted areas

  c. Stripping tape

   (1) Attach negatives to masking sheet

   (2) Block-out

Unit 91. Preparation and Layout for Stripping

A. Objectives

As a result of reading Unit 91, answering the appropriate questions, and engaging in activities, students will

 1. Internalize the attitude of carefully checking negatives prior to stripping a flat.

 2. Be able to accurately lay out a masking sheet for assembling a flat.

B. Instructor preparation

 1. Obtain DCA Education Products transparency *GA-21, Lithography—Laying Out the Flat*

 2. Collect the following items:

  a. Line and halftone negative

  b. Magnifying glass and/or linen tester

  c. Goldenrods (masking sheets)

  d. Rule

  e. Pencil

  f. Tape

 3. Consider obtaining and using the following videotape from the GAT/GAERF Videotape Project: Number 019, *Advanced Film Assembly (Stripping)*.

C. Suggested teaching outline

 1. Preparation for stripping

  a. Examine negatives

   (1) Overall visual inspection

   (2) Magnification

  b. Consult original layout

   (1) Location of image on printed product

   (2) Size of paper

   (3) Treatment of product after printing

   (4) Placement of multiple negatives on the sheet

  c. Location of the lead edge

   (1) Accurate placement of negative

   (2) Masking sheet lead edge corresponds to printed sheet lead edge

          (3) Lead edge

              (a) Goes through the press first

              (b) Press gripper edge

              (c) Marked on some masking sheets

    d. Identifying gripper margins

          (1) Define

              (a) Distance between lead edge and first image print

              (b) 1/4 to 3/8 inches

              (c) Press part that holds paper

          (2) No image in gripper margin

    e. Locating sheet margins

          (1) Show position where located on masking sheet

          (2) Lead edge is one margin

          (3) Provides reference point

  2. Layout for stripping

    a. Mark masking sheet

          (1) Sheet margins

          (2) Image

    b. Purpose

          (1) Prevent errors

          (2) Increase efficiency

    c. Marking for single page

          (1) Material appears on only one page

          (2) Refer to procedures in Unit 91—see "Layout for Stripping"

    d. Marking for multiple pages

          (1) Placing multiple pages on one masking sheet

          (2) Requires additional page separation

          (3) Refer to Unit 91

Unit 92. Attaching Negatives to the Masking Sheet

A. Objectives

Students will, as a result of reading, answering appropriate questions from Unit 95, and participating in reinforcing activities, be able to

1. Accurately attach negatives to masking sheet using either the "emulsion side up" or "emulsion side down" method.

2. Open the image areas on a flat

3. Opaque negatives

B. Instructor preparation

Flats are prepared by taping negatives to masking sheets. This unit was planned to help students learn how to use two stripping techniques. The first is the emulsion side down and the second is the emulsion side up method.

The instructor must demonstrate the methods to students so that they can visualize how each method is accomplished. If possible, the instructor should locate a light table in a place where students can clearly see the methods being demonstrated. It is best if the instructor can give the demonstrations to small groups of students. Obviously, the instructor should practice the demonstrations until they can be done with precision.

The instructor will need all of the materials and equipment used for demonstrations in other units in this section. It is essential that the instructor have:

1. Sharp frisket knife

2. Stripping tape
3. Cellophane tape
4. T-square, triangles, and straight edge
5. Several negatives that can be attached to the masking sheets.

Unit 93. Combining Negatives and Proofing

A. Objectives

Students, as a result of completing Unit 93, will be able to

1. Combine halftone negatives and illustrations when clear windows are provided on the line negative.
2. Combine line and halftone negatives when windows must be cut in the line negative.
3. Recognize the importance of making proofs.

B. Instructor preparation

1. Have a masking sheet with the line negative properly located. The negative should have a clear window where the halftone or illustration is to be located.
2. Obtain the halftone negative or illustration negative to be located behind the window.
3. Have masking sheet with the line negative properly attached. The line negative should not have a window where the halftone or illustration is to be located.
4. Obtain the halftone that is to be combined with the line negative in 3 above and the layout that describes where the halftone is to be located.
5. Obtain lithographer's tape, cellophane tape, opaquing solution, and brushes.
6. Be sure to have a sharp frisket knife and good straight edge.

C. Suggested teaching outline

The outlines in the textbook should be followed in preparing for this demonstration.

Unit 94. Stripping for Multiple Exposures

A. Objectives

Students, as a result of activities related to Unit 94, will be able to

1. Understand the importance of accurate registration and be able to describe the procedures for accomplishing registration when stripping flats.
2. Prepare complementary flats.
3. Prepare a flat to be used for the flat mask technique.
4. Prepare multi-color flats.

B. Instructor preparation

This unit should help students understand that some printing jobs require the preparation of multiple flats. While this is most easily illustrated when preparing multi-color jobs, the student should understand that certain single-color jobs also need multiple flats.

It is recommended that the instructor give several demonstrations to show the various methods. However, the instructor should attempt to help students conceptualize the use of multiple flats. For example, the student should recognize the similarities of complementary flats and multi-color flats.

Possibly the most important learning that can be accomplished from this unit is to reinforce the idea of working at a high level of precision. The instructor must work with extreme accuracy to demonstrate the relationship between accurate registration and precise workmanship.

The instructor should have negatives prepared specifically for this demonstration. When possible, the instructor should have the comprehensive layout or a print of the negatives. This will save time and help students better visualize the processes.

If available, the instructor should have a register punch and register pins to demonstrate the use of pin registration. If a register punch is not available, the instructor should consider using a field trip to reinforce the concept of pin registration.

C. Suggested teaching outline

1. Registration methods
    a. Register punch and register pins
       (1) Punch holes
           (a) Masking sheets
           (b) Plates
           (c) Pin fit holes
           (d) Hold masking in register with
               1) Other masking sheets
               2) Plates
2. Complementary flats
    a. Used when two or more flats are exposed on the same plate
    b. Line over halftone
    c. Line over tint
    d. Halftone close to line copy
3. Step and repeat
    a. Same image repeated on same sheet
    b. Items cut apart after printing
    c. Exposing one flat several times on one plate
    d. Must be precisely located
4. Masking method
    a. Multi-color plates from one negative
    b. Images must not overlap
    c. Procedure
       (1) Cover second color image
       (2) Make first plate
       (3) Cover first color images
       (4) Make second plate
5. Color stripping
    a. Colors overlap
    b. Similar to complementary flats
    c. Make window masks for halftones
6. Proofing
    a. Make proofs to check accuracy
    b. Customers should approve proofs

SECTION 12
LITHOGRAPHIC IMAGE CARRIERS

Section Goal: To provide information for students to learn about commercial-type lithographic image carriers (plates) and to learn how to prepare both direct image and pre-sensitized plates.

Section Description: Emphasis is placed on preparing plates for offset lithography duplicators. It is recognized that many industrial plants use kinds of plates other than those discussed in this section; but, the major instructional laboratories will deal primarily with those included here.

No attempt was made to include all the materials and equipment provided by the many manufacturers. The authors expect that instructors will adjust procedures described in the textbook to conform to their equipment and the specifications provided by the manufacturer of the plate used in the laboratory. The students' understanding can be expanded by referring them to the technical literature available from manufacturers and by encouraging students to visit local printers.

Units 96 and 97 could be combined in a single lesson and Units 98, 99, 100, and 101 should be included for one demonstration. Unit 102 has been included as an enrichment unit, and class discussion could be expanded by field trips.

Unit 96. Introduction to Lithographic Image Carriers

A. Objectives

The students, upon completing the reading, questions, and classroom discussion, will be able to

1. Identify and explain the purpose of the plate in the lithographic printing process.
2. Categorize lithographic printing plates by material and preparation procedure.

B. Instructor preparation

1. Secure several kinds of plates, including at least direct-image and presensitized.
2. Obtain a layout, copy, flat, and plate to show the sequence of operations to produce a plate.
3. Prepare the printing press/duplicator to show how the plate is used.
4. Consider obtaining and using the following videotape from the GAT/GAERF Videotape Project: Number 016, *Offset Platemaking*.

C. Suggested teaching outline

1. Show plates to students
   a. Direct-image
   b. Pre-sensitized
   c. Others
2. Use plates on the press
   a. Explain inking process
   b. Show image transfer

Unit 97. Kinds of Plates

A. Objectives

Students, as a result of reading Unit 97, answering the questions from Unit 102, receiving demonstrations, and engaging in the activities, will be able to

1. Classify the major kinds of lithographic image carriers.
2. Describe the characteristics of lithographic image carriers.

B. Instructor preparation

This unit should set the stage for subsequent units. Most instructors will not use all of the kinds of plates described in Unit 97. The instructor should try to collect examples of the plates not used in the laboratory. In most cases a discussion of the kinds of plates can be followed by demonstrations about how to prepare the plate.

An important outcome of the unit should be that students clearly understand what happens to make a lithographic plate produce an image. That is, they should understand that certain parts of the plate accept water and certain parts reject water (accept ink).

C. **Suggested teaching outline**
1. Plate groups
   a. Surface
   b. Deep etch
2. Surfaces
   a. Smooth
   b. Grained
3. Laser-imaged plates
   a. Applied directly to the plate
   b. No copy, film, or stripping
   c. Saving in time, material, and labor
4. Surface plates
   a. Pre-sensitized
      (1) Additive
      (2) Subtractive
   b. Direct image
   c. Electrostatic
   d. Diffusion-transfer
   e. Photo-direct
   f. Direct image
5. Deep-etch plates

Unit 98. Exposing Pre-Sensitized Plates

A. **Objectives**

Students will, as a result of reading Unit 98, answering questions from Unit 102, and completing appropriate activities, be able to
1. Recognize and use platemaking equipment.
2. Establish proper plate exposure.
3. Properly handle and expose pre-sensitized plates.

B. **Instructor preparation**

The information contained in Unit 98 is the procedure for exposing plates with specific kinds of equipment. If the instructor has different equipment, adjustments will have to be made in the procedure given in the textbook.
1. Obtain and organize the following:
   a. Flat to be used for exposing a plate
   b. Pre-sensitized plates
   c. Platemaker's sensitivity guide (gray scale)
2. Clean and prepare the platemaker. Some instructors prefer to clean the platemaker as part of the demonstration to illustrate the total procedure. This emphasizes that the platemaker should be cleaned regularly.

C. Suggested teaching outline

1. Plate material
   a. Base materials
      (1) Metal
      (2) Plastic
      (3) Paper
   b. Coating
      (1) Light-sensitive
      (2) Safe in subdued light
   c. Others
      (1) Press size
      (2) Attachment methods
      (3) Surface durability
2. Exposure frame (platemaker)
   a. Vacuum frame
      (1) Rubber blanket
      (2) Glass cover
      (3) Compresses flat to plate
   b. Light source
      (1) Point source (single light)
      (2) Ultraviolet
          (a) Mercury vapor
          (b) Pulsed xenon
          (c) Metal halide
3. Plate exposure
   a. Platemaker's sensitivity guide
      (1) Transparent gray scale
      (2) Obtain optimum exposure time
      (3) Attached to the flat
          (a) Developed with image
          (b) Consult manufacturer's specificiations
   b. Plate exposure procedure
      Consult Unit 98 for accurate procedure or use manufacturer's specifications.

Unit 99. Processing Pre-Sensitized Plates

A. Objectives

Students, as a result of reading Unit 99, answering questions from Unit 102, and engaging in reinforcing activities, will be able to

1. Display an attitude reflecting systematic procedure toward processing pre-sensitized plates.
2. Accurately and efficiently process pre-sensitized plates.

B. Instructor preparation

This unit will usually be combined with Units 98 and 100 to provide a complete and sequential lesson. As with the other units in this section, Unit 99 uses illustrations for only one kind of plate. Instructors should alter the information to be consistent with the kind of plate used in the laboratory or printing plant.

1. Prepare platemaking table or sink. This will vary from situation to situation.
2. Secure the following items:
   a. Exposed plate

b. Sponge

c. Dryer

d. Clamps

e. Chemicals for processing plates

C. Suggested teaching outline

The procedures given in Unit 99 are for specific brands of additive and subtractive plates. If you do not use these plates in your laboratory, substitute the instructions from the manufacturer of the plate that is used in your laboratory.

Unit 100. Preparing Diffusion-Transfer, Direct Image, and One-Step Photographic Plates

A. Objectives

After reading Unit 100, answering the appropriate questions from Unit 102, and engaging in the related activities, students will be able to

1. Identify kinds of plates that can be prepared without the need of a flat.

2. Prepare direct image and diffusion transfer plates.

3. Understand the process for preparing one-step plates.

B. Instructor preparation

Every laboratory should be able to demonstrate direct image plates. However, since diffusion-transfer and one-step photographic plates require special equipment and supplies, it may not be possible to demonstrate how to prepare these kinds of plates. It is important that instructors devote time to at least discuss diffusion-transfer and one-step photographic plates. The instructor can reinforce the discussion with a field trip to a plant where the processes are used.

The material necessary to demonstrate how to prepare the three kinds of plates discussed in Unit 100 will depend on which ones the instructor is able to illustrate. The direct image plate will require the following materials and equipment:

1. Carbon ribbon typewriter

2. Materials

   a. Direct image plates

   b. Grease pencil

   c. Nonreproducing pencil

   d. Reproducing pencil

   e. Ball-point pen

   f. Eraser

   g. Drawing instruments

C. Suggested teaching outline

The outline given below is for direct image plates. The instructor should consult manufacturer instructions to develop an outline for diffusion-transfer and one-step photographic plates.

1. Nature of direct-image plates

   a. Paper-base

   b. Water-resistant coating

   c. Accepts grease image

      (1) Ink receptive

      (2) Repels water

   d. Image applied mechanically to the surface

2. Plates

   a. Made for duplicators

     b. Guidelines
        (1) Drawing
        (2) Typing
        (3) Will not print
     c. Kinds of ends
        (1) Straight
        (2) Pinbar
        (3) Slotted

3. Image-producing methods
     a. Must be ink-receptive (grease) image
     b. Typewriter
     c. Pencils and pens
     d. Ball-point pens
     e. Drawing

4. Typing on direct-image plates
     a. Easy as paper
     b. Prepare typewriter
        (1) Clean roller
        (2) Typewriter characters
     c. Place ribbon in typewriter
        (1) Suitable for direct-image plates
        (2) Sometimes different from regular ribbon
     d. Place plate in typewriter
        (1) Hold by edges
        (2) Adjust carefully
     e. Adjust pressure
        (1) Must be even
        (2) Not too heavy
        (3) Not too light

5. Drawing on direct-image plates
     a. Kinds
        (1) Pencils
            (a) Grease
            (b) Reproducing pencil
            (c) Nonreproducing pencil
        (2) Pens
            (a) Ball-point
            (b) Ink
     b. Use drawing board
     c. Draw guidelines
        (1) Nonreproducing pencil
        (2) Use drawing instruments
        (3) Could be freehand
     d. Go over guidelines
     e. Avoid fingerprints

Unit 101. Correcting, Preserving, and Storing Pre-Sensitized Plates

A. Objectives

Students, after reading Unit 100, completing appropriate questions from Unit 102, and engaging in related activities, will be able to

1. Make simple corrections in pre-sensitized plates.
2. Adequately preserve plates for later use on presses.
3. Store plates for protection and later reference.

B. Instructor preparation

This is the culminating unit in a series dealing with pre-sensitized plates. Most instructors will want to include the information in this unit with the previous units to ensure a complete demonstration.

1. Secure the following items:
   a. Processed plates with errors. If there are no errors, the instructor can fabricate situations for demonstrations.
   b. Deletion fluid
   c. Eraser
   d. Scratch awl, knife, or needle
   e. Plate tusche
   f. Gum arabic
2. Prepare and organize table or sink where plate work is done.

C. Suggested teaching outline

1. Making corrections
   a. Deletions
      (1) Remove unwanted image
      (2) Done on the press
      (3) Done before press
      (4) Eraser (soft rubber)
      (5) Deletion fluid (large areas)
   b. Additions
      (1) Scratching
         (a) Repair broken lines
         (b) Damaged letters
      (2) Tusche
         (a) Holes in sold areas
         (b) Done before preserving
   c. Avoid correcting plates when possible
2. Preserving plates
   a. Prevent oxidation
   b. Prevent scratches
   c. Purpose
      (1) Later use
      (2) Reuse
   d. Gum arabic used
3. Storing plates
   a. Protect
   b. Later identification
   c. Hang rather than stack
   d. Place in envelopes
   e. Store in cool dry place

SECTION 13
LITHOGRAPHIC IMAGE TRANSFER

Section Goal: To introduce the students to lithography theory and to the operational procedures of a common litho press/duplicator.

Section Description: The first two units (Units 103 and 104) give the students needed background information. This information should help them to better understand the duplicator or press they might be working on in the school laboratory or in a commercial plant. Hopefully, this information also will be beneficial to students in preparation for a field trip that you might arrange to a commercial printing plant within your locality. The schematics shown of the cylinder and roller arrangements of several of the duplicators and presses may help students to understand more thoroughly what is happening when they see a machine operating in a commercial plant.

Unit 105, Safety with the Offset Lithography Duplicator/Press, is designed to suggest safety practices and procedures which you and your students should observe, if a safe laboratory is to be maintained. Units 106–111 are concerned with the operation of a litho duplicator.

The feeding and delivery systems include aspects that closely resemble commercial presses and do allow for close registration of multi-color work. Other features of this duplicator are similar to other brands of equipment of the same size that are on the market today; therefore, there is little difference in operating procedures with the inking, dampening, and cylinder systems. If you have an offset lithography duplicator/press in your laboratory different from the one shown in these units, it would be appropriate to have your students study the operational procedures of this machine since, basically, all machines operate the same way. If a person thoroughly learns operating procedures for one machine, he or she should be capable of transferring this knowledge to a different machine with little difficulty.

Unit 112 entitled Learning Experiences is designed to assist you and your students by providing key terms, study questions and suggested activities that students may become involved in to help them better understand the broad area of litho presswork. As in the previous learning experience units you may desire to select the terms, questions and activities you wish your students to become involved in. Many terms, questions and several activities were provided purposefully to allow you the opportunity for flexibility in your teaching.

Unit 103. Introduction to Offset Lithography Presswork

A. Objectives

Upon reading, defining the key terms, and answering the study questions relating to this unit, students should be able to

1. Locate and describe the function of each of the five systems of a litho duplicator or press.
2. Illustrate the three following offset lithography press designs: three-cylinder, two-cylinder, and four-cylinder press design
3. Distinguish between lithography presswork and letterset presswork.

B. Instructor preparation

1. Obtain and use the following DCA Educational Products transparencies *GA-25, Offset Lithography Duplicator—Two Cylinder Design; GA-26, Offset Lithography Duplicator—Three Cylinder Design; GA-27, Offset Lithography Press;* and *GA-79, Offset Lithography Press Systems.*
2. Prepare a transparency of Fig. 103–6, in which a heavy-duty press design is shown, and a transparency of Fig. 103–8, which shows the schematics of an offset lithography and letterset press. See Appendix M, Visual Masters 7 and 8. These illustrations are not available from commercial transparency sources, and it is likely that you will desire to discuss these press designs in class presentations of this unit.
3. Request advertising materials from various duplicator and press manufacturers that will be appropriate to show your students during a presentation and/or have them review the materials during their independent study time.

C. Suggested teaching outline

1. Offset lithography press systems
   a. Feeding system
   b. Cylinder system (printing)
   c. Dampening system
   d. Inking system
   e. Delivery system
2. Press designs
   a. Three-cylinder design
   b. Two-cylinder design
   c. Four-cylinder design
3. Offset lithography and letterset press design

Unit 104. Offset Lithography Duplicators and Presses

A. Objectives

Upon reading, defining the key terms, and answering the study questions relating to this unit, students should be able to

1. Distinguish between a litho duplicator and a litho press.
2. Recognize some of the common litho duplicators and presses that are available and being used in schools, offices, and commercial printing facilities.

B. Instructor preparation

1. Obtain and use the several transparencies from DCA Educational Products entitled *GA-80, Two Color Sheet Fed Offset Lithography Press Design; GA-81, Offset Lithography Perfecting Press; GA-82, Web Offset Newspaper Press; GA-83, Multi-Unit and Level Offset Web Press;* and *GA-84, Three Color Web Offset Press Unit.* These transparencies can be used by you during a class presentation and made available to the students for independent study purposes.
2. As with Unit 103, obtain advertising brochures on an many litho duplicators and presses as possible; then use the brochures to illustrate the many different manufacturers, sizes, and capabilities of machines that are available. Also, allow the students to look through these brochures as part of their independent study.
3. Consider obtaining and using the following videotape from the GAT/GAERF Videotape Project: Number 003, *Operating a Medium-Size Sheet-Fed Press.*

C. Suggested teaching outline

1. Litho duplicators and presses
   a. What makes the difference
   b. Precision machines
   c. Several manufacturers
2. Office duplicators
   a. Designed for simple and fast operation
   b. Table-top and floor models available
   c. Single lever control
   d. Program control
3. Form and job duplicators
   a. Web-fed multiple units
   b. Single and multiple color units
4. Commercial presses
   a. Used for high quality
   b. Single and multiple color units

    c. Publication presses

    d. High speed, multi-unit, and complex

  5. Lithographic proof presses

    a. Designed to simulate the production press

    b. Single color—flat bed design

    c. Four-color, rotary design

Unit 105. Safety with the Offset Lithography Duplicator/Press

This unit has been prepared and positioned within this section with a single primary thought. That thought is to assist you and your students with personal safety. The introductory paragraphs provide a small amount of background information, with the remaining content being concerned with safety practices. Be sure your students study this unit very thoroughly prior to working on laboratory assignments relating to litho presswork.

Unit 106. The Offset Lithography Duplicator/Press

A. Objectives

Upon reading, defining the key terms, and answering the study questions relating to this unit, students should be able to

1. Identify and discuss the purpose of the feeding system controls for a litho duplicator/press.

2. Identify and discuss the purpose of the cylinder system controls for a litho duplicator/press.

3. Identify and discuss the purpose of the dampening system controls for a litho duplicator/press.

4. Identify and discuss the purpose of the ink system controls for a litho duplicator/press.

5. Identify and discuss the purpose of the delivery system controls for a litho duplicator/press.

B. Instructor preparation

1. Obtain and use DCA Educational Products transparencies *GA-28, Lithography Press Dampening System* and *GA-29, Lithography Press Inking System*. If this type of litho duplicator/press is not available in your laboratory, you may wish to use the instruction manual for your machine.

2. See Appendix M, Visual Master 9 for an illustration of the AB Dick integrated dampening and inking system. Make a transparency of this illustration if it will properly serve your needs.

C. Suggested teaching outline

1. Feeding system controls

    a. Speed-control lever

    b. Left and right jogger control knobs

    c. Air-blow control

    d. Vacuum control

    e. Back paper feed control

    f. Paper platform handwheel

    g. Left and right paper stack side guides

    h. Paper stack back guide

2. Cylinder system controls

    a. Handwheel

    b. Manual plate-to-blanket impression control

    c. Vertical positioning control knob

3. Dampening system controls

    a. Dampener fountain roller control knob

    b. Dampener volume control

      c. Form roller control lever

      d. Auxiliary dampener form roller control knob

  4. Ink system controls

      a. Ink fountain roller control knob

      b. Ink volume control

      c. Ink fountain manual-control lever

  5. Delivery system controls

      a. Delivery sheet stop

      b. Delivery lock release

      c. Delivery paper feed control

      d. Delivery pile handwheel

      e. Delivery rate lowering control

      f. Automatic copy counter

  6. Miscellaneous controls and devices

      a. Delivery light

      b. Delivery side guide control knobs

      c. Delivery board

      d. Drive motor switch

      e. Air vacuum pump switch

      f. Paper platform

Unit 107. Preparing the Offset Lithography Duplicator/Press

A. Objectives

Upon reading, answering the study questions, and completing the activities relating to this unit, students should be able to

1. Perform the process of properly adjusting the feeding system of the litho duplicator/press.
2. Perform the process of properly adjusting the delivery system of the litho duplicator/press.
3. Ink the duplicator/press according to the procedures outlined in the unit.
4. Prepare the dampening system of the litho duplicator/press according to the procedures outlined in the unit.

B. Instructor preparation

1. Assess the condition of the duplicator/press that will be used for the class demonstration. If any maintenance is needed, take care of this well in advance of the actual demonstration date so necessary repair parts can be secured and installed.
2. Obtain all necessary materials needed to demonstrate the procedures involved in preparing the litho duplicator/press for the actual printing operation.

C. Suggested teaching outline

1. Preparing the feeding system

      a. Lower the paper plateform

      b. Set the paper stack guide

      c. Set the front paper guides

      d. Adjust the suction feet

      e. Adjust the air-blow

      f. Insert the paper

      g. Adjust the back and side guides

h. Raise the paper pile

i. Adjust the feedboard and joggers

2. Preparing the delivery system

a. Raise the delivery board

b. Adjust the side guides

c. Adjust the back jogging guide

d. Lower the pile

3. Preparing the inking system

a. Inspect and clean the ink rollers

b. Fill the ink fountain

c. Adjust the ink fountain

d. Adjust the ink flow

4. Making ready the dampening system

a. Dampening rollers, inspection and cleaning

b. Mix the fountain solution

c. Add the fountain solution

d. Moisten the dampening rollers

Unit 108. Operating the Offset Lithography Duplicator/Press

A. Objectives

Upon reading, defining the key term, answering the study questions, and completing the activities relating to this unit, students should be able to

1. Attach and securely fasten a prepared plate (image carrier) to the plate cylinder of the duplicator/press.

2. Perform the necessary steps required to starting the duplicator/press and printing a few sheets of paper.

3. Analyze the printed sheets to determine the necessary vertical, horizontal, and diagonal adjustments that are necessary to achieve proper printing position.

4. Compare the ink coverage with a properly printed product to determine whether more, or less, ink is needed for desired results.

B. Instructor preparation

1. Analyze the condition of the duplicator/press to determine whether maintenance work will be needed prior to the demonstration and student use.

2. Secure all supplies and tools necessary for the demonstration of the machine.

3. Organize the chemicals, ink, wiping pads, and other necessary supplies around the machine; then students will know where the needed materials are located and where to return them following their use. In other words, prepare the area for neat and safe operation of the duplicator or press.

4. Consider obtaining and using the following videotape from the GAT/GAERF Videotape Project: Number 001, *Operating A Small Offset Press.*

C. Suggested teaching outline

1. Attaching and securing the plate (image carrier)

2. Starting the duplicator/press

a. Wipe down the plate

b. Turn on the power

c. Lower the dampening roller

d. Lower the inking rollers

e. Begin the paper feed

3. Stopping the duplicator/press
    a. Turn off the paper feed
    b. Raise the ink rollers
    c. Raise the dampening roller
    d. Turn off the power
4. Printing position adjustments
    a. Vertical
    b. Horizontal
    c. Diagonal

Unit 109. Offset Lithography Duplicator/Press Adjustments

A. Objectives

Upon reading, defining the key terms, answering the study questions, and completing the activities relating to this unit, students should be able to

1. Determine and accomplish the necessary adjustments to the feeding system, which are needed to ensure that the paper feed is accurate.
2. Solve necessary adjustments appropriate to the delivery system.
3. Analyze inking system adjustments and to position all ink rollers properly.
4. Analyze the dampening system adjustments and to position all dampening rollers properly.
5. Perform the required adjustments and settings among the plate, blanket, and impression cylinders.
6. Install a blanket on the blanket cylinder according to the guidelines presented in this unit.
7. Summarize the construction of a blanket and to perform the necessary steps in preserving a blanket.

B. Instructor preparation

1. Thoroughly practice these various machine adjustments prior to demonstrating and/or asking the students to complete them. In this way you will detect whether the machine is operating and functioning properly.
2. Obtain the various materials needed to make press adjustments. Also, have a new or reconditioned blanket available for attachment to the blanket cylinder.
3. Consider obtaining and using the following videotape from the GAT/GAERF Videotape Project: Number 002, *Small Offset Press Adjustments and Preventive Maintenance.*

C. Suggested teaching outline

1. Feeding system adjustments
    a. Double-sheet eliminator
    b. Elevator control knob
    c. Printing speed
2. Delivery system adjustments
    a. Delivery rate lowering control
    b. Jogging guides
3. Inking system adjustments
    a. Form rollers
    b. Other ink rollers
4. Dampening system adjustments
    a. Form roller
    b. Oscillator roller
    c. Ductor roller

5. Cylinder system adjustments
   a. Plate-to-blanket impression
   b. Blanket-to-paper impression
6. Blanket installation
   a. Removal of old blanket
   b. Attachment to the lead clamp
   c. Attachment to the blanket tail clamp
   d. Securing the blanket
7. Blanket construction and preservation

Unit 110. Lithographic Printing Problems

A. Objectives

Upon reading, defining the key terms, answering the study questions, and completing the activity relating to this unit, students should be able to

1. Diagnose the printing problems associated with operating a litho duplicator/press.
2. Remedy the printing problems as diagnosed.

B. Instructor preparation

1. Keep a file of printed sheets that are less than the desired results. Group these samples according to specific problems and keep a written record of how the problem was solved or possibly not solved. Use these examples in your class presentation and/or for display purposes.
2. Learn to know your litho duplicator and preses quite well; then you will be more able to assist your students in solving printing problems which may occur as they are using the equipment.
3. Consider obtaining and using the videotape titled *Duplicator Press: Problems & Solutions* from Sunshine Enterprises, Spokane, WA.

C. Suggested teaching outline

1. Quality results
   a. How to recognize quality
   b. How to achieve quality
2. Printing problems
   a. How to diagnose a problem
   b. How to solve the problem
3. Common printed sheet problems
   a. Background dirty scumming
   b. Gray washed out, dirty background
   c. Too dark
   d. Weak spots
   e. Non-image area filling
   f. Image breaks down while plate is running

Unit 111. Cleaning the Offset Lithography Duplicator/Press

A. Objectives

Upon reading, defining the key terms, answering the study questions, and completing the activity relating to this unit, students should be able to

1. Thoroughly clean the dampening system of the litho duplicator/press.
2. Thoroughly clean the inking system of the litho duplicator/press.
3. Completely remove all foreign material from the cylinder system of the litho duplicator/press.

4. Secure the machine for the down period.

B. Instructor preparation

1. Obtain all necessary materials and supplies needed to thoroughly clean the entire duplicator/press following a printing operation. Such materials are ink solvent, wiping cloths, cleanup mats, and other small items.

C. Suggested teaching outline

1. Demonstration—Cleaning the dampening system
2. Demonstration—Cleaning the inking system
3. Demonstration—Cleaning the cylinder system
4. Demonstration—Securing the total duplicator/press.

SECTION 14
GRAVURE PRINTING PROCESS

Section Goal: To present a major printing process known as gravure through words, illustrations, photographs, and actual experiences.

Section Description: The gravure printing method is one of the four major methods of reproducing graphic products. It s hould be treated with the same time and effort as the other three major methods of reproduction—letterpress, lithography, and screen printing. Unfortunately, it is difficult to give students practical experiences with this method because of the unique methods necessary to produce an image carrier. Also, the commercial-size equipment used to reproduce images (printing press) is so large that one machine would more than fill most graphic arts educational laboratories.

Commercial appliations of the gravure printing method are presented in Units 113, 114, and 115. Content that can be conducted in the educational setting has been grouped in Units 117, 118, and 119. As in previous units where laboratory experiences are suggested with the use of equipment or etching and cutting materials, the safety unit (Unit 116) contains information valuable to you and to your students.

Several key terms and questions have been designed to self-test the student on his or her knowledge of the material contained in this section. These are presented in Unit 120, "Learning Experiences." The four suggested activities should give the students some practical experiences in the gravure area. They also should help them better understand this important process of reproducing graphic materials.

Your attention is drawn to the page immediately following the learning activities unit which is entitled "The Printed Page Can Live Forever." The content included in this page is a tremendous example showing the importance of the printed word. Require your students to read this page, since it is a true example of how the printed page "can live forever."

Unit 113. Introduction to the Gravure Printing Process

A. Objectives

Upon reading, defining the key terms, answering the study questions, and completing the activity related to this unit, students should be able to

1. Define the term "gravure" and explain how the gravure method of printing differs from the other major methods of reproducing graphic images.

2. Identify and collect products that have been printed via the gravure process.

3. Summarize the several advantages and disadvantages of the gravure printing method.

4. Generalize the historical development of the gravure printing process.

B. Instructor preparation

1. Review the entire Section 14 "Gravure Printing Process" to become very familiar with its content. In this way you will have a better understanding of what the students will be reading, thereby limiting your discussion in this unit basically to the content contained in it.

2. Develop a file of products which have been produced by the gravure printing method. Show these products during the class presentation of this unit and use them for a display board that you might prepare on the gravure printing process.

3. Lay the foundation and make specific plans to take your class on a field trip to a commercial printing plant that uses the gravure printing method.

4. Consider obtaining and using the following videotape from the GAT/GAERF Videotape Project: Number 014, *The Rotogravure Printing Process*.

C. Suggested teaching outline

1. The gravure printing process
   a. Gravure defined

      b. Intaglio defined

      c. Comparison to the other major printing processes

  2. Products produced by gravure

      a. Reading materials

      b. Packaging materials

      c. Specific products

      d. Currency and stamps

  3. Advantages and disadvantages

      a. Advantages

      b. Disadvantages

  4. Historical highlights

      a. Invented by Karl Kleitsch

      b. Invented in 1880's and 1890's

      c. First commercial use—1914 by the New York Times newspaper

Unit 114. Gravure Image Carriers

A. Objectives

Upon reading, defining the key terms, answering the study questions, and completing the activity relating to this unit, students should be able to

1. Name and tell the uses for each of the three main types of gravure image carriers.

2. Explain the preparatory steps necessary to engraving a gravure cylinder.

3. Summarize the engraving, proofing, and finishing procedures for a gravure cylinder.

B. Instructor preparation

1. Obtain commercial examples of flat plate and wraparound plate gravure image carriers. It is nearly impossible to obtain a gravure image carrier cylinder, although there are small laboratory-model gravure presses available. Small cylinders must be prepared for this style of unit; therefore, it may be possible to obtain a small gravure cylinder. Allow your students to carefully inspect these gravure image carriers with a magnifying glass, to better understand the nature of the printing surface.

2. Write to various gravure equipment manufacturers to obtain literature about the various pieces of equipment that are needed to prepare gravure image carriers. Place these in a convenient file which is accessible to your students and suggest that they review this material as part of their independent study.

C. Suggested teaching outline

1. Types of gravure image carriers

      a. Flat plate

      b. Wraparound plate

      c. Cylinder

2. Gravure cylinder preparation

      a. Copy preparation

      b. Readying the cylinder surface

      c. Engraving the cylinder

      d. Proofing and correcting the cylinder

      e. Finishing the cylinder

Unit 115. Gravure Printing Presses

A. Objectives

Upon reading, defining the key terms, answering the study questions, and completing the activity relating to this unit, students should be able to

1. Summarize the original use of color gravure presses and to note their speeds and sizes.
2. Name recent developments that have improved the reproduction quality of gravure printing presses.
3. Describe the operating principles of a gravure printing press.

B. Instructor preparation

1. Obtain and use DCA Educational Products transparencies *GA-88, Gravure Press Schematic* and *GA-89, Gravure Press Printing Unit*. These two transparencies definitely will assist you in presenting the content of this unit, and it will assist the students with their independent study.
2. Obtain advertising literature from several gravure press manufacturers and encourage your students to review this material, until they become familiar with equipment that is being used in the industry. Since it is nearly impossible to have this kind of equipment in a school setting, it will be necessary to rely upon the material found in the textbook, in the manufacturer's brochures, audiovisual materials, and field trips for an understanding of the gravure printing method.

C. Suggested teaching outline

1. Gravure printing presses
   a. First use of color presses
   b. Press speeds
   c. Electrostatic assist
   d. Computer applications
2. Gravure press operation
   a. The basic principle
   b. The printing unit
   c. Multiunit presses
   d. The doctor blade
3. Gravure proof presses
   a. Operation very similar to a regular press
   b. Corrections based upon the proofed image

Unit 116. Safety When Etching and Engraving

A. Objectives

This unit has been prepared and placed in this position within this section with a single primary thought in mind. That thought is to assist you and your students with personal safety. The introductory paragraphs provide a small amount of background information, with the remaining content being concerned with safety practices. Be sure your students study this unit very thoroughly prior to working on laboratory assignments relating to etching and engraving.

Unit 117. Flat-Plate Gravure Etching

A. Objectives

Upon reading, defining the key terms, answering the study questions, and completing the activity relating to this unit, students should be able to

1. Produce a simulated flat-plate gravure etching.
2. Proof and analyze problems that might be apparent.

B. **Instructor preparation**

1. Obtain the necessary materials to demonstrate and/or have the students produce a flat-plate gravure etching.

2. Practice this suggested procedure of preparing a flat-plate gravure etching and make necessary alterations according to the plate material, the light-sensitive material, the etching solution, the equipment, and other variables that might be present in your situation.

C. **Suggested teaching outline**

1. Making the plate
   a. Obtaining the materials
   b. Cleaning the plate surface
   c. Making the plate surface light sensitive
   d. Exposing the plate
   e. Etching the plate
   f. Flushing the prepared plate
   g. Immerse the plate into developer again
   h. Dry the plate with compressed air

2. Proofing the plate
   a. Placing ink into the image areas
   b. Removing ink from the non-image areas
   c. Pulling the proof
   d. Analyzing noted problems

Unit 118. Hand Engraving and Printing

A. **Objectives**

Upon reading, defining the key terms, answering the study questions, and completing the activity relating to this unit, students should be able to

1. Distinguish between the words "engrave" and "etch."

2. Summarize the use of copper and steel hand engravings.

3. Produce a dry-point engraving and to achieve several acceptable reproductions from the engraving.

B. **Instructor preparation**

1. Build a file of samples that have been reproduced from hand engravings. Display these to your students either in a class presentation or on a classroom display board.

2. Visit a commercial engraving establishment and obtain sample engraved plates. As with the printed examples, use them to help your students better understand this method of producing images.

3. Obtain the necessary materials to produce and print a dry-point engraving. Also, ready the necessary tools and equipment prior to demonstrating and having students complete this activity.

C. **Suggested teaching outline**

1. Etching and engraving
   a. Engraving defined
   b. Etching defined

2. Copper and steel hand engravings
   a. How made
   b. Products produced

3. Dry-point engraving and printing
   a. Selecting the copy
   b. Preparing the plate
   c. Reproducing the prints

Unit 119. Thermography

A. Objectives

Upon reading, defining the key terms, answering the study questions, and completing the activity relating to this unit, students should be able to

1. Define the word "thermography" and to recognize products that have been produced via the thermography method.
2. Perform the production procedure necessary to achieve raised printing (thermography)
3. Choose the appropriate type for thermography printing and to combine the proper powder and ink to produce the highest quality job.

B. Instructor preparation

1. Gather several samples of products which have been produced via the thermography method. Allow your students to thoroughly inspect these samples to obtain a good understanding of the value of this special technique.
2. Obtain the necessary equipment, powders, and special items that are needed to accomplish thermography printing in the school laboratory.

C. Suggested teaching outline

1. Thermography
   a. Its definition
   b. Materials and equipment needed to produce thermography printing.
2. Production procedure
   a. Printing
   b. Applying the powder
   c. Removing the excess powder
   d. Heating the powder
   e. Handling the completed product
3. Design limitations
4. Powders and inks

SECTION 15
SCREEN PRINTING

Section Goal: To introduce the students to the screen printing method which is one of the four major printing processes.

Section Description: This section contains fifteen units which makes it the longest section in the textbook. An attempt has been made to present sufficient content to provide the students with an understanding of the industrial screen printing methods, as well as the application of screen printing in the graphic arts laboratory. Entire books have been written on this single major graphic reproduction method; therefore, no claim is being made that the content in this section is complete in itself. It will, however, provide information and experiences to give students a solid understanding of this reproduction method.

Introductory information about the screen printing method is presented in Unit 121. Industrial equipment and a general review of industrial production methods are shown and discussed in Unit 122. The remaining units are designed specifically to provide information and experiences for the classroom, although these methods do not vary appreciably when they are used within industrial settings. Since this section includes considerable information regarding screen printing, you may desire to utilize only a few of the units.

This, of course, depends upon the course objectives and also the time, equipment, and supplies available. For example, Unit 125, entitled Building a Screen Printing Press, may not be appropriate for your situation, since screen printing units usually are already available. It is believed that this content should be presented for those students desiring to produce their own frames for use outside the classroom. After the students have experienced this reproduction method in the classroom, many of them will desire to prepare their own printing unit for use in their own homes.

The key terms, study questions and suggested activities in Unit 136 are designed to help both you and the students to get involved immediately into some "doing activities." Have the students complete the key terms, and study questions you deem appropriate and require them to complete the activities that are most timely and valuable for them.

Unit 121. Introduction to Screen Printing

A. Objectives

Upon reading, defining the key terms, answering the study questions, and completing the activity relating to this unit, students should be able to

1. Compare the screen printing graphic reproduction method with the other major reproduction methods of letterpress, lithography, and gravure.
2. Summarize the historical highlights of screen process printing.
3. Distinguish screen printed products from other methods of graphic reproduction.
4. Name three basic methods used to prepare screen printing image carriers.

B. Instructor preparation

1. Obtain a complete screen printing unit which is used for hand production. Also, obtain a hand-cut film image carrier. Use these materials to explain the basic reproduction process of screen printing.
2. Build a file of products that has been printed by the screen process printing method. As with other examples that you have in your laboratory, use these in your class presentation and for display purposes.
3. Review this entire section very thoroughly; then it will be possible for you to brief your students on the content they are expected to read and the activities they will be completing.
4. Obtain and use DCA Educational Products transparencies *SP-1, Screen Printing; SP-2, This is*

Screen Printing; SP-3, *A Basic Screen Printing Unit;* SP-4, *How Screen Printing Works;* and *SP-11, Overview of Screen Stencils.*

5. Consider obtaining and using the following videotape from the GAT/GAERF Videotape Project: Number 012, *Basic Screen Printing.*

C. Suggested teaching outline

1. Screen printing
    a. Known by various names
    b. The image-transfer principle
    c. Components necessary for printing
2. Historical highlights
    a. Screen printing done in ancient times
    b. First use in Europe
    c. First use in United States
    d. Recent events
3. Products
    a. Two-dimensional
    b. Three-dimensional
    c. Cylindrical objects
4. The three categories of image carriers
    a. Knife-cut film
    b. Photographic
    c. Washout (tusche)

Unit 122. Industrial Equipment and Production Methods

A. Objectives

Upon reading, defining the key terms, answering the study questions, and completing the activity relating to this unit, students should be able to

1. Name and briefly describe the four styles of screen process printing machines.
2. Recognize commercial screen printing units.
3. Explain the purpose and use for drying equipment that is needed with screen printing.

B. Instructor preparation

1. Write to several screen printing equipment manufacturers to obtain their latest literature. Encourage your students to review this literature, to become aware of current equipment and practices utilized within the commercial industry.
2. Obtain and use DCA Educational Products transparencies *GA-90, Screen Process Press Schematic* and *SP-28, Some Commercial Screen Printing Equipment.*
3. Obtain and use audiovisual materials, such as 16mm films and 8mm single-concept films, in the group presentation and for individual study. Slide tape series also may be available; therefore, search the AV catalogues and audiovisual sections of professional organizational literature.

C. Suggested teaching outline

1. The various screen principles
    a. Rotary screen
    b. Rocker-type machine
    c. Bottle-printing machines
    d. Flat-bed type machines

2. Printing machines for commercial use
    a. Hand-operated
    b. Flat-bed
    c. Cylinder
    d. Rotary
    e. Specialty
3. Drying Equipment
    a. Wood or metal drying racks
    b. Wicket dryers
    c. Drying ovens
    d. Continuous conveyor-belt dryers
    e. Ultraviolet (UV) Curing Units

Unit 123. Screen Printing Equipment for Hand Production

A. Objectives

Upon reading, defining the key terms, answering the study questions, and completing the activity relating to this unit, students should be able to

1. List necessary screen printing eqiupment for hand production.
2. Select the correct screen fabric for the kind of job that will be printed.
3. Select the squeegee that will serve the best purpose for the product being printed.
4. Recognize the common film-cutting tools and will know their applied use.
5. Build necessary drying equipment either for two-dimensional flat objects or for textile materials.

B. Instructor preparation

1. Inventory your supply of screen process materials and tools. If any items need repair, replacing, or must be purchasd, it would be beneficial to obtain these items well in advance of your students' needs.
2. After completing suggestion 1, you may desire to browse through one or more screen process supply and equipment catalogues. Quite likely, you will spot one or more items that would be beneficial to have available in your laboratory.
3. Obtain and use DCA Educational Products transparencies *SP-5, The Squeegee*; *SP-6, The Frame*; and *SP-7, Screen Printing Fabrics*.
4. Determine whether it is possible to obtain additional supplies, tools, or equipment with your present budget. If possible, select items that would augment your present supplies, tools, or equipment. If your budget will not permit additional spending for screen process materials this year, it is suggested that you make a list in rank order of the items needed most. Price them and when it comes time to place orders for the succeeding year, you will have a jump on the whole system.

C. Suggested teaching outline

1. Equipment for hand production
    a. Frame
    b. Screen fabric
    c. Squeegee
    d. Film-cutting tools
    e. Drying equipment
2. The screen fabric
    a. Materials used
    b. Typical mesh counts of silk

3. The squeegee
   a. Its purpose
   b. Basic structure
   c. Various blade angles
4. Film-cutting tools
   a. Single-blade knives
   b. Circle cutters
   c. Line cutters
5. Drying equipment
   a. For flat objects
   b. For textile materials and products

Unit 124. Safety With Screen Printing Equipment and Materials

This unit has been prepared and placed in this position within this section with one primary thought in mind. That thought is to assist you and your students with personal safety. The introductory paragraphs provide a small amount of background information with the remaining content being concerned with safety practices.

Be sure your students study this unit very thoroughly prior to working on laboratory assignments relating to screen printing. Consider obtaining and using the filmstrip or slide set titled *Art Hazards Alert: An Introduction*, available from the International Film Bureau, Inc.

Unit 125. Building a Screen Printing Press

A. Objectives

Upon reading, defining the key terms, answering the study questions, and completing the activity relating to this unit, students should be able to

1. Construct a hand-operated screen printing unit, including the frame and base.
2. Attach and properly secure the screen fabric to the screen printing frame.

B. Instructor preparation

1. If screen printing units are needed in your laboratory, it will be necessary for you to obtain the required supplies for their construction. Supplies needed will be wood, hinges, screen fabric, cord, wing-nut bolts, and masking tape. Make arrangements with your colleague in the materials processing laboratory to use the equipment necessary to construct the screen printing units. If you have students constructing these units, it is suggested that only one or two students work together; therefore, there will be less need for direct supervision in one laboratory while you are holding regular graphic arts classes in your own laboratory.
2. If you should choose not to construct the screen printing units yourself, make arrangements for this to be done in a materials processing or manufacturing class. Sometimes an activity like this will work well for a production activity, and it is likely the graphic arts class could reciprocate by producing a printed product that could be utilized in the materials processing or manufacturing laboratory.
3. Obtain and use DCA Educational Products transparencies *SP-8, Stretching Fabric: Staple Method; SP-9, Stretching Fabric: Cord & Groove Method;* and *SP-10, Finishing the Screen.*

C. Suggested teaching outline

1. Frame construction
   a. Commonly used woods
   b. Screen and image size ratio
   c. Construction procedure

2. Base construction
   a. Commonly used materials
   b. Screen and base size ratio
   c. Construction procedure
3. Attaching the screen fabric
   a. Various methods possible
   b. Cutting the fabric to correct size
   c. Stretching and securing the fabric
4. Taping the frame

Unit 126. Artwork for Screen Printing

A. Objectives

Upon reading, defining the key terms, answering the study questions, and completing the activity relating to this unit, students should be able to

1. Select and/or prepare artwork appropriate for use with one or more of the several methods of producing a screen image carrier.
2. Prepare artwork for multiple-color reproduction.

B. Instructor preparation

1. Obtain several art books or clippings that are appropriate for one of the different methods of preparing screen process image carriers. Arrange this collection of artwork in a location within the laboratory where students can browse through the material and use it for their individual or group activity. Make very attempt to keep this artwork in good order and condition, and add to it as additional artwork is identified.
2. Prepare an example set of artwork showing the three different methods for dividing four-color. Use these examples in your class presentation or display them where students can carefully study them prior to preparing their own multiple-color artwork.
3. Obtain and use DCA Educational Products transparency *SP-16, Artwork for Photostencils.*

C. Suggested teaching outline

1. Artwork for screen printing
   a. Hand-cut film
   b. Direct photosensitive screens
   c. Indirect photographic screen film
   d. Paper stencil
   e. Washout screens
2. Multiple-color artwork
   a. Artwork with an overlay sheet
   b. Artwork with full color
   c. Artwork with overlays

Unit 127. Lacquer-Soluble Hand-Prepared Film

A. Objectives

Upon reading, defining the key terms, answering the study questions, and completing the activity relating to this unit, students should be able to

1. Cut hand-prepared lacquer-soluble screen printing film.
2. Prepare the fabric using a mechanical treatment and a degreasing to accept the stencil.
3. Adhere lacquer-soluble hand-prepared film to the screen fabric.
4. Remove lacquer-soluble film from the screen, following the printing operation.

B. **Instructor preparation**

    1.   Obtain the necessary artwork, cutting tools, film, adhering liquid, and cloths necessary to produce, and adhere lacquer-soluble hand-prepared film. Also, remember the fabric preparation materials.

    2.   It is suggested that you determine a basic size or a limited number of basic sizes of hand-cut lacquer film that can be precut to size for convenient dispensing to the students. If it is necessary for you to charge the students for supplies used, it will be easier to calculate the prices of standard sizes of lacquer film than to calculate the price each time for a different size that will be used. Also, by cutting standard sizes of film, there will be less waste on the large roll of material.

    3.   Practice cutting an entire piece of lacquer film; use it for demonstration purposes, especially when adhering the film to the screen. Actually, it is not necessary to demonstrate the entire cutting of an illustration during a film-cutting demonstration. Much time can be saved if a piece of film is precut.

    4.   Obtain and use DCA Educational Products transparency *SP-14, Making Hand-Cut Stencils*.

C. **Suggested teaching outline**

    1.   A description of lacquer-soluble hand-prepared film

    2.   Demonstration—Cutting the film

        a.   Securing the artwork

        b.   Securing the lacquer film

        c.   Cutting procedures

        d.   Removing the film from image areas

        e.   Replacing film if corrections are needed

        f.   Safety—knives

    3.   Fabric preparation

        a.   Mechanical treatment

        b.   Degreasing

    4.   Adhering the film

        a.   Preparing the screen

        b.   Lacquer film placement

        c.   Applying the adhering liquid

        d.   Absorbing the excess adhering liquid

        e.   Removing the backing sheet

        f.   Safety—ventilation

    5.   Removing film from the screen

        a.   Preparation and supplies needed

        b.   Dissolving the lacquer

        c.   Safety—ventilation and fire

Unit 128. Water-Soluble Hand-Prepared Film

A. **Objectives**

Upon reading, defining the key terms, answering the study questions, and completing the activity relating to this unit, students should be able to

    1.   Cut hand-prepared water-soluble screen printing film.

    2.   Adhere water-soluble hand-prepared film to the screen fabric.

    3.   Remove water-soluble film from the screen following the printing operation.

B. **Instructor preparation**

    1.   Obtain the necessary artwork, cutting tools, film, adhering liquid, and cloths necessary to produce, and adhere water-soluble hand-prepared film.

2. It is suggested that you determine a basic size or a limited number of basic sizes of hand-cut water-soluble film that can be precut to size for convenient dispensing to the students. If it is necessary for you to charge the students for supplies used, it will be easier to calculate the prices of standard sizes of water-soluble film than to calculate the price each time for a different size that will be used. Also, but cutting standard sizes of film, there will be less waste on the large roll of material.

3. Practice cutting an entire piece of water-soluble film; use it for demonstration purposes, especially when adhering the film to the screen. Actually, it is not necessary to demonstrate the entire cutting of an illustration during a film-cutting demonstration. Much time can be saved if a piece of film is precut.

4. Obtain and use DCA Educational Products transparency *SP-14, Making Hand-Cut Stencils.*

C. **Suggested teaching outline**
1. A description of water-soluble hand-prepared film
2. Demonstration—Cutting the film
   a. Securing the artwork
   b. Securing the water-soluble film
   c. Cutting procedures
   d. Removing the film from image areas
   e. Replacing film if corrections are needed
   f. Safety—knives
3. Fabric preparation
4. Adhering the film
   a. Preparing the screen
   b. Water-soluble film placement
   c. Applying the adhering liquid
   d. Absorbing the excess adhering liquid
   e. Removing the backing sheet
   f. Safety—ventilation
5. Removing film from the screen
   a. Preparation and supplies needed
   b. Dissolving the water-soluble film
   c. Safety—ventilation and fire

Unit 129. Direct Photographic Screens

A. **Objectives**

Upon reading, defining the key terms, answering the study questions, and completing the activity relating to this unit, students should be able to
1. Note the advantage of using photographic screen methods over the use of hand-prepared image carriers.
2. Name several printed products that are produced by the direct emulsion photographic screen printing method.
3. Perform operations involved in sensitizing, exposing, and reclaiming the screen.

B. **Instructor preparation**
1. Inventory your supply of direct emulsion photographic supplies. If you are short of materials, as listed in Unit 129, obtain a sufficient supply for demonstration and student purposes.
2. Prepare a direct emulsion photographic screen in its entirety. Use this screen in your class demonstation to show the students exactly how the finished product should look. Also, obtain several products that have been printed by using the direct emulsion photoscreen method and show them the quality of work which actually can be accomplished.

3. Obtain and use DCA Educational Products transparencies *SP-15, Making Photostencils*; *SP-17, Sensitizing the Photostencil*; *SP-18, Washout*; and *SP-21, The Direct Photostencil*.

4. Prepare all materials, tools, and the screen in readiness for the class demonstration. If you personally have not worked with direct emulsion photoscreen for some time, be sure to experiment with it prior to the classroom demonstration.

5. Consider obtaining and using this video from Ulano: *Ulano Direct Emulsion System Video*.

C. **Suggested teaching outline**

1. The photographic screens
   a. Direct emulsion photographic screen method
   b. Indirect photographic screen printing film method
   c. Direct presensitized film method

2. Use of direct emulsion photosensitive screens
   a. For long printing runs
   b. Typical products

3. Demonstration—Sensitizing the screen
   a. Materials needed
   b. Preparing the emulsion
   c. Coating the screen
   d. Storing sensitized dry screens

4. Demonstration—Exposing the screen
   a. Materials needed
   b. Exposing procedure
   c. Developing procedure
   d. Washing out the image

5. Demonstration—Reclaiming the screen
   a. Materials needed
   b. Procedure to follow

Unit 130. Indirect and Direct Photographic Stencil Film

A. **Objectives**

Upon reading, defining the key terms, answering the study questions, and completing the activity relating to this unit, students should be able to

1. Recognize indirect photographic screen printing film.

2. Prepare the copy and a film positive according to specified procedures in earlier units of the textbook.

3. Expose, develop, adhere, and remove the pre-sensitized film.

4. Successfully attach and print with direct (capillary) stencil film.

B. **Instructor preparation**

1. Inventory the supply of chemicals, film, and other necessary materials needed to prepare the photographic screen printing film. If any materials are needed, be certain to stock them prior to demonstrating and making any assignment involved with this method of reproducing a screen image carrier.

2. Go through the entire process of preparing a screen with the photographic film. Determine the necessary exposure time and water temperature for both developing and removing the film from the screen.

3. Obtain and use DCA Educational Products transparencies *SP-19, The Indirect or Transfer Stencil*; *SP-20, Adhering the Indirect Stencil*.

4. Consider obtaining and using these two videos from Ulano: *Ulano Indirect System Photographic Film Video* and *Ulano CDF (TM) Direct-Film System Video.*

5. Gather the necessary materials such as a film positive, the pre-sensitized screen film, the developing solutions, the piece of glass, and the unprinted newsprint paper. Also, of course, obtain a ready stretched screen printing frame and the powder cleanser for use in thoroughly cleaning the screen prior to adhering the film. Arrange these materials in an order appropriate for a classroom demonstration.

C. **Suggested teaching outline**

1. Photographic screen printing film
   a. Its makeup
   b. How to handle

2. Preparing the copy
   a. Layout work
   b. Obtaining the actual copy
   c. Making the film positive

3. Demonstration—Preparing the photographic screen image carrier
   a. Exposing the pre-sensitized film
   b. Developing the film
   c. Adhering the film to the screen
   d. Removing the film from the screen
   e. Safety practices

4. Direct Film Stencils
   a. Concept of direct (capillary) stencil film
   b. Adhering direct stencil film
   c. Exposing direct stencil film
   d. Preparing direct stencil film for printing

Unit 131. Masking the Non-Printing Areas

A. **Objectives**

Upon reading, defining the key terms, answering the study questions, and completing the activity relating to this unit, students should be able to

1. Explain the purpose of masking the non-printing areas of the screen.
2. Perform the screen masking operations of top-paper masking, bottom-paper masking, liquid masking, and tape masking.

B. **Instructor preparation**

1. Inventory your screen supplies to determine whether there are sufficient quantities of masking tape, scrap paper, and liquid masking material. If sufficient quantities of these items are not available, obtain them prior to demonstrating and allowing the students to work in this area.

2. Obtain and use DCA Eduational Products transparency *SP-23, Blockout.*

3. In preparation for the demonstration on masking the screen, it is suggested that you prepare the two masking examples of top-paper masking and bottom-paper masking. By observation of the completed mask, it should be possible for the students to prepare their own. Your demonstration can consist of the procedure involved in liquid masking, using both the brush and the paperboard squeegee for application purposes.

4. Ready all materials in preparation for a demonstration on screen masking techniques. Materials needed will be paper, tape, liquid mask—either lacquer-base or waterbase, brush, paperboard or metal squeegee, and a container to hold the liquid mask. Obviously, it will be necessary to have several screens on which image carriers already have been attached.

   This would be a fine place to use examples of different methods of screen preparation.

C. Suggested teaching outline

1. The purpose of screen masking
2. Demonstration—Paper masking
   a. Top-paper masking
   b. Bottom-paper masking
3. Demonstration—Liquid masking
   a. Brush application
   b. Squeegee application
4. Demonstration—Tape masking

Unit 132. The Screen Printing Operation

A. Objectives

Upon reading, defining the key terms, answering the study questions, and completing the activity relating to this unit, students should be able to

1. Select the appropriate ink for the product being printed.
2. Accomplish the screen printing operation according to the procedures outlined in this unit.
3. Adapt the screen printing unit when it is necessary to print on three-dimensional and cylindrical objects.

B. Instructor preparation

1. Inventory the supply of screen printing ink. Be sure there are sufficient colors in the various kinds or categories of ink that will be needed, according to the products produced in the laboratory. Obtain the necessary inks prior to demonstrating or having your students complete an activity involved with the printing operation.
2. Obtain a supply of small containers, such as juice cans or small paper cups that can be used to mix and to hold the ink during the printing operation. It is unwise to use the ink directly from the ink container can, since the ink will dry out readily, thereby causing considerable waste. No mention was made in the unit regarding the mixing of ink. Special thinners are available for the various kinds of ink; but, for the regular oil base ink, it is possible to use turpentine as the thinner. For normal printing, the ink should be approximately the consistency of cake batter; therefore, in most instances, it will be necessary to thin the ink when taken from the can.
3. Obtain and use DCA Educational Products transparencies *SP-25, Register; SP-26, Screen Printing on Textiles;* and *SP-27, Screen Printing on Non-Flat Surfaces.*
4. Consider obtaining and using the following videotape from the GAT/GAERF Videotape Project: Number 015, *Screen Printing II: Materials and Supplies.*

C. Suggested teaching outline

1. Screen printing ink
   a. Water-base
   b. Oil-base
   c. Synthetic enamel
   d. Lacquer-base
   e. Plastisol
   f. Ultraviolet (UV)
   g. Special formulations
2. Demonstration—Printing procedure
   a. Attaching the frame to the base
   b. Securing the paper guides
   c. Applying the ink

     d. Pulling the squeegee—making a printed copy

     e. Making the flood stroke

     f. Removing the printed copy

     g. Printing multiple copies

  3. Printing on special materials

     a. Thick, flat objects

     b. Cylindrical objects

Unit 133. Screen Cleanup Procedures

A. Objectives

Upon reading, answering the study questions, and completing the activity relating to this unit, students should be able to

1. Recognize the importance of proper screen cleanup and housekeeping procedures.
2. Remove the ink, masking, and image carrier from the screen fabric.
3. Replace the screen printing units and all the supplies and materials used during the screen printing operation in their correct location according to the established laboratory arrangements.

B. Instructor preparation

1. Inventory your supply of newspapers, cleaning rags, and solvents in preparation for the screen cleanup demonstration. Obtain any materials that are in low supply.
2. Secure all the necessary materials and solvents in preparation for the demonstration on screen cleanup procedures. If not done previously, arrange the screen printing area so all tools, supplies, and solvents have a specific location, thereby giving the students the opportunity to learn where the items belong. Labeling each item location will provide considerable assistance for the student and will reduce cleanup and organizational work for you.
3. Obtain and use DCA Educational Products transparency *SP-24, Stencil Removal*.

C. Suggested teaching outline

1. Screen cleanup—its purpose
2. Demonstration—Cleaning the screen
     a. Removing the excess ink
     b. Removing all traces of ink
     c. Removing the mask
     d. Removing the image carrier
3. Storage
     a. Screen
     b. Solvents
     c. Tools and other supplies

Unit 134. Paper Stencil and Washout Screens

A. Objectives

Upon reading, defining the key terms, answering the study questions, and completing the activity relating to this unit, students should be able to

1. Prepare and print copies, using the stencil method of screen printing.
2. Prepare and print copies, using the washout method of preparing the screen.

B. Instructor preparation

1. Obtain the necessary materials for stencil and washout screen preparation and printing.
2. Obtain and use DCA Educational Products transparencies *SP-12, Making Paper Stencils*; and *SP-13, Making Tusche Stencils*.

3. Ready the materials in preparation for demonstrations on both the stencil image carrier method and the washout screen method. Have the necessary artwork prepared for both methods; then the demonstration can proceed smoothly and rapidly.

C. **Suggested teaching outline**
    1. The paper stencil
        a. Preparation of the stencil
        b. Printing with the stencil
        c. Cleanup procedures
    2. The washout screen
        a. Selection/preparation of the copy
        b. Filling in the image area
        c. Masking the non-printing area
        d. Removing the liquid tusche from the image area
        e. The printing operation
        f. Cleaning the screen

Unit 135. Multi-Color Screen Production

A. **Objectives**

Upon reading, answering the study questions, and completing the activity relating to this unit, students should be able to

1. Prepare multi-color copy for one or more methods of preparing the screen image carrier.
2. Reproduce multi-color screen printed products, according to the registration requirements, as prescribed by the original copy.

B. **Instructor preparation**

1. Prepare or obtain several examples of multi-color illustrations that will be appropriate for one or more methods of screen printing. Use these examples for illustrative purposes either for your class demonstration or for diaplay-board purposes.
2. Prepare all material and screens in readiness for a demonstration regarding the production of a printed product with two or more colors.

C. **Suggested teaching outline**
    1. Demonstration—Multi-color copy presentation
        a. Examples of multi-color copy
        b. Dividing for color
        c. Placement of register marks
    2. Preparing the film or screen
        a. Cutting or photographing each color
        b. Printing each color
        c. Cleanup procedures

SECTION 16
PHOTOGRAPHY

Section Goals:

1. To introduce students to the importance of photography as a communication technique.
2. To expose students to common materials, equipment, and facilities unique to photographic processes.
3. To permit students to learn how to produce black and white photographic negatives and prints.

Section Description: This section was prepared for the purpose of presenting only the basic information required to produce black-and-white prints. The authors recognize that the section is not extensive enough to provide the basis for an in-depth study of photographic procedures. If the instructor wants students to expand their competence in the area of photography, they should consult other sources. There are excellent books totally devoted to photography, and most manufacturers provide excellent information with their materials and equipment.

Units 137 and 138 are concerned with general, but very important, information and could easily be treated in one session of class. Unit 139 is related to Unit 140 and could be treated together. However, Unit 140 introduces several abstract and difficult concepts. The instructor is advised to devote multiple class sessions to the content in Unit 140. Some instructors may want to treat Units 139 and 141 together because of the obvious relationships.

Units 142 and 143 are clearly related to each other. The instructor will probably want to treat Unit 142 as a discussion unit and Unit 143 as a demonstration unit. The authors feel that it is important for Unit 142 to precede Unit 143 so that students will have a foundation to better understand the content in Unit 143.

Unit 137. Introduction to Photography

A. Objective

Students will be able to express the importance of photography in the everyday lives of all people.

B. Instructor preparation

Unit 137 was planned for the purpose of helping students understand the importance photography has for each individual and to identify some special applications. Students also should recognize that photography is an advantage that has become available to nearly every person within approximately the last forty years.

1. Collect as many examples of photographic prints as possible; attempt to find as many unique examples as possible. While printed examples will show unique kinds of situations, try to identify actual photographs if possible.
2. Identify local sources where students can see examples of photography in action.
3. Secure the following items:
   a. Camera
   b. Negatives
   c. Prints
4. Obtain and use DCA Educational Products overhead transparencies: *PHO-1—What is Photography; PHO-2—Photography: A Communications Medium; PHO-3—Photography: A Career;* and *PHO-4—Photography: Fun.*

C. Suggested teaching outline

1. Origin of photography
   a. Man's desire to capture events
      (1) Cave drawings
      (2) Paintings
   b. Photography invented
      (1) Mid 1800's

        (2)   Daguerre

        (3)   George Eastman

        (4)   Continued improvement

2. Influences people's lives

   a. Newspaper

   b. Scientific

   c. Engineering

   d. Others

3. Photography for everyone

   a. Improvement for everyone

   b. Standardized film

   c. Economically accomplished

4. Avocational and occupational implications

Unit 138. The Camera

A. Objectives

Students will be able to

1. Distinguish, by name, among several kinds of commonly available cameras.

2. To identify the important parts of various cameras.

B. Instructor preparation

1. Obtain several kinds of cameras—box, twin-lens reflex, 35mm or smaller, single-lens reflex, press, or view—if available.

2. Secure enough film to illustrate how cameras are loaded. In some instances, this will ruin the film, but it can be re-used for other demonstrations.

3. Obtain and use DCA Educational Products overhead transparencies: *PHO-5, The Basic Camera*; *PHO-6, Viewfinder Camera*; *PHO-7, Twin-Lens Reflex Camera*; *PHO-8, Single-Lens Reflex Camera*; *PHO-9, View Camera*; *PHO-10, The Parallax Problem*; *PHO-11, Focusing: 3 Methods*; and *PHO-12, The Range Finder Principle*.

C. Suggested teaching outline

1. Simple Cameras

   a. Box camera

   b. Cartridge cameras

        (1)   Fixed focus

        (2)   Fixed aperture

        (3)   Fixed focus

        (4)   126 size film

        (5)   110 size film

2. Twin-lens reflex

   a. Two duplicate lenses

        (1)   Top for view

        (2)   Lower for exposure

   b. Problem with close-ups

   c. Choice of many professionals

        (1)   Small

        (2)   Good lens

        (3)   Adequate film size—120

3. Rangefinder cameras

   a. Focusing mechanisms

        (1)   Double image

        (2)   Split image

    b. Fixed focal length lens

    c. Most have light meter

    d. 35mm film

4. Single-lens reflex cameras

    a. Most common kind of 35mm camera

    b. Also made for 120 film

    c. Image viewed through viewfinder

    d. Several focusing mechanisms

    e. Interchangeable lenses

    f. Built-in light meters

    g. Other special attachments

5. Press cameras

    a. Large

    b. Sheet film

    c. Built for rough treatment

    d. Ground-glass focus

6. View cameras

    a. Ground-glass viewing

    b. Changeable lens

    c. Large

    d. Not too mobile

    e. Large film size

    f. Sheet film

    g. Used in studio

Unit 139. Photographic Films

A. Objectives

As a result of studying this unit, answering the appropriate questions in Unit 145, and participating in the related activities, students will be able to

1. Identify different kinds of film and describe the characteristics.

2. Properly load film into cameras.

B. Instructor preparation

The instructor should obtain, for display purposes, several examples of film including:

1. ISO (ASA) speeds

    a. Slow

    b. Medium

    c. Fast

2. Sizes

    a. Sheet film

    b. Roll film

        (1) 120

        (2) 35mm

        (3) 126

        (4) 110

3. Obtain and use DCA Educational Products overhead transparencies: *PHO-38, Panchromatic Photographic Film*; *PHO-39, Photographic Film & Light*; *PHO-40, Film Emulsion Ratings*; and *PHO-43, Sensitometry: The Characteristic Curve (H & D)*.

C. Suggested teaching outline

1. Kinds of film
   a. Panchromatic
   b. Orthochromatic
   c. Infrared
2. Structure of film
   a. Base
   b. Emulsion
   c. Antihalation dye
3. Latent image
4. Film speeds
   a. ISO (ASA)
   b. Fast film
   c. Medium film
   d. Slow film
5. Grain
6. Film sizes
   a. 110
   b. 126
   c. 35mm
   d. 120
   e. Sheet film
   f. Bulk film
7. Loading film
   a. 35mm cameras
   b. 120 cameras

Unit 140. Making the Exposure

A. Objectives

Students, as a result of reading Unit 140, answering the questions from Unit 145, and participating in the activities will be able to

1. Describe what constitutes properly exposed film.
2. Explain the importance of light in achieving a good exposure.
3. Identify and explain common apertures and how they are adjusted to achieve good exposures and predict depth of field.
4. Name common shutter speeds and show the relationship between apertures to achieve proper exposures.
5. Explain the purpose of light measurement.
6. Demonstrate the law of reciprocity.
7. Properly hold the camera to avoid blur.

B. Instructor preparation

Unit 140 is possibly the most important in Section 16. It is also the most difficult for students to understand and typically generates less interest than other units. Students must learn to obtain good exposures if they are to have good negatives. Also, until students are able to manipulate the variables associated with making exposures, they will have difficulty dealing with various subjects.

The concept of depth of field and the law of reciprocity are particularly difficult for most students to understand. The authors recommend that instructors develop several teaching aids and prepare examples to illustrate these concepts and principles. The instructor should not expect students to grasp the concepts in one exposure to the material. Repeated review and reinforcement is usually necessary before students are able to internalize the learning.

Obtain and use DCA Educational Products overhead transparencies: *PHO-13, Exposure Control Variables; PHO-14, Balancing Lens Apertures with Shutter Speeds; PHO-15, 1-Stop and Exposure Time Comparisons; PHO-16, Camera Shutters: Location; PHO-17, Shutters: Motion and Light Control; PHO-18, Shutter Speed; PHO-19, Photoelectric Exposure Meters; PHO-20, Photoelectric Exposure Meter Scale; PHO-21, Using the Photoelectric Exposure Meter; PHO-22, The Visible Light Spectrum; PHO-23, Light Refraction Principle; PHO-24, Lenses: Simple and Multiple Element; PHO-25, Circle of Confusion; PHO-26, Depth of Field Principle; PHO-27, Depth of Field: Two Controlling Principles; PHO-28, The f-Number of a Lens; PHO-29, Lenses: Types and Relative Speeds; PHO-30, Focal Length: Effect on Image Size; PHO-31, Lenses: Focal Lengths and Angles of Coverage (35mm Cameras); PHO-32, Lenses: Focal Lengths and Areas of Coverage (35mm Cameras); PHO-33, Lenses: Zoom and Fisheye Types (35mm Cameras); PHO-34, The Filter Principle (Panchromatic Film); PHO-35, Common Filters and Characteristics (Panchromatic Film); PHO-36, The Polarizing Filter; PHO-37, Filter Factors; PHO-53, Reflected Light Principle; PHO-54, Inverse Square Law; PHO-55, Flash Synchronization: Focal Plane Shutters; PHO-56, Flash Synchronization: Between-the-Lens/Leaf Shutters; PHO-57, Flash Guide Numbers;* and *PHO-58, Portrait Lighting.*

Any effort that the instructor can provide to reinforce the importance of obtaining accurately exposed film will be helpful. Students will be able to see immediate improvement in the appearance of their prints if they improve their negatives.

Most instructors will want to devote several class sessions to this unit. Below are items that will be needed in nearly every session:

1. Cameras
    a. 35mm
    b. 120 (if possible)
2. FIlm
    a. 35mm
    b. 120
    c. Various speeds
3. Light meter
4. Flash unit
5. Data sheets from film package

C. Suggested teaching outline

1. Image areas of photograph
    a. Highlights
    b. Shadows
    c. Middletones
2. Film speeds
    a. ISO (ASA)
    b. Fast
    c. Medium
    d. Slow
3. Light
    a. Natural
    b. Artificial
        (1) Flash bulbs
        (2) Flash cubes and bars
        (3) Electronic flash

      c. Natural light measured with meter
         (1) In camera
         (2) Exposure meter
  4. Apertures
      a. Sizes—f/numbers
      b. Depth of field (Depth of focus)
  5. Shutter speeds
      a. Range of speeds
      b. Influence on motion
  6. Holding the camera
      a. Hand-held techniques
      b. Use of tripod

Unit 141. Film Processing

A. Objectives

As a result of the activities associated with Unit 141, students will be able to

1. Identify proper equipment and materials to develop film.
2. Develop film using the tank method.

B. Instructor preparation

Next to obtaining the proper exposure, Unit 140, the content of Unit 141 is the most important in Section 16. Like Unit 140, the activities are not as exciting as making photographic prints. However, without carefully processed negatives, the quality of the photographic prints will be reduced.

Careful and accurate procedures must be followed to obtain quality negatives. The instructor must impress the importance of establishing a routine that will yield quality negatives. Many of the problems students encounter when making prints can be traced to improperly developed film.

1. Collect the following equipment and materials in the proper location to demonstrate film development:
   a. Developing tanks
   b. Developer
   c. Stop bath (if used)
   d. Fixer
   e. Film
   f. Thermometer
   g. Graduate
   h. Funnel
   i. Timer
2. Identify some rolls of film for students to use in practicing to load loading tanks.
3. Review the loading procedure for demonstration.
4. Obtain and use DCA Educational Products overhead transparencies: *PHO-41, Processing Roll Film*; and *PHO-42, Machine Film Processing*.
5. Consider obtaining and using the filmstrip or slide set titled *Health Hazards in Photography*, available from the International Film Bureau, Inc.

C. Suggested teaching outline

1. Latent image
   a. Exposed silver halides
   b. Becomes visible upon development
      (1) Dark where light strikes
      (2) Clear where no light strikes

    c. Film exposed by relected light
2. Development chemicals
    a. Select chemicals
        (1) Compatible with film
        (2) Become familiar with
    b. Developer
        (1) Silver halide to metallic silver
        (2) Reducers
        (3) Kinds
            (a) Fine-grain
            (b) Medium
            (c) Coarse-grain
        (4) Fine-grain developers work slower
        (5) Coarse-grain developers work fast
    c. Stop-bath
        (1) Mild acetic acid
        (2) Water sometimes used
        (3) Stop developing action
    d. Fixers
        (1) Remove unexposed silver halides
        (2) Remove undeveloped silver halides
        (3) Harden emulsion
        (4) Light-safe after fixing
    e. Wash
        (1) Clear water
        (2) Remove chemicals
    f. Wetting agent
        (1) After washing
        (2) Prevents water spots
3. Developing film
    a. Done in total darkness
        (1) Tray development
        (2) Tank development
    b. Equipment
        (1) Tanks
        (2) Thermometer
        (3) Graduate
        (4) Funnel
        (5) Timer
    c. Tanks
        (1) Rubber
        (2) Stainless steel
        (3) Plastic
        (4) Sizes
            (a) One size
            (b) Adjustable
        (5) Simplify development process

4. Loading roll film
    a. Total darkness
    b. Some loaded from the center of reel
    c. Some loaded from outside—ratchet action
    d. Be sure film does not touch
    e. Organize parts in darkroom
5. Processing film
    a. Follow manufacturer recommendations
    b. Primary factors
        (1) Development time
        (2) Chemical temperature
        (3) Agitation
    c. Procedure
        (1)   Collect chemicals
        (2)   Bring chemicals to same temperature
        (3)   Adjust running water to correct temperature
        (4)   Load film into tank
        (5)   Fill tank with water
            (a) Wets film
            (b) Prevent air bubbles
        (6)   Pour out water
        (7)   Fill tank with developer
            (a) Do quickly
            (b) Rap tank to eliminate bubbles
        (8)   Agitate film in developer
            (a) Can turn some tanks
            (b) Shake others
        (9)   Agitate according to recommendations
        (10) Pour out developer
            (a) Some developer is saved
            (b) Some discarded
        (11) Pour in stop bath
            (a) Mild acetic acid
            (b) Clear water
        (12) Pour out stop bath
        (13) Pour in fixer
            (a) Follow recommendations
            (b) Agitate vigorously
        (14) Pour out fixer—save
        (15) Remove tank cover
        (16) Wash as recommended
        (17) Apply wetting agent
        (18) Dry
            (a) Dust free
            (b) Quickly

    NOTE: *Try to reduce the time that the film is wet. This will help to keep the grain size to a minimum.*

Unit 142. Photographic Papers

A. Objectives

Students, as a result of studying Unit 142, answering the appropriate questions in Unit 145, and engaging in the activities will be able to

1. Identify various kinds of photographic papers and describe the characteristics of each.

2. Select the best kind of paper to enhance the photographic print.

B. Instructor preparation

Secure several kinds of photographic paper for illustration to students. Manufacturers of photographic paper usually have samples of paper on which photographs have been printed. These usually include samples of surfaces, colors, bases, and emulsion contrasts. Examples of items the instructor should have are:

1. Weights
    a. Single-weight (SW)
    b. Double-weight (DW)
    c. Medium-weight (MW)—resin-coated (RC)

2. Emulsion
    a. Various speeds
    b. Variable contrasts
    c. Graded

3. Finishes
    a. Glossy
    b. Matte
    c. Silk
    d. Others

4. Obtain and use DCA Educational Products overhead transparencies: *PHO-44, Basic Printing Techniques*; and *PHO-45, Photographic Paper.*

C. Suggested teaching outline

1. Bases
    a. White
    b. Withstand development
        (1) Chemicals
        (2) Water
        (3) Rapid drying
        (4) Age
    c. Weights
        (1) Single-weight (SW)
            (a) Economical
            (b) Withstand little abuse
            (c) Quick drying
        (2) Double-weight (DW)
            (a) For larger prints
            (b) Slow drying
            (c) Display purposes
        (3) Middle-weight (MW)
            (a) Resin coated
            (b) Easy to dry

2. Emulsions
   a. Light-sensitive cyrstals
   b. Suspended in gelatin
   c. Silver chloride emulsion
      (1) Least sensitive
      (2) Used mainly for contact printing
   d. Silver bromide emulsions
      (1) More light sensitive
      (2) Enlarging—projection printing
   e. Chlorobromide emulsion
      (1) Medium speed
      (2) Either enlarging or contact
   f. Can be used in red light
3. Emulsion contrasts
   a. Contact printing grades
      (1) Compare with negative contrast
      (2) Range from 0–5
   b. Projection paper
      (1) Number system (not uniform)
      (2) Low number—indicates high contrast negatives
      (3) Medium numbers—average negatives
      (4) High numbers—low contrast (flat) negatives
   c. Variable-contrast paper
      (1) Single kind of emulsion
      (2) Use filters to compensate
4. Paper finishes
   a. Glossy
   b. Semi-matte
   c. Matte
   d. Linen
   e. Silk
   f. Other

Unit 143. Photographic Printing

A. Objectives

As a result of reading Unit 143, answering questions from Unit 145, completing the appropriate reinforcement activities, students will be able to

1. Identify appropriate equipment and materials needed for making contact and projection prints.
2. Describe the principles and concepts underlying the contact and projection printing.
3. Make contact and projection prints.
4. Identify and correct defects in contact and projection prints.

B. Instructor preparation

The instructor may want to include both contact and projection printing in the same discussion/demonstration. Refinement in projection printing techniques can be demonstrated later. Because most black and white photography done today is on 35mm film or smaller, the unit will focus on making contact prints for the purpose of proof sheets.

1. Identify the equipment and tools necessary to make contact and projection prints.

2. Collect and prepare the following equipment and materials needed for making contact and projection prints.

    a. Contact printer or printing frame

    b. Enlarger

    c. Paper and data sheets

    d. Negatives to be printed

    e. Chemicals and trays

        (1) Developer

        (2) Stop bath

        (3) Fixer

        (4) Wash

    f. Thermometer

    g. Timer

    h. Drier or ferrotype plate

    i. Enlarging easel(s)

3. Review the procedure for making a test strip and print prior to the demonstration.

4. Obtain and use DCA Educational Products overhead transparencies: *PHO-46, Determining Exposure When Enlarging; PHO-47, Processing Photographic Prints; PHO-48, Types of Enlargers; PHO-49, Enlarger Nomenclature; PHO-50, Cropping the Enlargement; PHO-51, Printing-in & Dodging;* and *PHO-52, Vignetting & Distortion Control.*

C. Suggested teaching outline

1. Contact printing

    a. Negative between light and paper

        (1) Clear negative areas=dark print areas

        (2) Gray negative areas=gray print areas

        (3) Dark negative areas=light print areas

    b. Negative in contact with printing paper

    c. Same size print as negative

    d. Simplest method

    e. Produces small print

2. Contact printing devices

    a. Printing frame

        (1) Base side of negative against glass

        (2) Emulsion of paper against emulsion of film

        (3) Paper and negative pressed together

        (4) Placed in front of light source

    b. Contact printer

        (1) More elaborate

        (2) Box with glass

        (3) Light below glass

        (4) Platen holds paper and film

3. Make the contact print

    a. Organize the negatives

    b. Clean the contact printer

    c. Organize the trays

    d. Prepare the development solutions

    e. Make a test strip

    f. Make the print

4. Principles of projection printing
   a. Often called enlarging
   b. Light passes through the negative to print paper
   c. Use enlarger
   d. Vary distance between lens and paper
   e. Lens focuses image on the paper
   f. Provides print that is larger than negative
   g. Can control contrast in specific areas
   h. Control distortion
   i. Produce special effects
   j. Increases visible grain structure
5. Enlargers
   a. Parts
      (1) Light source
      (2) Negative carrier
      (3) Lens
      (4) Base
   b. Different sizes
   c. Different qualities
   d. Image focus—distance between lens and negative
   e. Size is determined—distance between lens and paper
6. Making projection print
   a. Clean enlarger
   b. Select paper
   c. Prepare chemicals
   d. Examine negatives
   e. Place negative into carrier
      (1) Emulsion toward lens
      (2) Avoid scratches
   f. Adjust easel to print size
   g. Turn out white light
   h. Adjust enlarger
      (1) Focus
      (2) Size
      (3) Crop
   i. Adjust the lens aperture
   j. Make test exposure
   k. Evaluate test exposure
   l. Place sheet of paper in easel
   m. Make exposure
   n. Process exactly as test strip
   o. Dry the print

Unit 144. Finishing and Mounting Prints

A. Objectives

As a result of reading Unit 144, participating in related activities, and completing the questions from Unit 145, students will be able to

1. Identify photographic paper that will yield the desired finish on the photograph.
2. Dry photographs, using the correct procedure to obtain the proper finish on the print.
3. Mount prints on mounting board using dry mounting tissue.

B. Instructor preparation

Activities associated with Unit 144 usually occur as a followup of Unit 143. That is, after demonstrating how to make a print (either contact or projection print), a natural continuation is to show how to dry and apply a finish to the print. In some instances, it may not be appropriate or there may insufficient time to demonstrate the drying and mounting processes. The following preparation will assume that drying, finishing, and mounting will be a separate demonstration from the demonstration on making a print.

1. Have prints ready to be dried. If possible papers requiring both gloss and dull finishes should be available for class demonstration.
2. Collect the following items:
    a. Print dryer or ferrotype plate
    b. Squeegee
    c. Print roller
    d. Print blotter
    e. Mounting board
    f. Tacking iron
    g. Dry mount tissue
    h. Mounting press
3. Obtain and use DCA Educational Products overhead transparencies: *PHO-59, A Good Photograph*; *PHO-60, Arrange the Subject: The Rule of Thirds*; *PHO-61, Balance: The Key to Good Composition*; *PHO-62, Vertical and Horizontal Lines*; *PHO-63, Diagonal and S-Curve Lines*; *PHO-64, Circular and Zig-Zag Lines*; and *PHO-65, Framing, Foreground and Horizon Guidelines*.

C. Suggested teaching outline

1. Purpose of finishing
    a. Determined by kind of paper
    b. Influenced by the intended use
2. Drying
    a. Prepare the print
        (1) Should contain only water
        (2) Free of chemicals and dirt
    b. Methods
        (1) Air
        (2) Heat
3. Gloss surface
    a. Print surface against ferrotype plate
    b. Protect ferrotype surface
        (1) Fingerprints
        (2) Scratches
        (3) Dirt
        (4) Rust pits
    c. Dryers have ferrotype drums
    d. Clean ferrotype surface
        (1) Flush with clean water
        (2) Dry with soft dustfree cloth

e. Rub hand over wet print
   (1) Remove bubbles
   (2) Eliminate dirt
f. Hold print by adjacent corners
g. Slowly lower print to plate
   (1) Print should roll onto plate
   (2) Prevents air bubbles
h. Squeegee or roll print on ferrotype
   (1) Remove excess water
   (2) Ensure good contact
i. Permit print to dry until it pops off

4. Dull surface
   a. Similar to gloss
   b. Print surface against blotter
   c. Back of print against ferrotype on print dryers

5. Mounting photographs
   a. Place print on heavier material
      (1) Frequent handling
      (2) Display
   b. Commonly placed on mounting board
   c. Dry-mount method most satisfactory
   d. Attach dry-mount tissue
      (1) Back of print
      (2) Same size as print (sometimes slightly larger)
      (3) Tack with tacking iron
   e. Trim dry-mount tissue
   f. Mark location of print on mounting board
   g. Place print on mounting board
      (1) Locate accurately
      (2) Tack at three points
   h. Place into dry-mounting press
   i. Household iron can be used

SECTION 17
DUPLICATING AND SPECIAL PRINTING PROCESSES

Section Goal: To provide the opportunity for students to become knowledgeable about duplication techniques and to learn about the concepts and principles underlying inkjet and heat transfer printing.

Section Description: In many business situations, it is necessary to transmit information in limited quantities and in a short period of time. In most instances, time is of more importance than the quality of the material; in other situations, these methods are much more economical than conventional printing methods.

Many graphic arts laboratories do not contain the equipment necessary to demonstrate the techniques. However, the equipment and materials for the processes usually can be found somewhere in the institution or in a local business. If the equipment is not in the laboratory, the instructor should arrange to have the equipment moved to the laboratory or plan to give the demonstration at the site where the equipment is located. In most instances, the preparation of masters can be done in the laboratory.

Some instructors tend to take these methods lightly or even eliminate them from the course of study. When this is done, the students are deprived of the knowledge of functional communication devices.

This section does not include all the possible duplication and copying methods available. In many instances, changes are taking place so rapidly that the equipment is obsolete before it is delivered.

Inkjet printing and heat transfer processes are recent innovations that do not clearly fit into any of the other printing categories in the book. They have limited applications but permit printing to be accomplished where other processes cannot be used effectively.

Unit 146. Introduction to Duplicating and Special Printing Processes

A. Objectives

As a result of studying Unit 146, students will be able to

1. Explain the importance and applications of limited copy duplication and copying methods.
2. Distinguish between "duplicating" and "copying."

B. Instructor preparation

This unit should serve as the basis for introducing Units 147, 148, and 149. Instructors may want to use the information in Unit 146 to begin a day's activity to be followed with demonstrations relating to Units 147, 148, or 149.

1. Assemble the following items:
    a. Spirit masters, including blank masters and masters which have been printed. It would be helpful to have copies of the printed master for distribution to students.
    b. Mimeograph stencils, including stencils which are blank, prepared, and already used. Duplicated copies of the used masters should be available for distribution to students.
    c. Original and copies from several different copying techniques including the thermographic process, transfer-electrostatic, and direct-electrostatic processes.
    d. Examples of inkjet printing and samples of heat transfer process printing.
2. Review the purposes and techniques for duplicating and copying.

C. Suggested teaching outline

1. Purposes of limited copy duplicating and copying
    a. Rapid distribution of information
    b. Speed more important than quality
    c. Economy

2. Distinguish between duplicating and copying
   a. Duplicating
      (1) Produce copies from image carrier
      (2) Multiple copies made from master (image carrier)
         (a) Offset lithography
         (b) Spirit
         (c) Mimeograph
   b. Copying
      (1) Accurate prints from originals
      (2) No image carrier needed
3. Decision to use duplicating or copying methods
   a. How soon it is needed
   b. Kind of equipment available
   c. Economy of each copy
   d. Number of copies
   e. Repeat uses
   f. Preciseness of original

Unit 147. Spirit and Mimeograph Duplication

A. Objectives

As a result of reading Unit 147, engaging in associated activities, and completing related questions from Unit 150, students will be able to

1. Verbally and/or pictorially describe the principles of spirit and mimeograph duplication.
2. Prepare spirit and mimeograph masters.
3. Duplicate copies on spirit and mimeograph duplicators.

B. Instructor preparation

1. The instructor should secure and organize the following items for use in discussion and demonstration:
   a. Spirit duplicator. Since many graphic arts laboratories do not have this machine as a regular piece of equipment, instructors may have to locate one in another place in the school.
   b. Mimeograph duplicator. Instructors will have the same problem locating a mimeograph duplicator as a spirit duplicator.
   c. Typewriter
   d. Spirit and mimeograph masters
   e. Drawing instruments
   f. Razor blades for spirit masters
   g. Correction fluid for mimeograph masters
2. Obtain DCA Education Products, transparencies *GA-95, Spirit Duplicating Principle* and *GA-94, Mimeograph Duplicating Principle*.
3. Check duplicators to be sure they are operating properly.

C. Suggested teaching outline

1. Principle of spirit duplication
2. Master (image carrier)
   a. Master sheet (actual image carrier)
   b. Carbon
      (1) Not actually carbon
      (2) Aniline dye

c. Protective sheet
   (1) Between master sheet and carbon
   (2) Prevents carbon transfer
d. Impression paper absorbs duplicating fluid
e. Carbon dissolves on damp paper
f. Colors
   (1) Blue
   (2) Black
   (3) Red
   (4) Green
   (5) Purple

3. Preparing masters
   a. Remove protective sheet
   b. Typing
      (1) Most common preparation method
         (a) Manual
         (b) Electric
      (2) Type on master sheet (not on carbon)
      (3) Keen even pressure
   c. Drawing
      (1) Place on hard surface
      (2) Draw guidelines
         (a) Very light
         (b) Leave protective sheet in place
      (3) Remove protective sheet
      (4) Make final lines

4. Making corrections
   a. Remove error
      (1) Back of master sheet
      (2) Scrape away carbon
   b. Correct error
      (1) Cut small piece of carbon
      (2) Place behind error
         (a) Carbon toward back of master sheet
         (b) Be sure carbon is in correct place
      (3) Make the correction

5. Duplicate copies
   a. Load paper
   b. Fill fluid container
   c. Dampen fluid applicator
   d. Clamp master on cylinder
   e. Feed sheets
   f. Stop fluid flow to applicator
   g. Remove master
   h. Remove duplicated sheets

6. Principles of mimeograph duplication
   a. Image placed on stencil
   b. Principle similar to screen process
   c. Ink passes through holes in the stencil

7. Stencil
   a. Determines quality of print
   b. Core
      (1) Fibrous material
      (2) Porous
      (3) Tissue thin
   c. Coated
      (1) Wax material
      (2) Both sides
      (3) Prevents ink passage
   d. Making image
      (1) Pressure
      (2) Striking
      (3) Wax surface moved to side
   e. Parts
      (1) Film protective sheet
      (2) Stencil sheet
      (3) Typing cushion
      (4) Backing sheet
      (5) Markings on stencil sheet
          (a) 8½″×11″ guide
          (b) 8½″×14″ guide
          (c) Postcard guide
          (d) Typing guide
8. Preparing stencil
   a. Methods
      (1) Typing
      (2) Handwriting
      (3) Drawing
   b. Typing
      (1) Place in typewriter
      (2) Stencil sheet toward typist
      (3) Set typewriter on stencil—no ribbon
      (4) Correct errors
          (a) Roll up stencil in typewriter
          (b) Rub or burnish error with paperclip
          (c) Paint over burnished error with correction fluid
          (d) Make correction
9. Handwriting
   a. Done with stylus or ball point pen
   b. Place writing sheet between stencil sheet and typing cushion
      (1) Hard surface
      (2) Matte surface
   c. Roll stylus in fingers
10. Drawing
    a. Use illuminated stencil drawing board
    b. Place sheet on board
    c. Stencil sheet toward artist

      d. Place sketch between stencil sheet and cushion

      e. Make drawing using stylus or ball point pen on stencil

11. Electronically prepared stencils

      a. Prepare an original on plain paper

      b. Place copy on appropriate cylinder

      c. Attach special stencil to stencil cylinder

      d. Duplicates copy on stencil

12. Mimeograph inks

      a. Fluid

      b. Kind depends on machine

      c. Absorbed in paper

      d. Black and colors

13. Mimeograph paper

      a. Bond

      b. Absorbent

      c. Certain card stocks

      d. Store in cool dry location

14. Mimeograph duplicator

      a. Parts

          (1) Cylinder

          (2) Impression roll

          (3) Ink pad

          (4) Feed mechanism

      b. Cylinder

          (1) Has holes

          (2) Ink pad covers

          (3) Ink placed inside cylinder

          (4) Clamp holds stencil

      c. Impression roll

          (1) Located below cylinder

          (2) Presses paper against stencil

      d. Hand or electrically operated

      e. Procedure

          (1) Clamp stencil to cylinder

              (a) Smooth

              (b) Nonreadable side toward operator

          (2) Load paper

          (3) Feed paper

          (4) Remove paper

          (5) Remove stencil

          (6) Cover cylinder with protective cover

Unit 148. Office Copying Methods

A. Objectives

As a result of studying Unit 149, students will be able to

1. Name several kinds of office copiers.

2. Explain the image producing principles of thermograhic, transfer-electrostatic, and direct-electrostatic copiers.

B. Instructor preparation

1. Obtain as many copiers as possible. If certain copiers are not available in the school, local businesses should be consulted to determine where students can observe the process.

2. Prepare copy (straight typing or paseteup with illustrations) to be duplicated by the copiers. To adequately demonstrate the potential results of copiers, prepare the copy to have fine lines, solids, and halftones. Be sure that some images are made with carbon-base material to demonstrate the thermographic process. Also, use different colors to prepare the copy.

3. Secure DCA Education Products transparencies *GA-91, Electrostatic Copying Machine; GA-92, Multi-Color Electrostatic Printing Machine;* and *GA-93, Electrostatic Stencil Printing Principle.*

C. Suggested teaching outline

1. Kinds
   a. Thermographic
   b. Transfer-electrostatic
   c. Direct-electrostatic

2. Thermographic
   a. Produces image by heat
   b. Copy image must be black carbon
   c. Print paper specially treated
      (1) Sensitive to heat
      (2) Produces colored image
   d. Copy and treated paper placed in contact
   e. Infrared light creates heat
      (1) Causes carbon image to get hot
      (2) Heat causes paper image

3. Transfer-electrostatic copiers
   a. Selenium plate (drum)
      (1) Holds electrical charge in dark
      (2) Electrical conductivity varies with light intensity
   b. Process
      (1) Coat plate with positive charge
      (2) Coating done in dark
      (3) Expose plate to copy through lens system
      (4) Positive charge leaves plate where light strikes
      (5) Toner spread over plate
         (a) Has pigment (black)
         (b) Negative charge
      (6) Toner sticks to image area
      (7) Sheet placed over plate and toner
         (a) Positive charge
         (b) Plain paper
      (8) Toner transfers to bond with paper
      (9) Toner heated to bond with paper

4. Direct-electrostatic copiers
   a. Image produced on treated paper
      (1) Coating placed on paper
      (2) Zinc oxide
      (3) Heavier than regular paper
   b. Paper given negative electrical charge in total darkness

    c. Exposed to copy

    d. Image areas retain negative charge

    e. Developer positively charged

    f. Negatively charged areas attract develoer

    g. Image made permanent by heat

Unit 149. Inkjet Printing and Heat Transfer

A. Objectives

As a result of reading Unit 149, answering the questions in Unit 150, and completing the associated activities, students will be able to

1. Describe the principles and concepts of inkjet printing and heat transfer processes.

2. Identify applications of inkjet and heat transfer processes.

B. Instructor preparation

This unit is intended to be primarily an information unit. Some laboratories may have the capabilities to do heat transfer, however, most instructors will have to use field trips to show students actual applications. The instructor should collect as many samples to help students see where the two processes are used.

C. Suggested teaching outline

1. Inkjet printing

    a. Sprays tiny drops of ink

    b. Controlled by electronics

    c. Can be done without machine touching material

    d. Characters similar to typewriter

    e. Can be programmed to form many different characters

    f. Often controlled by computer or word processor

    g. Can be used on uneven surfaces

    h. Often used when material must be sterile

2. Heat transfer

    a. Is not a new printing process

    b. Can be done by several printing processes

    c. Image is printed on paper with special dye

    d. Image is transferred to cloth by heat and pressure

    e. Dye vaporizes and is deposited in cloth

    f. Sometimes call sublimation

SECTION 18
FINISHING AND BINDING

Section Goal: To introduce the students to the finishing and binding techniques and the processes used in hand and mechanized finishing and binding in both school and commercial applications.

Section Description: This section consists of nine units, plus the Learning Experiences unit. The first unit contains historical highlights of finishing and binding procedures, and Unit 152 includes several suggested safety practices that must be followed within the finishing and binding area if safe conditions are to exist. Units 153–156 contain information that will directly assist the students in becoming involved in finishing and binding methods. These units contain background and procedural information which will assist them in completing a finishing or binding operation.

Commercial case binding operations are presented in Unit 157. Procedural information for hand binding and hardcover (casebound) books is given in Unit 158. In the final unit (Unit 159), microstorage and retrieval systems are explained in sufficient depth for students to gain a sound introduction to this important storage and retrieval method. When these methods of storing and retrieving information first became available, it was said that binding, as we presently know it, would soon be replaced and that there would be little need for the books that line our library shelves. This, of course, has proven false, since there is a definite place for both major systems in our society.

Unit 160, entitled Learning Experiences: Finishing and Binding, includes key terms, study questions, and a few activities which can be completed as a result of the information learned in this section. Keep in mind that you should be selective in assigning the learning experiences since all do not necessarily need to be completed for a particular course. In other words, make your course content relevant to the needs of your students.

Unit 151. Introduction to Finishing and Binding

A. Objectives

Upon reading, defining the key terms, answering the study questions, and completing the activity relating to this unit, students should be able to

1. Note the purposes of finishing and binding.
2. Review the historical highlights of binding books.

B. Instructor preparation

1. Review the entire section, thereby becoming familiar with its contents.
2. Obtain examples of some early bound books. This probably will be a difficult task, since old books in good condition are collector's items and, therefore, are worth a considerable amount of money. As a substitute, you may desire to make a scroll that would represent one of the earliest forms of books. Also, have someone in the fine arts area prepare a clay tablet that represents the oldest form of books.
3. Search local libraries to determine whether they have an old book collection. If you can locate an early book collection, you may desire to take your entire class on a field trip to this library or suggest that your students visit the library on their own.

C. Suggested teaching outline

1. Purpose of finishing and binding
2. Books
    a. Historical development
    b. Importance—yesterday and today
    c. Early book binderies
3. Modern finishing and binding methods

Unit 152. Safety in Finishing and Binding

This unit has been prepared and placed in this position within this section with a single primary thought in mind. That thought is to assist you and your students with personal safety. The introductory paragraphs provide a small amount of background information, with the remaining content being concerned with safety practices. Be sure your students study this unit very thoroughly prior to working on laboratory assignments relating to finishing and binding.

Unit 153. Finishing Methods

A. **Objectives**

Upon reading, defining the key terms, answering the study questions, and completing the activities relating to this unit, students should be able to

1. Describe the following ten finishing operations: cutting, folding, scoring, perforating, gathering, punching, drilling, die-cutting, hot-stamping, and laminating.
2. Perform the finishing operations, as named in Objective 1, following demonstrations on the appropriate equipment.

B. **Instructor preparation**

1. Obtain brochures and advertising literature of equipment utilized in the finishing operations. Use these brochures during your class presentation to emphasize specific details of this equipment. Allow your students to utilize these materials as part of their independent study.
2. Establish a file where samples of the various finishing methods can be gathered. Use these during a class demonstration or for classroom display purposes.

C. **Suggested teaching outline**

1. Common finishing operations
   a. Cutting and trimming
   b. Folding
   c. Scoring
   d. Perforating
   e. Gathering
   f. Collating
   g. Punching and drilling
2. Other finishing procedures
   a. Die-cutting
   b. Hot stamping
   c. Laminating

Unit 154. Paper-Cutting Procedures

A. **Objectives**

Upon reading, defining the key terms, answering the study questions, and completing the activities relating to this unit, students should be able to

1. Prepare a cutting chart and determine the number of needed stock sheets based upon a predetermined number of press sheets.
2. Identify the parts of the hydraulic, power operated paper cutter.
3. Accurately and safely use the power paper cutter to cut press sheets from stock sheets.

B. **Instructor preparation**

1. Set up several problems for use either on the chalkboard or on overhead transparencies showing the procedure to determine the number of press sheets needed to end up with the required number of printed finished sheets, and the number of stock sheets necessary to cut for the required press sheets. For some of your students this may be a difficult concept for them to grasp; therefore, teaching aids of several varieties may be of value in presenting this content.

2. Obtain or prepare a slide tape or film loop on the operation of the lever-operated paper cutter. Make these AV's available to students for self-instructional purposes.

3. Prepare overhead transparencies of a Press Sheet Calculation (Appendix M, Visual Master 10) and of a Cutting Order Layout (Appendix M, Visual Master 11). Use these teaching devices in your class lecture on "Planning and Cutting Paper for Printing."

4. Thoroughly inspect the paper cutter available in your laboratory for student use. Make sure it is operating properly and safely. Also, inspect the paper-cutter knife to determine whether it should be exchanged for a sharp knife.

5. Lubricate and clean the paper cutter as necessary.

C. **Suggested teaching outline**

1. The primary rule—"Think and Practice Safety"
2. Planning for cutting
    a. Determining needed press sheets
    b. Determining the number of stock sheets
    c. Making a cutting chart
3. The power paper cutter parts and purposes
    a. Table
    b. Backgage
    c. Backgage handwheel
    d. Backgage indicator
    e. Clamp
    f. Clamp control
    g. Cutting stick
    h. Knife
    i. Knife control buttons
    j. Light switch
    k. Power switch
    l. Pressure gauge and controls
4. Demonstration—Paper-cutter operation
    a. Backgage adjustment
    b. Positioning the paper
    c. Clamping the paper
    d. Cutting the paper
    e. Removing the cut paper and/or trimmings
5. Special cuts
    a. Booklets
    b. Angle cutting

Unit 155. Basic Binding Methods

A. **Objectives**

Upon reading, defining the key terms, answering the study questions, and completing the activities relating to this unit, students should be able to

1. State the purpose of binding sheets of paper together in book form.
2. Identify the twelve specific methods of binding sheets of paper together.

B. **Instructor preparation**

1. Obtain one or more examples of each of the twelve specific binding methods. Utilize these samples in your class presentation or for classroom display purposes.

2. Obtain and use DCA Educational Products transparencies *GA-30, Mechanical Binding Methods; GA-31, Loose-leaf Binding Methods; GA-32, Wire Staple Binding Methods;* and *GA-33, Sewn Binding Methods.*

C. **Suggested teaching outline**

1. Binding—its purpose
2. Mechanical binding methods
   a. Spiral wire
   b. Plastic cylinder
3. Loose-leaf bindings
   a. Ring binder
   b. Post binding
   c. Base-and-prong
   d. Friction
4. Wire staple binding
   a. Saddle-wire
   b. Side wire
5. Perfect binding
6. Sewn bindings—soft or hard cover
   a. Saddle sewing
   b. Flat sewing
   c. Signature to signature sewing
7. Welding

Unit 156. Soft-Cover Binding

A. **Objectives**

Upon reading, defining the key terms, answering the study questions, and completing the activities relating to this unit, students should be able to

1. Bind one or more books or booklets, using plastic-cylinder binding, post binding (loose-leaf), saddle-wire stitching, side-wire stitching, and padding methods.
2. Operate the necessary equipment to complete any one or all of the binding methods named in Objective 1.
3. Perform the necessary steps in the preparation of library and nicked corners.

B. **Instructor preparation**

1. Inventory the necessary supplies for each of the five binding methods, as listed in this unit. If the needed supplies are in low quantity, purchase the needed materials prior to assigning activities relating to these binding methods.
2. Check the equipment which will be used to bind the books or booklets, according to the five methods as shown in this unit. As with the supplies, if any of the pieces of equipment need repair or general maintenance, be certain to accomplish this prior to making any student assignments.
3. Since it is somewhat difficult for students to learn the proper techniques involved in making library and nicked corners, it is suggested that you prepare a sample set of examples in step-by-step form for each of the two corner methods. Use the same steps, as noted in Figs. 156–5 and 156–7. Place these samples on a display board and label them properly, so students can make observations during the construction of their book covers.

C. **Suggested teaching outline**

1. Demonstration—Plastic-cylinder binding
   a. Materials needed
   b. Operating the punch

    c. Operating the plastic cylinder opening device

    d. Attaching the sheets and attaching the plastic cylinder

2. Demonstration—Post binding

    a. Materials needed

    b. Operating the bar cutter or broad shears

    c. Fastening the binder's board to the binding cloth

    d. Constructing the library corner

    e. Constructing the nicked corner

    f. Operating the hot-stamping press

    g. Punching holes

    h. Assembling the book

3. Demonstration—Saddle-wire stitching

    a. Materials needed

    b. Folding the sheets by hand or with a paper folder

    c. Gathering the signatures

    d. Operating the power stitcher

    e. Trimming the booklets

4. Demonstration—Side-wire stitching

    a. Materials needed

    b. Gathering the sheets or signatures

    c. Operating the side-wire stitching machine

    d. Applying the book cloth to the backbone

    e. Trimming the book

5. Demonstration—Padding

    a. Materials needed

    b. Gathering the sheets

    c. Preparing the binding

    d. Applying the adhesive

    e. Trimming the pads

Unit 157. Case Binding

A. Objectives

Upon reading, defining the key terms, answering the study questions, and completing the activity relating to this unit, students should be able to

1. Identify the parts of a case-bound book.

2. Summarize the production steps necessary in the manufacture of case-bound books.

B. Instructor preparation

1. Personally visit a binding facility which manufactures case-bound books. Obtain samples of different stages of a case-bound book. Use these samples to better explain the construction of case bindings.

2. Obtain samples of case-bound books that have been sewn by each of the three methods—saddle-sewn, flat-sewn, and signature-to-signature.

3. Obtain and use DCA Educational Products transparencies *GA-33*, *Sewn Binding Methods* and *GA-34*, Parts of a Book.

4. Obtain advertising literature from companies that manufacture case-binding and sewing equipment. Use this literature to help explain further the processes involved in case bindings. Also, allow the students to utilize this material for their outside or self-study.

C. **Suggested teaching outline**
1. Parts of a book
    a. Body
    b. Case
    c. End sheets
    d. Backbone
    e. Super
    f. Binder's board
    g. Book cloth
    h. Backing paper
    i. Lining
    j. Headbands
    k. Gummed tape
    l. Thread
2. Case-binding procedures
    a. Gathering the body content
    b. Sewing the signatures
    c. Forwarding
    d. Cover preparation
    e. Casing-in
    f. Pressing the books
    g. Attaching the jackets and shipping

Unit 158. Hand Case Binding

A. **Objectives**

Upon reading, defining the key terms, answering the study questions, and completing the activity relating to this unit, students should be able to
1. Assemble the materials, tools, and equipment necessary for binding a group of saddle-stitched journals together via the hand case binding method.
2. Bind a group of saddle-stitched journals into a case-bound edition according to the procedures outlined in this unit.

B. **Instructor preparation**
1. Survey the list of materials, tools, and equipment, as listed in the unit. Determine whether there is need for replenishing the supply of these materials or servicing of the tools and equipment available in your laboratory.
2. Obtain one or more examples of hand-case bindings of a group of journals. If these cannot be obtained, it is suggested that you as an instructor not only prepare a case-bound group of journals but also prepare samples of each step, so that the students can inspect and learn the procedure involved in each stage of hand case binding.

C. **Suggested teaching outline**
1. Needed materials, tools, and equipment
2. Demonstration—Hand case binding
    a. Preparatory steps
    b. Sewn the signatures
    c. Forwarding the book study
    d. Preparing the case
    e. Casing-in

Unit 159. Microstorage and Retrieval Systems

A. **Objectives**

Upon reading, defining the key terms, answering the study questions, and completing the activity relating to this unit, students should be able to

1. Clarify the advantages and uses for microstorage and retrieval systems.
2. Compare the four common microform storage methods.
3. Summarize the several retrieval methods and devices that are utilized with the four common microform storage methods.
4. Discuss the value of videodisks for storing Information.
5. Summarize briefly the historical development and use of microstorage and retrieval systems.

B. **Instructor preparation**

1. Obtain samples of the four common microform storage methods. Use these samples during your classroom presentation or for display purposes.
2. Check with your school library to determine the extent of use these four common methods enjoy in your locality. Make arrangements to take your class on a field trip either to your local school library or to a public or private library in your geographical area for the purposes of showing the students the actual applications of these methods.
3. Obtain an example of a videodisk from a manufacturer or distributor. Permit the students to inspect this very useful information storage device.
4. Cooperate with your industrial education colleague who is teaching Mechanical Design Drafting courses. It may be possible for both of you to develop a cooperative program, whereby purchased equipment could be utilized by both the graphic communication areas of graphic arts and drafting.

C. **Suggested teaching outline**

1. Purposes and uses of microstorage and retrieval systems
2. Microfilm storage methods
   a. Roll film
   b. Film magazines or cartridges
   c. Aperture cards
   d. Microfiche cards
3. Microfilm retrieval
   a. Screen projection
   b. Hard copy prints
4. Videodisk storage and retrieval
5. Historical highlights

SECTION 19
PULP AND PAPER MANUFACTURING

Section Goal: To provide information and experiences relating to one of the most important commodities available to the civilized world—paper.

Section Description: This section is designed to serve as an informational group of units, with the exception of Unit 166, which suggests laboratory experience involving the making of paper by hand. Without question, paper is a commodity that the civilized world could not do without. In fact, as pointed out in Unit 161, the living index not only of the United States but also of other countries and the production and consumption of paper products are nearly parallel.

Within the units of this section, every attempt has been made to emphasize the importance of paper, the amount of raw material and work hours needed to make a ton of paper, the processes involved in making pulp, and the actual process of making the usable paper. The many kinds, weights, and sizes of paper along with information on purchasing and determining cost of paper are presented in Units 164 and 165. Finally, a limited experience of making paper by hand is explained and illustrated in Unit 166.

The need for reuse and recycling of paper is only lightly presented in this section. This is because of the space limitation. It is suggested that you, as a respected leader of your students, take appropriate time to emphasize the need for reusing and recycling a product that is in shorter supply than it should be. One way in which this can be accomplished is to demonstrate the different ways paper can be reused or used to its fullest—by utilizing both sides of the sheet and filling the entire sheet within the limits of good design, instead of placing only one or two lines on a full sheet of paper and then discarding it immediately after someone has taken only a few seconds to read it.

A worthwhile activity that you may desire to have your students become involved in might be a recycling program for the school or possibly the entire school district. If a program of this kind would be organized through your graphic arts facility or program, this would certainly provide a certain amount of favorable publicity which, in turn, would likely reap many benefits. Besides the immediate benefits to your graphic arts program, the students and yourself could take great pride in contributing to a patriotic campaign that is gaining considerable favor throughout our country today.

Learning experiences involving pulp and paper manufacturing are presented in the final unit of this section. Select key terms and study questions from those listed which you believe appropriate for your students. Do the same in regard to the six activities listed in the unit. Keep in mind that these learning experiences are made available only as suggestions; therefore, your personal ingenuity or creativity is likely to increase the value of this unit and the entire section. Do not be afraid to provide alternate experiences for your students.

Unit 161. Introduction to Pulp and Paper Manufacturing

A. Objectives

Upon reading, defining the key terms, answering the study questions, and completing the activity relating to this unit, students should be able to

1. List ten or more paper products, other than the common sheet of paper, that are used for printing and writing purposes.

2. Cite facts and explain the relationship between the amount of paper used and the living index of a country.

3. Summarize historical highlights of paper.

4. Review the highlights of the Tree Farm System which has made it possible to produce much of the raw material—trees—that is needed and used in making paper.

5. List the basic ingredients needed to produce a ton of paper.

B. Instructor preparation

1. Obtain samples of the paper products listed in the first part of this unit. Use these materials for developing interest in studying pulp and paper manufacturing.

2. Obtain the most recent figures available on the per capita consumption of paper not only in the United States but also in other countries. This information is available from the American Paper Institute and from the United States Department of Labor. It will be necessary to obtain current figures each year.

3. Most libraries contain information in regard to paper and its production. You may desire to search not only your school library but also the public libraries within your geographical area and determine the numbers of books available on this important product and possibly become involved in reading one or more of them.

4. Prepare a transparency entitled "Materials Needed to Make One Ton of Paper." See Appendix M, Visual Master 12, for an illustration that you can use to make an overhead transparency. This informational illustration should be very useful when leading a discussion on this important topic.

5. Consider obtaining and using the slide/audio series titled *Milestones in Papermaking*, from the Graphic Arts Technical Foundation.

C. Suggested teaching outline

1. Paper manufacturing—a basic industry
2. Paper products
   a. Paper bags
   b. Paper for cigarettes
   c. Gun cartridges
   d. Diapers
   e. Drinking cups
   f. Many others
3. Paper and the living index
   a. United States consumption
   b. Sweden and Canada
   c. Soviet Union
   d. China
   e. Other countries
4. Historical highlights
   a. Ancient graphic materials
   b. Papyrus
   c. Invention of paper in China
   d. Invention of paper in the western world
   e. The papermaking machine
   f. Early papermaking in the United States
5. Paper and raw materials
   a. The American Tree Farm System
   b. Trees—the basic raw material
   c. Fresh water—an essential for making paper
   d. Other necessary ingredients

Unit 162. Pulp Manufacturing

A. Objectives

Upon reading, defining the key terms, answering the study questions, and completing the activities relating to this unit, students should be able to

1. List the major sources of wood which are used for paper pulp.
2. Name and describe the pulping stages of debarking, chipping, and pulping.
3. Also, name and describe the pulping processes of bleaching, beating and refining, adding the additives, and cleaning.

B. Instructor preparation

1. Write to the United States Forest Service and request the latest information on the number of acres of pulpwood. Ask them to identify the number of acres of pulpwood that are government-owned land and those that are private and company-owned lands.
2. Obtain a sample set of small glass jars containing wood chips, brown stock pulp, bleached pulp, and dyed pulp. Most paper companies will furnish samples of this kind for educational purposes, if you will provide the small glass jars. One known source for these samples is Hammermill Papers, Memphis, Tennessee.

C. Suggested teaching outline

1. Pulpwood
   a. Kinds of trees
   b. Percentage of wood used in papermaking
   c. Transportation and handling
2. Debarking
3. Chipping
4. Pulping
   a. Chemical
   b. Mechanical
   c. Chemical-mechanical
5. Bleaching
6. Beating and refining
7. Additives
8. Cleaning
   a. By screening
   b. Centricleaner

Unit 163. Paper Manufacturing

A. Objectives

Upon reading, defining the key terms, answering the study questions, and completing the activities relating to this unit, students should be able to

1. Summarize the total process of forming the sheet of paper once the pulp reaches the papermaking machine.
2. Identify and explain the two methods of producing watermarks.
3. Describe the processes involved in water removal and drying the newly made paper during its travel through the papermaking machine.
4. List the three principal methods of manufacturing paper and paperboard.
5. Generalize the finishing operations once the paper leaves the papermaking machine.
6. State the important of research in the papermaking industry.

B. **Instructor preparation**

1. Write to several paper companies, the United States Forest Service or the American Paper Institute and request posters, charts, and other literature which helps to explain the total process involved in the production of paper. Many materials are available from these sources and, in most instances, can be obtained at no cost merely by making a written request.

2. Obtain one or more of the 16mm films and videotapes available from papermaking companies that present the papermaking process. One excellent film, titled *Seeds of Wonder*, is available from Hammermill Papers, Memphis, TN.

C. **Suggested teaching outline**

1. Forming the paper
2. Adding the watermark
    a. The dandy roll method
    b. The rubber stamp roll method
3. Water removal and drying
4. Methods of manufacturing paper and paperboard
    a. The Fourdrinier
    b. The cylinder
    c. The inverform
5. Finishing
    a. Inspecting
    b. Sheeting
    c. Special finishing
    d. Packaging
6. Paper research
    a. The people
    b. Purpose
    c. Findings

Unit 164. Kinds, Weights, and Sizes of Paper

A. **Objectives**

Upon reading, defining the key terms, answering the study questions, and completing the activities relating to this unit, students should be able to

1. Clarify the terms "Weights" and "Sizes" in relationship to paper as used for printing purposes.
2. Compare the ten basic papers of bond, book, bristol, cover, ledger, offset, text, newsprint, duplicator, and mimeograph.
3. Discuss the defintion of recycled paper, as defined by the federal government.
4. Determine the caliper of a specified weight of different kinds of paper according to the table listed in this unit.
5. Compute the weight of special sizes and kinds of paper according to the table in this unit.

B. **Instructor preparation**

1. Obtain samples from a paper supply house of each of the ten basic papers, as listed in this unit. Use these samples during your discussion of each kind of paper and also allow your students to study the samples freely during their individual study time.
2. Also, obtain samples of special papers such as onion skin, tracing vellum, kraft wrapping paper, paperboard, and other papers that are not considered of the common printing varieties. Use these samples in the same way as suggested in No. 1 above regarding basic papers.

3. If possible, determine from the American Paper Institute or from one or more of the several paper companies the extent to which recycled paper is being made throughout the country. Ask them to provide you as much information as possible on recycled paper, so you may not only explain this to your students but also attempt to encourage them to develop a reuse and recycle program for one of our most important commodities.

4. Make transparencies of Figures 164–2 and 164–3. See Appendix M, Visual Masters 13 and 14. These two textbook figures have been enlarged for your convenience in making overhead transparencies. Use these transparencies to help your students understand the relationships involved with "calipers and weights" of paper and the "constant weight factor schedule" for the different kinds and weights of paper.

C. Suggested teaching outline

1. Basic weights and sizes of paper
2. Basic printing papers
   a. Bond
   b. Book
   c. Bristol
   d. Cover
   e. Ledger
   f. Offset
   g. Text
   h. Newsprint
   i. Duplicator
   j. Mimeograph
3. Recycled paper
   a. Not a new idea
   b. Definition of recycled paper
   c. Grades of waste paper
4. Calipers and weights of paper
   a. Relationship between calipers and weights
   b. Reading the calipers and weights table
5. Weights of special paper sizes
   a. Using the "constant factor schedule"
   b. The MW system of detemining basis—weight

Unit 165. Buying and Finding Cost of Paper

A. Objectives

Upon reading, answering the study questions, and completing the activities relating to this unit, students should be able to

1. Name the several methods of packaging paper for sale and shipment to the purchaser who is usually a commercial printer or an in-plant operation.
2. Determine the package breaking point for specified papers according to the table listed in this unit.
3. Compute the cost of a specified kind, weight, and basic size of paper according to information found in a typical paper supply house pricing catalogue.

B. Instructor preparation

1. Obtain a pricing catalogue from a paper supply company. Allow your students to study this catalogue thoroughly, and encourage them to determine the cost of paper according to the 1000-sheet system. There is little need to have them determine the cost of paper per pound, but there may be special cases where this knowledge could be of some assistance.

2. Develop some typical problems or situations where the cost of paper must be determined. Place this information either on an overhead transparency or on the chalkboard; then help the students understand the method of determining paper cost. Also, you may desire to set up several problems, duplicate them, and give the students some opportunity to work the problems as part of their normal homework.

C. **Suggested teaching outline**
   1. Packaging methods for printing papers
      a. Package
      b. Carton or bundle
      c. 4-carton or 4-bundle
      d. 16-carton or 16-bundle
      e. Carton assortments
      f. Wrapped goods
   2. Paper breaking points
   3. Determining cost of paper
      a. By the 1000-sheet system
      b. By the pound system

Unit 166. Making Paper by Hand

A. **Objectives**

Upon reading, answering the study questions, and completing the activities relating to this unit, students should be able to
   1. Assemble the necessary equipment and supplies necessary for making paper by hand.
   2. Produce an acceptable sheet of paper, according to the procedure outlined in this unit.

B. **Instructor preparation**
   1. Obtain the necessary tools and supplies for the production of hand papermaking. Papermaking kits can be obtained from The American Paper Institute or from Hammermill Papers.
   2. Have several sheets of hand-made paper available for students to study and observe prior to having them prepare hand-made paper.

C. **Suggested teaching outline**
   1. Equipment and supplies necessary for hand papermaking
      a. A fine-meshed wire screen
      b. A metal pan such as an old biscuit pan, refrigerator tray, aluminum frozen-food container, or similar shape
      c. A forming rack or mold. This can be made from a second pan that will fit inside the first. Cut out the entire bottom, leaving only the sides.
      d. A basin that will hold at least 10 quarts of water
      e. Thirty sheets of facial tissue, not the wet-strength kind
      f. Two sheets of blotting paper, pan size
      g. Laundry starch. One tablespoon of instant starch to two cups of water provides what commercial papermakers call "size."
      h. An egg beater or blender and a rolling pin
      i. A household electric iron
   2. Papermaking procedure
      a. Preparation stages
      b. Preparing the pulp
      c. Forming the sheet
      d. Drying the sheet
      e. Finishing the sheet

SECTION 20
PRINTING INK MANUFACTURING

Section Goal: To introduce students to terminology associated with inks, composition of inks for various printing processes, printing ink difficulties, and methods of mixing inks.

Section Description: This section has been included in the textbook to help students understand a major material used in the printing process. While the information has been placed in a separate section of the book, it has application to many other units. Some instructors will want to treat the section as a unit of study, and others will want to integrate the information with appropriate units. The authors recommend that the units be taught as separate topics. Other units relating to image transfer can be used to reinforce the concepts in Section 20. The unit also can be used for reference purposes throughout your course.

Unit 168. Introduction to Printing Inks

A. Objectives

Students, as a result of reading Unit 168 and completing the questions in Unit 174, will be able to

1. Describe multiple uses of printing inks.
2. Identify the development of printing ink manufacturers.

B. Instructor preparation

1. Collect as many different samples of printed products representing different kinds of printing processes as possible.
2. Secure several different inks to show to students.
3. Show the 35mm slide audio series *Introduction to Lithographic Ink*, available from the Graphic Arts Technical Foundation.

C. Suggested teaching outline

Unit 168 is an introductory unit and will nearly always be combined with subsequent units to make a complete lesson.

1. Printing process
   a. Coat one material onto another
      (1) Ink most common material
      (2) Ink placed on substrate
   b. Many different kinds of substrate
   c. Each substrate requires special ink
   d. Different processes require different inks
   e. Product uses determine kinds of inks
2. History
   a. Chinese
      (1) Third century B.C.
      (2) Block printing
   b. Today
      (1) Large chemical industry
      (2) 600 million dollars per year

Unit 169. Formulation of Printing Inks

Students, after reading Unit 169, engaging in associated activities, and completing the appropriate questions from Unit 174, will be able to identify the main ingredients in printing inks.

B. Instructor preparation

If possible, students should observe the effects of various ingredients included in printing inks. Many school laboratories use only prepared inks and do not stock many ingredients or additivies for printing inks. In those instances, arrangements might be made with a local printing establishment to view the effects of printing ink ingredients.

1. When available, collect ingredients for inks that can be shown to students.
2. Review the material for discussion purposes.

C. Suggested teaching outline

1. Main printing materials
   a. Substrate
      (1) Material on which printing is done
      (2) Wide variety of materials used for substrate
      (3) Different characteristics
   b. Inks
      (1) Many kinds
      (2) Different colors
      (3) Matches printing process or substrate material
2. Ingredient categories
   a. Vehicles
   b. Pigments
   c. Others
      (1) Driers
      (2) Waxes
      (3) Greases (lubricants)
3. Vehicles
   a. Body of ink
   b. Establishes ink character
   c. Kinds
      (1) Nondrying oil vehicles
      (2) Drying oil vehicles
         (a) Dry by oxidation
         (b) Oxygen hardens ink
         (c) Letterpress and lithographic inks
         (d) Kinds of oil
            1. Linseed oil
            2. Lithographic varnish
            3. Chinawood oil
            4. Castor oil
            5. Cottonseed oil
            6. Fish oil
         (e) Linseed oil varnishes
            1. Distribute well
            2. Transfer well to substrate
         (f) Litho varnish numbered
            1. Identifies viscosity
            2. 00000—very thin
            3. 10—very heavy (body gum)

(3) Solvent-resin vehicles
    (a) Elements
        1. Resin
        2. Oil
        3. Solvent
    (b) Solvent absorbed by substrate
    (c) Dry coat of resin and oil on surface of the substrate
    (d) Quick-setting inks
    (e) Letterpress and lithographic inks

(4) Other kinds of vehicles
    (a) Glycol
    (b) Resin-wax
    (c) Water-soluble

4. Pigments
  a. Give color to ink
  b. Kinds
    (1) Black
      (a) Carbon
      (b) Special chemicals
    (2) White
      (a) Opaque white
        1. Cover substrate and other pigments
        2. Titanium dioxide
        3. Zinc oxide
        4. Zinc sulfide
        5. Used directly on substrate
        6. Mixed with other inks
      (b) Transparent white
        1. Light passes through
        2. Color below shows through
        3. Aluminum hydrate
        4. Magnesium carbonate
        5. Calcium carbonate
        6. Clays

5. Other ingredients
  a. Driers
    (1) Speed oxidation
    (2) Drier should match vehicle
    (3) Problems resulting from driers
      (a) Drying on press
      (b) Halftone fill-in
      (c) Excessive sticking
    (4) One ounce per pound will dry ink in 4 to 8 hours
  b. Waxes
    (1) Combat setoff
    (2) Improve abrasion resistance
    (3) Kinds
      (a) Paraffin wax
      (b) Carnauba wax

    c. Greases or lubricants
        (1) Reduces sticking
        (2) Increases drying
        (3) Kinds
            (a) Cup grease
            (b) Wool grease
            (c) Petroleum jelly

Unit 170. Manufacture of Printing Inks

A. Objective

Students, as a result of reading Unit 170 and completing the appropriate questions from Unit 174, will be able to describe the printing ink manufacturing process and use the terminology associated with printing ink manufacturing.

B. Instructor preparation

This unit was planned to be an informational unit. It was expected that few laboratories will be able to provide demonstrations or activities for students. The instructor should be thoroughly familiar with the unit. In most instances, the information in Unit 170 will be combined with other units in Section 20.

C. Suggested teaching outline

1. Manufacturer
2. Mixing pigments and compounds—"wetting down"
3. Prepare by "batch" method
   a. One quantity mixed
   b. Equipment cleaned
4. Continuous process
   a. Mixing always in operation
   b. Produce standardized inks—newsprint
5. Ink ground after mixing
   a. Reduces size of solid particles
   b. Distributes pigments and compounds
   c. Grinding methods
      (1) Three-roll mill
      (2) Ball mills
      (3) Colloid mills
      (4) Sand grinders
      (5) Turbine grinder
   d. Fineness used to measure grinding

Unit 171. Kinds of Printing Inks

A. Objective

After completing activities associated with Unit 171 and answering the related questions from Unit 174, students will be able to identify the correct ink to be used for various printing situations.

B. Instructor preparation

1. Secure samples of several kinds of inks. If there is not an adequate variety of inks in the laboratory, attempt to borrow some samples from printers in the community.
2. Obtain samples of many kinds of printed materials. Include materials that have different substrate and represent several printing processes.

C. Suggested teaching outline

1. Printing inks developed for various printing processes
   a. Letterpress
      (1) Specific presses require certain ink characteristics
      (2) Platen
         (a) Short
         (b) Tacky
      (3) Cylinder
         (a) Long
         (b) Good flowability
   b. Lithographic
      (1) Cover flat surface
      (2) Long
      (3) Viscous
      (4) Resistant to water
   c. Gravure
      (1) Good body
      (2) Printing method determines
         (a) Length
         (b) Drying speed
   d. Screen process
      (1) Greatest variety
      (2) More fluid
      (3) Pass through screen
      (4) Substrate determines ink
2. Use of printed item
   a. Must be consideration
   b. Examples
      (1) Abrasion
      (2) Weather
      (3) Sanitary
3. Substrate
   a. Ink matches substrate
      (1) Paper
         (a) Newsprint
         (b) Uncoated
         (c) Coated
      (2) Nonpaper
         (a) Glass
         (b) Plastic
         (c) Wood
         (d) Metals
   b. Irregular surfaces
4. Types of inks
   a. Heat-set ink
      (1) High-speed press
      (2) Vehicle evaporates with heat
      (3) Pigment remains on surface

b. Quick-set oil inks
   (1) Vehicle
       (a) Oil
       (b) Resin
   (2) Oil penetrates surface
   (3) Letterpress and lithographic
c. Gloss inks
   (1) Little penetration
   (2) Pigment gives high gloss
   (3) Not appropriate for certain papers
d. News ink
   (1) Dry by absorption
   (2) Generally very thin
   (3) Designed for high-speed presses
e. Metallic inks
   (1) Metal powder pigment
   (2) Aluminum for silver
   (3) Bronze for gold
   (4) Usually mixed before printing
f. Magnetic inks
   (1) Pigment can be magnetized
   (2) Used for electronic recognition
   (3) Must be perfectly formulated
g. Sublimable inks
   (1) Use in heat transfer
   (2) Printed on paper
   (3) Transferred to cloth
   (4) Transferred by heat and pressure
   (5) Works well on cotton
h. Ultraviolet curing inks
   (1) Ultraviolet light dries ink
   (2) Used on high speed

Unit 172. Difficulties With Printing Ink

A. Objective

Students, after reading Unit 172 and answering appropriate questions from Unit 174, will be able to recognize common printing ink problems and recommend possible solutions.

B. Instructor preparation

There are few illustrations included in Unit 172, because they are difficult problems. The instructor constantly must be aware of such problems. Ink problems often are attributed to other kinds of printing problems.

1. Collect samples of as many kinds of printing ink problems as possible.
2. Be prepared to refer students to specific parts of Unit 172 when a problem occurs in the classroom.

C. Suggested teaching outline

1. Check all possible problems
   a. Inaccurate match of ink and substrate
   b. Poor press conditions
   c. Wrong additives

2. Off color
   a. Cause
      (1) Dirty press
      (2) Thickness of film
   b. Color formulation
      (1) Color to be duplicated
      (2) Sample of substrate
      (3) Draw-down
3. Setoff
   a. Ink transfers to back
   b. Occurs in delivery section
   c. Causes
      (1) Static electricity
      (2) Heavy ink film
      (3) Slow ink penetration
      (4) Improper handling
   d. Precautions
      (1) Minimum ink film
      (2) Eliminate static
      (3) Check kind of ink
      (4) Careful handling
      (5) Wax spray
      (6) Reduce paper stack size
4. Improper drying
   a. Ink dries too slowly
   b. Causes
      (1) Improper substrate
      (2) Old ink
      (3) Temperature
      (4) Humidity
   c. Remedies
      (1) Control atmospheric conditions
      (2) Use drier
5. Sticking
   a. Ink film holds together
   b. Causes same as for setoff
   c. Remedies same as for setoff
6. Chalking
   a. Inadequate binding
   b. Ink film dry
   c. Removed by light abrasion
   d. Remedies
      (1) Select another ink
      (2) Add varnish
      (3) Overprint clear coat
7. Specking
   a. Small dots
      (1) In halftone areas
      (2) Nonprinted areas

    b. Causes
       (1) Ink contamination
       (2) Heavy ink film
       (3) Excessive impression
       (4) Poor makeready
       (5) Poorly ground ink

8. Strike-through
    a. Ink goes through sheet
    b. Confused with setoff
    c. Causes
       (1) Ink dries slowly
       (2) Improper ink and substrate

9. Plate wear
    a. Improperly ground ink
    b. Too much pigment
    c. Excessive roller pressure
    d. Abrasive paper

Unit 173. Mixing Printing Inks

A. Objectives

As a result of reading Unit 173, engaging in related activities, and completing appropriate questions from Unit 174, students will be able to

1. Identify the tools required to mix inks.
2. Select proper ingredients for mixing inks.
3. Accurately mix inks for various situations.

B. Instructor preparation

1. Collect the tools needed for mixing inks, including:
    a. Slab—nonporous material like plate glass
    b. Knives or spatulas
    c. Scales
2. Secure ingredients for mixing inks, such as:
    a. Litho varnish, several weights
    b. Driers
    c. Waxes and compounds
    d. Two or more black inks
    e. Gray ink
    f. Transparent and mixing white inks
    g. Several strong colors

C. Suggested teaching outline

1. Purpose
    a. Obtain new colors
    b. Adjust ink characteristics
2. Mixing tools
    a. Slab
       (1) Nonporous material
       (2) Free of scratches

    b. Knives and spatulas
        (1) Blend ink and ingredients
        (2) Remove ink from containers
    c. Scales
        (1) Weigh ingredients
        (2) Increases accuracy
3. Ingredients
    a. Best done by ink formulator
    b. Ink and ingredient must match
    c. Minimum for letterpress and lithographic
        (1) Litho varnish
            (a) Several grades
            (b) Appropriate for ink
        (2) Driers
        (3) Waxes and compounds
        (4) Two or more kinds of black inks
        (5) Gray ink
        (6) Transparent and mixing white
        (7) Several strong colors
            (a) Blue
            (b) Yellow
            (c) Red
            (d) Green
            (e) Brown
4. Mixing
    a. Mixing situations
        (1) Match existing color
        (2) Adjust characteristics
        (3) Duplicate previous formula
            (a) Measure correct amounts
            (b) Blend the ingredients
    b. Considerations
        (1) Hue—shade
        (2) Value—lightness or darkness
        (3) Chroma—strength or grayness
    c. Compare with color chart
    d. Assemble tools
        (1) Be sure they are clean
        (2) Cleaning materials
    e. Select ingredients
    f. Mix the ingredients
        (1) Start with lightest
        (2) Add only little dark ink
        (3) Blend until streaks gone
        (4) Use separate spatulas for each color
    g. Test after mixing
        (1) Fingerprint test
        (2) Draw-down test

h. Manufacturer tests
   (1) Flow
   (2) Fineness of grind
   (3) Fading

SECTION 21
LEGAL CONSIDERATIONS FOR THE PRINTER

Section Goal: To explore the privileges and obligations of the publisher, the printer, and the citizen in regard to printed works and to provide information regarding copyright infringement and unethical practices.

Section Description: The content of this section is quite short in comparison to other sections. It does, however, contain some information which should be useful not only in an immediate sense but also should be beneficial to the students on a long-range basis. There has been, there still is, and there will always be problems with copyright infringement, pornography, counterfeiting, and unethical practices. If graphic arts educators can in a small way help to educate and hopefully reduce this amount of illegal practice, they will have made a contribution that will be beneficial to society.

This section may well be studied at the end of a particular course when the students are active in completing the laboratory assignments that have been made. The units are exceptionally short in comparison to previous units; therefore, it will take only a short time for the students to read a unit, and probably no more than 10–15 minutes will be needed to discuss and/or review the content in class. By taking a short time for both reading and discussion, students are not likely to become bored or unhappy with its content.

The key terms, study questions and activities suggested in Unit 181 should be beneficial in helping the students to understand the content of this section. The activities can be a considerable amount of fun and the students may be eager to complete all six activities instead of the lesser number that you might consider assigning.

Unit 175. Legal Restrictions of Printed Materials Production

A. **Objectives**

Upon reading, defining the key terms, and answering the study questions, students should be able to

1. Define the word "Copyright."
2. Summarize the rights and privileges of a copyright as specified by the current Federal Copyright Act.

B. **Instructor preparation**

1. Secure the latest information available regarding copyrights directly from the Copyright Office. They have some excellent materials in printed form which will help your students better understand this important law.
2. Check your local school library or city libraries to determine whether there is additional information available regarding copyright. If so, this information may be valuable to you in making a presentation on this topic.

C. **Suggested teaching outline**

1. Copyright defined
2. The Federal Copyright Act
   a. First initiated in 1790
   b. Present law
   c. Copyright length—28 years
3. Copyright benefits
   a. Prohibits reproduction of a product
   b. An exclusive right
   c. Economic benefits

Unit 176. How to Obtain a Copyright

A. Objectives

Upon reading, defining the key terms, answering the study questions, and completing the activities relating to this unit, students should be able to

1. Name the three primary rights of the copyright owner which are beyond the single exclusive right of copyrighted works.
2. Recognize the seven broad classes of work in which copyright may be claimed.
3. Know the steps necessary to secure a copyright and know the proper forms of displaying copyright notice.

B. Instructor preparation

1. Send for the paperwork necessary for application of copyright. Allow your students to study this document thoroughly, and display it on a display board which you have prepared concerning content in this entire section.
2. Obtain samples of publications which contain the three forms of displaying the copyright notice. These samples may interest your students in a way that they may become more aware of the copyright law and respectful of a published work.

C. Suggested teaching outline

1. The rights of copyright
   a. The exclusive right
   b. Other specific rights
2. The copyright
   a. Seven classes of work which can be copyrighted
   b. What cannot be copyrighted
   c. Copyright claims
   d. Obtaining the copyright
   e. The three forms of copyright notice

Unit 177. Copyright Infringement

A. Objectives

Upon reading, defining the key terms, study questions, and completing the activity related to this unit, students should be able to

1. Identify the statement found in the United States Constitution in which the copyright privileges are alluded to.
2. Help interpret the copyright law in respect to using a copying machine to duplicate parts of a copyrighted work.

B. Instructor preparation

1. From your school or public library, obtain a copy of the Constitution of the United States. Turn to the article in which the statement is made in regard to the protection of writings and discoveries. Ask your students whether they have ever noticed this part of the Constitution when they studied it in a social studies class.
2. Ask an attorney to make a presentation in your class in regard to copyright infringement. He or she likely will be able to give some excellent insights into some of the problems regarding the copyright law.

C. Suggested teaching outline

1. The United States Constitution and the copyright
   a. The constitutional statement
   b. Infringement and unlawful printing

2. Breaking the law
    a. Copying machine
    b. Libraries, schools and business establishments
    c. Copyright infringement solutions

Unit 178. Pornography

A. Objectives

Upon reading, defining the key terms, answering the study questions, and completing the activity relating to this unit, students should be able to

1. Define the word "pornography."
2. Discuss the role of a printer concerning the laws of obscenity.
3. Summarize the vulnerability of the publisher and distributor of pornographic materials.

B. Instructor preparation

1. It is obvious that you are not encouraged to gather pornographic materials for display to your class. You will, however, probably receive several requests and quite likely receive samples of pornographic materials from students as a result of studying this unit. You will have to use your own good judgment and common sense in handling these situations.
2. Talk with your local law enforcement authorities and determine the extent of problems within your geographical area in regard to pornography. Obtain data from these authorities which you can present to your class.

C. Suggested teaching outline

1. Pornography defined
2. The role of the printer
    a. Vulnerability
    b. Responsibility
3. The publisher and distributors
    a. More vulnerable to the obscenity laws
    b. The United States Supreme Court decision

Unit 179. Counterfeiting

A. Objectives

Upon reading, defining the key terms, answering the study questions, and completing the activity relating to this unit, students should be able to

1. Define the term "Counterfeiting."
2. Summarize the four important facts about United States currency.
3. List the penalties of counterfeiting and forgery.

B. Instructor preparation

1. Talk with your local law enforcement authorities about the problems that have been encountered in your local area regarding counterfeiting and forgery. Request a knowledgeable law enforcement authority to make a presentation to your class regarding problems encountered with counterfeiting and forgery in your own local area.
2. Obtain or borrow a strong magnifying glass or system by which the students can inspect the paper used for currency. Give each student the opportunity to inspect the paper thoroughly through the magnifying system.

C. Suggested teaching outline

1. Counterfeiting—defined

2. Facts about United States currency
    a. The use of special paper
    b. Paper contains red and blue fibers
    c. The use of engraved plates
    d. Important features of paper currency
3. Penalties for counterfeiting and forgery
    a. The fine
    b. Years in prison

Unit 180. Moral and Ethical Considerations

A. Objectives

Upon reading, answering the study questions, and completing the activity relating to this unit, students should be able to

1. Discuss the need and reasons for abiding by a code of ethics in regard to printing and distribution of graphic materials.
2. Clarify a statement such as: "Because it's printed, it must be the truth."

B. Instructor preparation

1. Visit with a commercial printer or publisher about the code of ethics which they have established and follow in regard to the printing of two-dimensional products. If possible obtain a copy of any guidelines they may have available to guide them in making decisions in regard to "Ethics."
2. Ask a commercial printer or publisher to visit with your class concerning any problems they may have or have had in regard to producing products that seem to be questionable in regard to the moral and ethical practices followed by the commercial printer and publishers.

C. Suggested teaching outline

1. The printer's and publisher's code of ethics
2. Printed material and the "truth"
3. Reprinting a product by another printer

SECTION 22
DESKTOP COMPOSITION

Unit 182. What Is Desktop Composition?

A. Objectives

Upon reading, defining the key terms, answering the study questions, and completing the one activity relating to this unit, students should be able to

1. Discuss the role of desktop composition in the total graphic arts.
2. Determine the hardware needs for a desktop composition system.
3. Classify the software used in a desktop composition system.

B. Instructor preparation

1. Determine the operating condition of the several hardware units within the desktop composition system available for student use. This equipment may be located in the graphic arts laboratory or in a separate computer laboratory. It is important that all units are functioning properly.
2. Become very familiar with the desktop composition software available for your students to use. When they have questions, it is important that you know how to help them solve their problems.
3. Arrange to have a computer expert make a presentation to your students regarding the latest advancements in computer hardware technology and computer graphics software programs.
4. Consider obtaining and using the following videotape from the GAT/GAEFT Videotape Project: number 018, *Desktop Publishing*.
5. Consider obtaining and using the videotape titled *Desk Top Publishing*, from Sunshine Enterprises, Spokane, WA.

C. Suggested teaching outline

1. What is desktop composition?
   a. Using computers and special software
   b. Integration of text and graphics
   c. Other names: electronic publishing and desktop publishing
   d. Creation of documents for printing
2. Required hardware and software
   a. Computer system with adequate memory
   b. Software, computer programs, designed for convenience to produce text and graphics
3. Hardware needs
   a. Computer CPU
   b. Monitor
   c. Keyboard
   d. Mouse
   e. Scanner
   f. Printer
4. Software
   a. DOS (Disk Operating System)
   b. Word processing
   c. Scanning programs
   d. Page makeup programs
   e. Graphics Programs

f. Raster graphics

g. Vector graphics

5. Summarization of the content

Unit 183. Input in Desktop Composition

A. Objectives

Upon reading, defining the key terms, answering the study questions, and completing the one activity relating to this unit, students should be able to

1. Explain how desktop composition systems work.

2. Describe the components of a desktop composition system.

3. Create a document by combining text and artwork into one unit.

B. Instructor preparation

1. Study the desktop composition software thoroughly. This will help you present the material to your students in a conceptual manner.

2. Photocopy the critical information on how to use desktop composition from the software reference manual. Make these pages available to your students for their independent study. If the software publication has been copyrighted, be sure and obtain formal permission to copy it directly from the publisher.

3. Arrange to have a computer store software expert give a demonstration to your students using the same software available for your students. Even though you may know the software very well, this is a good opportunity to bring in a guest speaker. It also gives you the opportunity to learn the latest developments about software, thus you are able to remain current in this ever-changing area.

C. Suggested teaching outline

1. How desktop composition systems work

    a. Transfer information

    b. Combine information

    c. Word processing features

2. Components of desktop composition software

    a. Menus

    b. Formats

3. Creating documents

    a. Begin with the copywriter's work

    b. Introduce the art director's work

    c. Combining text and art into one file

    d. Working with the artwork

    e. Positioning and sizing all copy

4. Summarization of the content

Unit 184. Page Layout and Output in Desktop Composition

A. Objectives

Upon reading, defining the key terms, answering the study questions, and completing the one activity relating to this unit, students should be able to

1. Explain how to lay out a page of text, art, and photographs using traditional and electronic layout methods.

2. Prepare acceptable page layouts by using appropriate type styles.

3. Make printouts on one or more of the several categories of output printers.

B. Instructor preparation

1. Review the content of Section 2, *Type Styles*, and Section 3, *Planning, Designing, and Layout*. Use this information when presenting the content of Unit 184 to your students. Remember that traditional methods of layout serve as a basis for content layout on a computer screen.

2. Obtain professionally prepared examples of printed products that have been "created" by using desktop composition software. These examples should serve as excellent stimuli for your students when you have them create desktop composition layouts.

3. Obtain desktop composition video demonstration programs from software companies. Show these to your students to "stretch" their creativity beyond what is possible to accomplish in the graphic arts classroom and laboratory.

C. Suggested teaching outline

1. Laying out a page
   a. Traditional page layout
   b. Electronic page layout
   c. Style sheets and templates

2. Type and page balance
   a. Choosing typefaces
   b. One-, two-, or three-column layouts
   c. Balancing content on the page
   d. Procedure to select type styles

3. Categories of output printers
   a. Dot matrix printers
   b. Ink jet printers
   c. Laser printers
   d. Post Script® laser printers
   e. Imagesetters

4. Service bureaus

5. Summarization of the content

SECTION 23
GRAPHIC ARTS CAREER OPPORTUNITIES

Section Goal: To introduce a number of graphic arts career opportunities which are available to the young men and women who are interested in joining an industry offering challenges and opportunities for advancement.

Section Description: This section serves as a capstone for all content in the book. During the course work in which informational and procedural content was studied in Sections 1–22, it has likely been your desire as well as the desire of the authors that several of the young people taking your course will become interested in choosing graphic arts for a career. Obviously, all people are not or should not choose this area; but by giving them the opportunity to have experiences in this area, it may help them to make a decision.

Information regarding the overall graphic arts industry is provided in Unit 186. Information on the pre-press jobs in the production preparation areas is given in Unit 187. Unit 188 contains content dealing with the actual printing and finishing of printed products. Management and sales opportunities, commonly called white collar jobs, are covered in Unit 189.

The authors, as educators, believed it important to include Unit 190, which contains information with regard to teaching opportunities in the graphic arts area. There seems to be a number of secondary and post-secondary teaching openings within the graphic arts area. From all indications, it appears the trend for maintaining and opening new graphic arts teaching facilities in both secondary and post high school institutions will continue, thereby creating an additional need for teachers within this area.

Opportunities in pulp and paper are covered in Unit 191. There are a wide variety of opportunities for both men and women in this important industry, just as there is a need for both men and women in the graphic arts industry. As an educator, you are challenged to encourage your students to consider an occupation or profession in the graphic arts and paper industries.

Two new units in the textbook and within this section are Unit 192, "Being a Successful Employee" and Unit 193, "Owning a Graphic Arts Business." Unit 192 has been included to serve as a guide to encouraging young people to be quality employees. Working for a company, whether it be small or large, demands responsibility on the part of the employee. As an educator, you have great opportunities to help your students gain and retain proper attitudes toward their current part-time employment and future full-time employment.

Most people have a dream of being financially successful in their adult life. The content of Unit 193 may help your students become involved in graphic arts entrepreneurship during their working lives.

As with all previous sections within the text, the last unit in this section and obviously the last unit in the textbook, Unit 194, is involved with learning experiences. Utilize these learning experiences in a way that will help your students dig into their pool of interests and abilities and to assess whether they should enter an area which you have chosen to teach. Good luck on being a successful career counselor. Your help is vital to the future of lifetime work of a number of young people.

Unit 186. Introduction to Careers in Graphic Arts

A. Objectives

Upon reading, defining the key terms, answering the study questions, and completing the activities relating to this unit, students should be able to

1. Summarize the opportunities and challenges available to students in the graphic arts industry.
2. Define the term "apprenticeship" and to clarify the features of the apprenticeship program.
3. Compare the earning and working conditions of production workers in the graphic arts industry to other manufacturing industries.
4. Name several of the specific opportunities that are available in the employment market of the graphic arts industry.

B. Instructor preparation

1. Consider obtaining and using the following two videotapes from the GAT/GAERF Videotape Project: Number 009, *Careers: Graphic Communications (Dear Student)* and Number 008, *Video Forum (Students Inquire—Industry Responds)*.

2. Obtain career booklets that are available from several different sources. One of these sources is the Graphic Arts Technical Foundation and another is the International Graphic Arts Education Association.

C. Suggested teaching outline

1. The Graphic Arts Industry
   a. Its opportunities
   b. Its challenges
2. Qualifications
   a. Apprenticeship
   b. Journeyman
   c. How to achieve needed qualifications
3. Earnings and working conditions
   a. The hourly pay
   b. The work-week length
   c. The stability of employment
4. Employment outlook
   a. Today's opportunities
   b. Opportunities in 5 to 10 years
   c. Operating a personal business

Unit 187. Opportunities in Pre-Press Preparation

A. Objectives

Upon reading, answering the study questions, and completing the activities relating to this unit, students should be able to

1. Assess their level of interest in pursuing a career involving the specific areas of graphic arts production known as design and layout, composition, photography, and image carriers.

2. Compare the advantages and disadvantages involved in each of the four previously named preparation production areas of the graphic arts.

B. Instructor preparation

1. Some associations make specific career publications available within certain areas. It will be to your advantage to write and request a list of items that they make available.

2. Companies producing equipment in primary areas of the graphic arts generally have some literature available regarding careers within that area. Be constantly on the search for this kind of information and obtain sufficient quantities to distribute to your students, especially to those who seem to have a flare for these areas of the graphic arts.

C. Suggested teaching outline

1. Design and layout
   a. The area of design origination
   b. People need artistic talent
2. Composition
   a. The compositor—a talented person
   b. Much mechanical training necessary

3. Photography
   a. Continuous-tone photography needs
   b. High-contrast photography needs
4. Image carriers
   a. People with a knowledge of chemistry desirable
   b. Many new materials within this area

Unit 188. Opportunities in Printing and Finishing

A. Objectives

Upon reading, answering the study questions, and completing the activities relating to this unit, students should be able to

1. Appraise the image-transfer area and determine their interest in pursuing this phase of the graphic arts.
2. Judge the amount of interest they have with regard to the finishing and binding areas of the graphic arts.

B. Instructor preparation

1. As with Unit 187, write directly to manufacturers of image-transfer equipment and finishing and binding equipment to request the literature that may be available within the career function. Some of the literature that companies can make available may not necessarily refer directly to the careers by title, but are likely to provide the kind of information that will be helpful to your students.
2. Look for different sources of audiovisual material that may have titles within these two specific graphic arts areas.

C. Suggested teaching outline

1. Image transfer
   a. The area by definition
   b. Personnel qualifications
   c. Working conditions
   d. Kinds and sizes of equipment available
2. Finishing and binding
   a. Finishing operations
   b. Personnel qualifications for the finishing area
   c. Binding operations
   d. Skills necessary for the binder

Unit 189. Opportunities in Management and Sales

A. Objectives

Upon reading, defining the key term, answering the study questions, and completing the activities relating to this unit, students should be able to

1. Analyze the qualities, as outlined in this unit, that people within the management and sales areas of the graphic arts must possess.
2. Appraise the known talents of themselves and the talents that have been beneficial for both management and sales personnel.

B. Instructor preparation

1. Visit management and sales personnel with whom you may have become acquainted during your teaching career. Ask these people to give you some ideas and thoughts in regard to the needs for management and sales personnel in the graphic arts industry within your geographical area. Quite likely, these people will be interested in making a presentation to your class about their personal thoughts and experiences.

2. Talk with your school counselor and determine whether he or she is aware of any audiovisual material that may attempt to depict management and sales opportunities within general business. It is likely that there are some excellent titles available.

C. **Suggested teaching outline**

1. Management and sales personnel
   a. Essential ingredients of all business enterprises
   b. Must be specialists in change
2. Management people
   a. Qualifications
   b. Complex work
3. Sales personnel
   a. An area of many challenges
   b. Qualities of a good salesperson

Unit 190. Opportunities in Teaching Graphic Arts

A. **Objectives**

Upon reading, answering the study questions, and completing the activity relating to this unit, students should be able to

1. Name several specific areas or levels of education in which teaching opportunities are available in graphic arts.
2. Summarize the several qualifications of an instructor.
3. Assess their interest in becoming an instructor within the technical area of graphic arts.

B. **Instructor preparation**

1. Write to the International Graphic Arts Education Association and request the most current information available on teaching opportunities within graphic arts. Also, request information concerning educational opportunities within companies or corporations that are considered part of the graphic arts industry.
2. Determine the number of secondary and post-secondary school programs within your state offering courses in graphic arts. This information can generally be obtained from the State Department of Public Instruction.
3. If a college or university industrial technology department within your state conducts a conference or exposition in which students are invited to participate, be certain to provide them with this opportunity. This will give them a chance to see and possibly become involved in a graphic arts program at the college/university level. Also, if there is an area vocational/technical school located in your geographical area offering graphic arts instruction, it would be greatly beneficial for your students to tour this facility and see its operation.

C. **Suggested teaching outline**

1. Graphic arts teaching opportunities
   a. Secondary schools
   b. Vocational high schools
   c. Area vocational-technical schools and institutes
   d. Junior colleges
   e. College/universities
2. Instructor qualifications
   a. Personality/ability traits
   b. Educational requirements

Unit 191. Opportunities in Pulp and Paper

A. Objectives

Upon reading, answering the study questions, and completing the activity relating to this unit, students should be able to

1. Identify the five possible areas of employment for people having a degree in industrial, civil, or mechanical engineering.
2. Summarize opportunities for people who have advanced formal degrees in the sciences and research.
3. Review the opportunities open to people interested in management, business, legal, and plant occupations—as related to the pulp and paper industry.
4. Clarify the opportunities for women and minorities within the pulp and paper industry.
5. Assess their own personal interests in relation to the kinds of opportunities and the qualifications necessary for people who are involved in the pulp and paper industry.

B. Instructor preparation

1. Write or visit a pulp or paper manufacturing facility, and request information on career opportunities available in this industry. Actually, several publications are available from many companies; therefore, you should have no problem in locating handout materials for your students.
2. If a paper facility is located within your geographical area, contact one of the management personnel and request someone to make a presentation to your class regarding career opportunities in this field. Usually, these people will be eager to talk to young people and attempt to encourage them to join an industry to which they are devoting their lives.

C. Suggested teaching outline

1. Pulp and paper manufacturing opportunities
   a. Engineering
   b. Scientific areas
   c. Research areas
   d. Management, business, and legal areas
2. Opportunities within the plant operations
   a. Production workers
   b. Maintenance personnel
   c. Semi-skilled personnel
3. Opportunities for women
   a. Areas of work
   b. Future opportunities

Unit 192. Being a Successful Employee

A. Objectives

Upon reading, defining the key terms, answering the study questions, and completing the one activity relating to this unit, students should be able to

1. Apply the steps involved in getting a job.
2. Explain the critical factors associated with keeping a job.
3. Write a letter of resignation for a simulated job setting.
4. Describe leadership and understand how to attain experiences in this important area.

B. Instructor preparation

1. Consult with a school guidance counselor and obtain literature or information that he or she may have on the topic of "Being a Successful Employee." The contents of this printed material may be helpful in preparing a class lecture.

2. Arrange to have a business personnel manager from a local company, preferably a graphic arts company, serve as a guest speaker in your graphic arts classes or for the Student Graphic Arts Club.

3. Ask the school audio-visual coordinator to help obtain a 16mm film or video program on the topic of maintaining employment which would be appropriate for showing to your students.

C. Suggested teaching outline

1. Getting a job
   a. Where to look
   b. Making contacts
   c. Interviewing for a job

2. Keeping a job
   a. Employees must benefit a company
   b. Employees should be fully informed
   c. Ability to get along
   d. Quality work performance
   e. Maintain competency

3. Changing jobs
   a. The right way
   b. Letter of resignation
   c. The wrong way

4. Developing leadership abilities
   a. Meaning of leadership
   b. Student leadership opportunities
   c. Employee leadership opportunities
   d. Citizen leadership opportunities

5. Summarization of the content

Unit 193. Owning a Graphic Arts Business

A. Objectives

Upon reading, defining the key terms, answering the study questions, and completing the one activity relating to this unit, students should be able to

1. Name key characteristics of a graphic arts business owner.
2. Explain the several graphic arts business types, financial considerations, and ownership options.
3. Discuss the various aspects of getting into business, the several regulations that must be considered, and managing a business.

B. Instructor preparation

1. Talk with a local or regional director of economic development. This person may be willing to give a talk to your students about graphic arts business opportunities.

2. Arrange to have an owner of a graphic arts company come and make a presentation to your students. This person could bring "real life" experiences into your classroom.

3. Write or telephone one or more of the agencies listed in the textbook unit. Request current information that they may have available about business ownership.

4. Prepare a display board using the information you have been able to acquire from one or more sources.

C. Suggested teaching outline

1. Business owner characteristics
   a. Being competitive
   b. Being motivated
   c. Being an entrepreneur

2. What kind of business?
    a. General commercial printing?
    b. Specialty product printing?
    c. Pre-press work?
    d. Which printing process?
3. Financial considerations
    a. How much money will be needed?
    b. Having adequate capital
    c. Maintaining reserve funds
    d. Using a financial planning form
    e. Sources of funds
4. Ownership options
    a. Sole proprietorship
    b. Partnership
    c. Corporation
    d. Sub-Chapter S corporation
5. Getting into business
    a. Starting a new business
    b. Buying an existing business
    c. Investing in a franchise
6. Regulations to consider
    a. Licensing
    b. Protection of the environment
    c. Fair labor standards
    d. Safety
    e. Taxes
    f. Insurance
7. Managing a business
    a. Importance of planning
    b. Structuring the company
    c. Record keeping
    d. Hiring and supervising employees
    e. Remaining competitive
    f. Sources of help
8. Summarization of the content

APPENDIX A

COMPREHENSIVE GRAPHIC ARTS COURSE OUTLINE
(4 credits/semester)

Major Goal

Develop a degree of skill in using several of the techniques and methods currently being practiced in the graphic arts field.

Objectives

Upon satisfactory completion of this course the student will be able to

1. Define the broad areas of graphic arts.
2. Illustrate basic concepts of layout and design as related to the graphic arts.
3. Identify the several methods of type and image composition.
4. Discuss the several aspects of photo conversion.
5. Note the various image carrier devices.
6. Describe the various methods of image transfer.
7. Recognize finishing and binding methods.
8. Review the production of selected raw materials used in the graphic arts industry.
9. Skillfully solve problems relating to methods of graphic reproduction.
10. Value and appreciate the contribution graphic arts has made to civilization and as a career alternative.

Activities

I. Orientation—The technical area and course
   A. Introduction to the course
   B. Introduction of department faculty
   C. Areas of graphic arts—the structure
   D. Graphic arts defined
      1. Civilization builder
      2. Communication media
      3. Form of technology
      4. Language
      5. Education
      6. Big business
      7. Money
      8. Employment
   E. Historical significance
      1. Early world development
      2. Early U.S. development

II. Design and Layout
   A. Alphabet and typefaces
   B. Design principles
   C. Layout procedures

III. Type and Image Composition
   A. Methods of composition
   B. Desktop composition
   C. Foundry-type composition
   D. Impact or strike-on
   E. Photographic
   F. Dry transfer
   G. Hand-mechanical
   H. Electronic typesetting

IV. Photo-conversion
   A. General area of photo-conversion
   B. Theory of photography
   C. Basic operation of cameras
   D. Photographing high-contrast, copy-line, and continuous-tone
   E. Processing of film
   F. Proper method of handling photographing materials
   G. Chemicals used in photography

V. Image carriers
   A. Letterpress image carriers
   B. Lithographic image carriers
   C. Screen image carriers
   D. Gravure image carriers
   E. Electrostatic image carriers
   F. Photographic image carriers
   G. Preparation to produce; stripping, opaquing, masking, etc.
   H. Chemicals used to produce each
   I. Duplicating methods

VI.	Image transfer
   A.	Different methods of placing images on receptors
      1.	Letterpress
      2.	Lithography
      3.	Screen
      4.	Gravure
      5.	Electrostatic
      6.	Photographic
   B.	Presses used with each image-transfer method
   C.	How to use the following presses/duplicators
      1.	Platen press
      2.	Litho duplicator
      3.	Screen (hand and power)
      4.	Office duplicators
      5.	Office copiers

VII.	Finishing and binding
   A.	Finishing operations
      1.	Cutting
      2.	Folding
      3.	Scoring
      4.	Perforating
      5.	Gathering
      6.	Laminating
      7.	Stamping
      8.	Punching and drilling
   B.	Binding procedures
      1.	Mechanical
      2.	Loose-leaf
      3.	Wire staple
      4.	Perfect
      5.	Sewn
      6.	Welding

VIII.	Graphic arts industry information
   A.	Raw materials
      1.	Paper manufacture
      2.	Ink manufacture
   B.	Economics
      1.	Size of graphic arts—ranking, dollar value, number of people employed
      2.	Trends—relationship of graphic arts and world culture
      3.	In-plant printing operations
   C.	Education and organizations
      1.	Other schools
      2.	Graphic arts education—past, present, future, visual communications
      3.	Technical organizations
      4.	Education organizations

Resource:

Text:	Dennis, E. A. and Jenkins, J. D., *Comprehensive Graphic Arts*. 3rd edition, 1991.

References:

1.	Various graphic arts journals
2.	Commercially available 16mm films and video programs
3.	Slides and transparencies

APPENDIX B

LESSON PLAN FORM

Course _____

Number _____   School Term _____

Class Session _____   Date _____

LESSON PLAN

Title _____

Materials Needed

_____

_____

_____

_____

_____

_____

Class Procedure

_____

_____

_____

_____

_____

_____

_____

APPENDIX C

CARD FOR TEST QUESTIONS

Front

T-F	M-C	Completion	Discussion	File......

Test Question:

Answer

Back

Question Used	Item	Reliability															
		Difficulty															
	Year																
	Term																
	Test Name																

Suggested Color Code
    Buff—True-False
    Salmon—Multiple choice
    Blue—Matching
    Cherry—Completion
    White—Discussion

APPENDIX D

SAMPLE LEARNING CONTRACT

CONTRACT FOR GRADE

In this course you have the opportunity to contract for your final course grade. Review the requirements as outlined and select the course grade that you believe attainable for yourself. The various requirements listed for each grade are based upon the material found in the course *laboratory manual*.

To achieve the selected grade, it will be necessary to meet the minimum requirements in the class activities and assignments. You may change your selected grade anytime during the course. Merely see your instructor and re-contract. You may have one additional opportunity to achieve the minimum requirements for your selected grade.

If you do not meet the requirements for your selected grade, a lower grade will be given. The lower grade will be determined on an individual basis and, when possible, in conference with you.

REQUIREMENTS FOR THE FINAL COURSE GRADE

A—grade

1. Complete lab assignments (1, 2, 3, 5, 6, 7, and 8, plus one open category) with 90% accuracy on total combined points.
2. Complete three lecture assignments of your choice with 90% accuracy on total combined points.
3. Complete the two major tests with 70% accuracy (sessions 16 and 32) on total combined points.
4. Complete the two announced quizzes with 80% accuracy on total combined points.
5. Complete a course evaluation questionnaire in its entirety.

B—grade

1. Complete lab assignments (1, 2, 3, 5, 6, 7, and 8, plus one open category) with 80% accuracy on total combined points.
2. Complete two lecture assignments of your choice with 90% accuracy on total combined points.
3. Complete the two major tests with 60% accuracy (sessions 16 and 32) on total combined points.
4. Complete the two announced quizzes with 70% accuracy on total combined points.
5. Complete a course evaluation questionnaire in its entirety.

C—grade

1. Complete lab assignments (1, 2, 3, 5, 6, 7, and 8) with 70% accuracy on total combined points.
2. Complete one lecture assignment of your choice with 90% accuracy.
3. Complete the two major tests with 50% accuracy (sessions 16 and 32) on total combined points.
4. Complete the two announced quizzes with 60% accuracy on total combined points.
5. Complete a course evaluation questionnaire in its entirety.

SPECIFIC ASSIGNMENT CRITERIA

SAMPLE LEARNING CONTRACT

LABORATORY	Point Guidelines	LECTURE	Point Guidelines
Name Tag (Possible 12)	A=11, B=10, C=8	Design and Layout—Alphabet (Possible 10)	A, B, or C=9
Memorandum Pad (Possible 17)	A=15, B=14, C=12	Design and Layout—Typeface Classifications (Possible 15)	A, B, or C=14
End Sheet (Possible 16)	A=14, B=13, C=11	Copy Preparation (Possible 12)	A, B, or C=11
Division Page (Possible 20)	A=18, B=16, C=14	Photo-Conversion (Possible 12)	A, B, or C=11
Title Page (Possible 16)	A=14, B=13, C=11	Image Carriers (Possible 12)	A, B, or C=11
Foreword Page (Possible 16)	A=14, B=13, C=11		
Open Category (Possible 16)	A=14, B=13	Image Transfer (Possible 14)	A, B, or C=13
Notebook Binding (Possible 20)	A=18, B=16, C=14	Finishing and Binding (Possible 15)	A, B, or C=14

QUIZZES AND TESTS	Point Guidelines
Quiz 1 (Possible 15)	A=12, B=11, C=9
Quiz 2 (Possible 15)	A=12, B=11, C=9
Test 1 (Possible 75)	A=53, B=45, C=38
Test 2 (Possible 75)	A=53, B=45, C=38

APPENDIX D (Cont'd)

NECESSARY POINT TOTALS	A	B	C
Laboratory Assignment (Possible 133)	120	106	93
Lecture Assignment	30	20	10
Quizzes (Possible 30)	24	21	18
Tests (Possible 150)	105	90	75
GRAND TOTAL	279	237	197

NOTE

You must meet subtotals and grand totals for a selected grade.

Example: If you desire an "A" final course grade, it is necessary to earn a minimum of:

Lab Assignments	120 points
Lecture Assignments	30 points
Quizzes	24 points
Tests	105 points
Minimum Total	279 points

Points cannot be transferred from one category to another.

CONTRACT FOR GRADE

(STUDENT'S COPY)

Student

I, _____, agree to contract for a grade of _____ for the course,

Graphic Arts, offered semester _____ of the 19_____–_____ school year by fulfilling the specified requirements.

NOTE: All course requirements must be completed by the designated due date or a point penalty will be imposed.

If the C grade requirements are not met by the end of the term, the grades of D or F will be given.

Signed _____ Date _____
         (Student)

Instructor

I agree to record a grade of _____ for the said course to _____

when the specified requirements have been fulfilled satisfactorily by the end of the said semester.

Signed _____
         (Instructor)

Date _____

Grade change (re-contract)

I wish to change my course grade from _____ to _____.

Signed _____
         (Student)

Signed _____
         (Instructor)

Date _____

APPENDIX D (Cont'd)

CONTRACT FOR GRADE

(INSTRUCTOR'S COPY)

Student

I, _____, agree to contract for a grade of _____ for the course,

Graphic Arts, offered semester _____ of the 19_____–_____ school year by fulfilling the specified requirements.

NOTE: All course requirements must be completed by the designated due date or a point penalty
      will be imposed.

If the C grade requirements are not met by the end of the term, the grades of D or F will be given.

Signed _____   Date _____
                        (Student)

Instructor

I agree to record a grade of _____ for the said course to _____

when the specified requirements have been fulfilled satisfactorily by the end of the said semester.

Signed _____
                        (Instructor)

Date _____

Grade change (re-contract)

I wish to change my course grade from _____ to _____.

Signed _____
                        (Student)

Signed _____
                        (Instructor)

Date _____

APPENDIX E

AUDIOVISUAL SOURCES

This is a partial listing of companies and associations that have one or more audiovisual items available for rental or purchase. You are encouraged to make contact with these sources and obtain their complete listings of audiovisual titles. Audiovisuals, if used correctly, can be used to deliver significant content to students at all educational levels.

AMERICAN PAPER INSTITUTE, INC.
260 Madison Avenue
New York, NY 10016-2499
A papermaking kit and literature about the papermaking industry.

DCA EDUCATIONAL PRODUCTS INC.
P. O. Box 338
Keller Church Road
Bedminster, PA 18910
Graphic arts overhead transparencies—GA-1 through GA-95; Photography overhead transparencies—PHO-1 through PHO-80; and Screen Printing overhead transparencies—SP-1 through SP-28.

GAT/GAERF PROJECT
Department of Graphic Arts Technology
Murray State University
Murray, KY 42071
Numerous video titles in several areas of graphic arts. Most titles are within 10 to 30 minutes long. Hands-on and philosophical content are found in the content of these video programs.

GRAPHIC ARTS TECHNICAL FOUNDATION
Order Department
4615 Forbes Avenue
Pittsburgh, PA 15213-3796
Graphic arts 35mm slide/audio series. Several titles centered around pre-press and press operations for the lithography printing process.

HAMMERMILL PAPERS
Publicity and Promotion
6400 Poplar Avenue
Memphis, TN 38197-7000
A papermaking kit plus a 16mm educational film titled, Seeds of Wonder.

INTERNATIONAL FILM BUREAU INC.
332 South Michigan Avenue
Chicago, IL 60604-4382
Videos, filmstrips, and slide/audio programs on several topics important in the study of graphic arts.

SUNSHINE ENTERPRISES
P. O. Box 13245
Spokane, WA 99213
A wide variety of video titles on many areas in graphic arts. New titles are produced each year.

ULANO
255 Butler Street
Brooklyn, NY 11217
Several video titles on the topic of screen printing stencil preparation for the three primary photographic methods utilized within the screen printing industry.

CAREER AND INFORMATION SOURCES

This listing of sources should be considered only as a beginning. You, as a resourceful educator, can very likely identify several other sources of excellent information which will improve the teaching and learning process.

American Paper Institute, Inc.
260 Madison Avenue
New York, NY 10016-2499

Graphic Arts Technical Foundation
Education Department
4615 Forbes Avenue
Pittsburgh, PA 15213-3796

International Graphic Arts Education Association, Inc.
4615 Forbes Avenue
Pittsburgh, PA 15213

Colleges and Universities offering graphic arts and graphic communications curricular programs. Contact the GATF for a booklet listing these programs and contact personnel.

Industry Organizations. See the listing in Appendix I of this *Instructor's Guide*.

APPENDIX F

AV AID INFORMATION

```
┌─────────────────────────────────────────────────────────────────────┐
│  ☐ File Under       AV AID INFORMATION                                │
│                                                                       │
│  Title: _____   Sound _____           │
│                                                                       │
│  Kind of Aid: _____   Silent _____         │
│                                                                       │
│  Subject-matter field: _____   B&W _____          │
│                                                                       │
│  Date Produced: _____   Color _____          │
│                                                                       │
│  Producer: _____   Reels _____          │
│                                                                       │
│  Available from: _____   Min. _____           │
│                                                                       │
│  _____    Sale price _____         │
│                                                                       │
│  _____    Rental fee _____         │
│                                                                       │
│  Short synopsis (by producer)    No. Slides _____  Free _____   │
│                                                                       │
│  (Place on back of card)              Grade Level G J S C A           │
└─────────────────────────────────────────────────────────────────────┘
```

AV AID EVALUATION

Evaluator: _____

Title: _____

Kind of Aid: _____ No. Slides: _____

Subject Matter Field: _____ Length: Reel(s): _____ Min: _____

Date Produced: _____

Producer: _____

Purchase Sources: _____

_____

Sound _____ B & W _____ Sale _____ Rental _____

Silent _____ Color _____ Price _____ Free _____

Recommended age level: Primary _____ Elementary _____ Junior High _____

Senior High _____ College _____ Adult _____

Synopsis: (About 75–100 words, as detailed as possible. Do not use producer's summary.)

_____

_____

_____

_____

_____

_____

_____

_____

_____

THE SHERMAN FILM EVALUATION PROFILE   **Developed by:** Mendel Sherman, Ed. D.
A-V Center, University of Indiana

	0	10	20	30	40	50	60	70	80	90	100
1. Relevancy to curriculum											
2. Accuracy and authenticity											
3. Organization of content											
4. Scope (Suitable number of concepts)											
5. Suitability of film length											
6. Coordination of picture and sound concepts											
7. Pupil interest											
8. Pupil comprehension											
9. Technical quality of picture											
10. Technical quality of sound											
11. Overall rating of film (NOT necessarily an average of the other points)											

APPENDIX H

SELECTED GRAPHIC ARTS TRADE JOURNALS

1. *American Printer*
   Maclean Hunter Publishing Co.
   29 N. Wacker Drive
   Chicago, IL 60606

2. *Electronic Publishing & Printing*
   Maclean Hunter Publishing Co.
   29 N. Wacker Drive
   Chicago, IL 60606

3. *Graphic Arts Monthly*
   The Cahners Publishing Company
   44 Cook Street
   Denver, CO 80602

4. *Graphic Arts Product News*
   Maclean Hunter Publishing Co.
   29 N. Wacker Drive
   Chicago, IL 60606

5. *Gravure*
   Gravure Association of America, Inc.
   90 Fifth Avenue
   New York, NY 10011

6. *High Volume Printing*
   Innes Publishing Co.
   425 Huehl Rd., Bldg. 11
   Northbrook, IL 60062-2319

7. *In-Plant Printer & Electronic Publisher*
   Innes Publishing Co.
   425 Huehl Rd., Bldg. 11
   Northbrook, IL 60062-2319

8. *Printing Impressions*
   North American Publishing Co.
   401 N. Broad St.
   Philadelphia, PA 19108

9. *Printing Manager*
   National Association of Printers
      and Lithographers
   780 Palisade Avenue
   Teaneck, NJ 07666

10. *Printing Views*
    Cahners Publishing Co.
    8328 N. Lincoln Ave.
    Skokie, IL 60077

11. *Print - Equip News*
    215 Allen Avenue
    P.O. Box 5540
    Glendale, CA 91221-5540

12. *Print News*
    Kimberley Press
    11071 Aurora Avenue
    Des Moines, IA 50322

13. *Publishing & Production Executive*
    North American Publishing Co.
    401 N. Broad St.
    Philadelphia, PA 19108

14. *Quick Printing*
    Coast Publishing, Inc.
    1680 SW Bayshore Blvd.
    Port St. Lucie, FL 34984

15. *Screen Printing*
    ST Publications, Inc.
    407 Gilbert Avenue
    Cincinnati, OH 45202

16. *World-Wide Printer*
    Deutscher Drucker Co.
    Stuttgart, Germany

APPENDIX I

SELECTED LIST OF GRAPHIC ARTS ORGANIZATIONS AND ASSOCIATIONS

1. **American Paper Institute**
   260 Madison Ave.
   New York, NY 10016
   Phone: (212) 340-0600

2. **Flexographic Technical Association (FTA)**
   900 Marconi Ave.
   Ronkonkoma, NY 11779
   Phone: (516) 737-6020

3. **Graphic Arts Technical Foundation (GATF)**
   4615 Forbes Ave.
   Pittsburgh, PA 15213
   Phone: (412) 621-6941

4. **Gravure Assn. of America**
   90 5th Ave.
   New York, NY 10011
   Phone: (212) 255-0070

5. **In-Plant Printing Management Assn.**
   1205 W. College Ave.
   Liberty, MO 64068
   Phone: (816) 781-1111

6. **International Assn. Printing House Craftsmen (IAPHC)**
   7599 Kenwood Rd.
   Cincinnati, OH 45236
   Phone: (513) 891-0611

7. **International Graphic Arts Education Association, Inc.**
   4615 Forbes Avenue
   Pittsburgh, PA 15213-3796
   Phone: (412) 682-5170

8. **National Association of Litho Clubs (NALC)**
   P.O. Box 1258
   Clifton, NJ 07012
   Phone: (210) 777-6727

9. **Nat. Assn. Printers and Lithographers (NAPL)**
   780 Palisade Ave.
   Teaneck, NJ 07666
   Phone: (201) 342-0707

10. **Nat. Assn. Printing Ink Manufacturers (NAPIM)**
    47 Halstead Ave.
    Harrison, NY 10528
    Phone: (914) 835-5650

11. **National Association of Quick Printers (NAQP)**
    One Illinois Center/Suite 600
    111 East Wacker Drive
    Chicago, IL 60601
    Phone: (312) 644-6610

12. **Nat. Printing Equipment and Supply Assn. (NPES)**
    1899 Preston White Dr.
    Reston, VA 22091
    Phone: (703) 264-7200

13. **Printing Industries of America (PIA)**
    1730 N. Lynn St.
    Arlington, VA 22209
    Phone: (703) 841-8100

14. **Printing Industry/Carolinas (PICA)**
    3601 Rose Lake Dr.
    P.O. Box 19889
    Charlotte, NC 28219
    Phone: (704) 357-1150

15. **Screen Printing Assn. International (SPAI)**
    10015 Main St.
    Fairfax, VA 22031
    Phone: (703) 385-1335

16. **Technical Assn. of the Graphic Arts (TAGA)**
    P.O. Box 9887
    Rochester, NY 14623
    Phone: (716) 272-0557

17. **Technical Assn., Pulp and Paper Ind. (TAPPI)**
    Technology Park/Atlanta
    P.O. Box 105113
    Atlanta, GA 30348
    Phone: (404) 446-1400

18. **Typographers International Association (TIA)**
    2266 Hall Place, N.W.
    Washington, DC 20007
    Phone: (202) 965-3400

APPENDIX J

ANSWERS TO SAFETY REVIEW QUESTIONS
FOUND IN THE *STUDENT WORKBOOK.*

Safety Review #1—Copy Preparation Safety

1. True	5. A	9. A	13. D
2. B	6. C	10. False	14. B
3. False	7. False	11. True	15. False
4. True	8. True	12. D	16. True

Safety Review #2—Camera and Darkroom Safety

1. True	6. True	11. False	16. C
2. A	7. D	12. C	17. False
3. C	8. B	13. True	18. True
4. True	9. D	14. False	
5. False	10. False	15. A	

Safety Review #3—Letterpress Printing Safety

1. False	6. True	11. C	16. D
2. B	7. D	12. False	17. True
3. True	8. A	13. A	18. False
4. C	9. False	14. False	19. B
5. True	10. True	15. False	20. True

Safety Review #4—Lithographic Printing Safety

1. False	6. A	11. False	16. True
2. B	7. C	12. B	17. A
3. C	8. True	13. False	18. False
4. True	9. A	14. False	19. True
5. D	10. D	15. C	20. True

Safety Review #5—Gravure Printing Safety

1. True	5. A	9. D	13. D
2. True	6. False	10. C	14. True
3. B	7. True	11. False	15. False
4. False	8. C	12. True	16. A

Safety Review #6—Screen Printing Safety

1. True	6. False	11. True	16. A
2. D	7. B	12. A	17. B
3. D	8. False	13. C	18. C
4. A	9. C	14. D	19. True
5. True	10. B	15. False	20. False

Safety Review #7—Finishing and Binding Safety

1. False	6. C	11. False	16. False
2. True	7. True	12. C	17. False
3. B	8. True	13. True	18. True
4. D	9. D	14. False	
5. A	10. False	15. B	

APPENDIX K

ANSWERS TO UNIT QUESTIONS
FOUND IN THE *STUDENT WORKBOOK.*

SECTION 1: THE GRAPHIC ARTS INDUSTRY

Unit 1

1. (B)   a producer of temporary visual images.
2. True
3. 80 percent
4. False
5. Any ten printed products will be correct.

Unit 2

6. True
7. Commercial
8. Design and layout, image carriers, copy preparation, image transfer, photoconversion, finishing and binding
9. True
10. A company that specializes in one phase of graphic arts such as typesetting or finishing and binding.

Unit 3

11. (D)   gestures and sounds
12. (G)   paper invented
13. (E)   used wood blocks for printing in A.D. 770
14. (K)   first book ever produced—done by Chinese
15. (B)   accomplished by the Chinese in A.D. 1100
16. (H)   developed movable method type in about 1450
17. (F)   first book produced in the American colonies by Matthew Daye
18. (J)   helped to start America's first paper mill
19. (A)   controversial printer-journalists
20. (I)   a typesetting machine developed by Ottmar Mergenthaler
21. (C)   inventor of the first papermaking machine
22. False
23. Satellite

Unit 4

24. Throughout every country of the world, plus every state of the United States.
25. 50,000
26. (C)   One million
27. U. S. Government Printing Office

Unit 5

28. (D)   Relief
29. False
30. (A)   Alois Senefelder

SECTION 2: TYPE STYLES

Unit 7

1. Typefaces
2. Alphabet
3. True
4. The design of lowercase letters causes them to blend well allowing the eyes to move rapidly from one letter to another.
5. Legibility, Readability, Appropriateness, Reproducibility, and Practicality
6. False
7. True
8. False

Unit 8

9. Memory
10. Pictograms, ideograms, phonograms
11. Hieroglyphics
12. False
13. Alpha, Beta
14. (B)   Phoenicians
15. (A)   2000 to 1000 B.C.
16. Scribes, writers, scholars

Unit 9

17. True
18. Strokes
19. Continuity
20. False
21. The letter relationships can be seen easily.

22. Unitizing
23. (C) Digital
24. (D) Arranges and selects type

Unit 10

25. Ascender
26. Descender
27. (C) Serif
28. (A) Light   (B) medium
29. True
30. (D) Type with the same general characteristics
31. To emphasize selected printed material

Units 11–16

32. False
33. (C) Roman
34. Text
35. (C) Wedding invitations, greeting cards, and religious publications
36. (F) Most newspapers and many books and magazines
37. (A) Some books, newspapers, and magazines
38. (B) Limited to headlines, letterheads, and advertisements
39. (D) Announcements, advertisements, and where the handwritten appearance is important.
40. (E) Advertisements, trade names of companies, and personalized publications

SECTION 3: PLANNING, DESIGNING, AND LAYOUT

Unit 18

1. True
2. Permits the graphic designer and customer to review and revise ideas while changes are still easy to make.
3. (B) pre-layout planning form
4. False
5.

Tools	Supplies
Pencils	Drawing paper
Straightedge or T-Square	Rubber cement
Drawing Board	Tape
Triangle	Grid paper
Measuring device	Tracing paper

Unit 19

6. Point

7. (A) Line gauge
8. (D) 108
9. (D) 4½ inches
10. Ascender, Descender
11. False
12. Ten
13. False

Unit 20

14. (D) All elements of a printed page positioned on a vertical center line
15. (B) Relationship of width to height
16. (G) Image elements belonging together
17. (E) Imaginary line slightly above the true vertical center
18. (A) Unused printed space
19. (I) Visual location of image elements
20. (C) An uninteresting page proportion
21. (H) Repetition of image elements develop a feeling of rhythm.
22. (F) All display is no display

Unit 21

23. To enhance the beauty of a printed product and to make the scene, such as a photograph, appear natural.
24. True
25. False
26. Analogous
27. False
28. (C) Two or more tones of any solid color
29. (B) Quieting

Unit 22

30. True
31. Helps determine size relationships and positioning of the image elements.

Unit 23

32. (A) Visually permits the comparison of two or more ideas.
33. True
34. False

Unit 24

35. True
36. False
37. 1. Kind, size, and style of type
    2. Location and size of illustrations
    3. Color(s) of ink to be used
    4. Kind of paper to be used (Plus several other items)

Unit 25

38. True
39. (C)   Signature
40. True

SECTION 4: TYPE AND IMAGE COMPOSITION

Unit 27

1. The setting or generation of characters and symbols and arranging them to communicate thoughts and ideas to other people.
2. True
3. Hot, cold
4. 1450
5. (C)   Mergenthaler
6. True
7. Facsimile

Unit 28

8. True
9. .918
10. Face, counter, serif, nick, feet
11. False
12. Banks
13. (B)   the square of the type size being used
14. False
15. (D)   Half-picas and picas
16. True
17. (A)   Away from the compositor

Unit 29

18. False
19. They serve as molds that help form the characters and lines of type.
20. Ludlow
21. (B)   Elrod

Unit 30

22. Dot matrix and Daisy wheel
23. 1867
24. True
25. (C)   Magnetic tape
26. Lettering machines are generally slower and designed to produce display type. Electronic typewriters produce body copy with high speed.
27. True

Unit 31

28. False
29. False
30. Users can create their own type characters and symbols.
31. Obtaining the correct spacing between letters and words.
32. (A)   Technical inking pen
33. Stencils, templates, pens, and brushes

Unit 32

34. 1950
35. Four
36. False
37. True
38. A beam of light is sent through a negative image (film font) onto light-sensitive paper. When the exposed paper is processed, visible images are formed.
39. (D)   Produces quality type
40. (1)   Input device
    (2)   Typesetting unit
    (3)   Processing unit
41. (D)   Kerning
42. False
43. True
44. Three

Unit 33

45. 2600
46. (A)   Use a laser to create the images.
47. True
48. False
49. True

Units 27–33

50. (D)   Matrix storage for line casting machines.
51. (A)   One of the several cold typesetting methods.
52. (G)   Fourth generation typesetting equipment.
53. (C)   Duplicate of graphic images.
54. (I)   Quality imaging possible but limited permanence.
55. (H)   Contact and projection methods used to create type.
56. (B)   System closely aligned with photographic and electronic typesetting.
57. (F)   Used the principle of the circulating matrix.

58. (E) Using carbon ribbon and relief characters to create images.

59. (K) Automated pre-press preparation of type, artwork, and photographs.

60. (J) Light amplification by stimulated emission of radiation.

SECTION 5: PROOFING TYPE AND IMAGE COMPOSITION

Unit 35

1. False

2. Reading proofs, reproduction proofs

3. 1st. Typesetter's proof—used only by typesetting firm
   2nd. Customer's proof—given to customer for final proofing

4. (D) Thumbnail sketches of job

5. True

6. False

Unit 36

7. True

8. (B) Grippers

9. To make high quality proofs from relief type that will be used in paste-ups.

10. Yellow, magenta, cyan, black

11. False

12. Brayer

Unit 37

13. False

14. True

15. Galley

16. (A) Original proof of the typeset material

17. Laser

18. False

Unit 38

19. 2

20. (C) Typos

21. Copyholder

22. True

23. True

24. (C) Let it stand

25. (D) Insert period

26. (G) Center the line

27. (B) Delete, take out

28. (H) Indent 1 em

29. (J) Transpose letters or words

30. (C) Close up, no space

31. (F) Quad left

32. (I) Wrong font

33. (K) Query to author

34. (A) Insert space

35. (E) Right margin even

Unit 39

36. (B) When type characters have a different set width

37. False

38. True

39. False

40. Computer terminal

SECTION 6: COPY PREPARATION FOR PROCESS PHOTOGRAPHY

Unit 41

1. True

2. Type matter and illustrations

3. False

Unit 42

4. (C) Red and black

5. White

6. True

7. These tools and equipment help the artist prepare quality camera-ready copy.

8. Airbrush

9. (B) Transparent tape

Unit 43

10. (D) Line and continuous tone

11. (A) Line reproduction

12. (D) Treated as continuous-tone copy and made with water paint.

13. (H) A printed reproduction of a photograph with the background removed.

14. (E) A light image printed in selected areas of a product.

15. (G) Most common kind of continuous-tone copy.

16. (B) The visual image is the same color as the paper with a dark background.

17. (F) A creative continuous-tone image made by spraying ink on a sheet.

18. (C) Using line and continuous-tone copy in the same printed reproduction

19. (I) Prepared with black India ink on white paper or art board.

20. (A) Treated as continuous-tone copy and made with charcoal.

Unit 44

21. False
22. (B) 5.2×6.5 inches (13.2×16.5 cm)
23. True
24. False
25. Another person will likely locate errors or problems because he or she is unfamiliar with the total content.

Unit 45

26. False
27. Borders (margins)
28. Proportional wheel, mathematical formula and diagonal line
29. 100 percent
30. (A) 2 to 4

Unit 46

31. True
32. Diffusion transfer
33. (D) Photograph
34. True
35. (B) Wax

Unit 47

36. Process, mechanical
37. Magenta
38. In a process camera, light is reflected from reflection copy to create an image on film whereas with transmission copy, light passes through it to create the film image.

Unit 48

39. (C) Technical production data and personal data
40. Write it directly in the margins of the paste-up, but be careful to not damage the image elements.

SECTION 7: PROCESS CAMERAS AND DARKROOM PROCEDURES

Unit 50

1. Lens, bellows, camera back, copyboard, lights
2. This reduces the aperture opening by one half, thus half as much light can pass through the lens.
3. True
4. (C) Pulsed xenon

Unit 51

5. (B) Gallery
6. False

Unit 52

7. Polyester
8. It absorbs excess light that passes through the film during exposure. This keeps the film from being double exposed by light reflecting back through the film.
9. False
10. False
11. (D) Fixer

Unit 53

12. True
13. Thermometers, graduates, funnels, timers, plus several other items.
14. True
15. False

Unit 54

No questions appear in the *Student Manual* for this unit. Refer to Safety Test 2 "Camera and Darkroom Safety" in Section 3 of the *Student Manual*. Answers to the questions for Safety Test 2 are found on the back pages of the *Instructor's Guide*.

Unit 55

16. (A) Developer, stop bath, fixer, water
17. Equal
18. False
19. (B) Inverted
20. (A) Emulsion
21. (D) Darkest areas on the original copy

Unit 56

22. True
23. True
24. Highlights, shadows, middle tones
25. Main
26. True
27. False
28. (B) Autoscreen

Unit 57

29. (C) Highlight
30. True
31. (A) Shadow
32. False

33. Duotone

Unit 58

34. Vacuum printing frame, point source light
35. True
36. False
37. (D) The vacuum glass
38. 1. To give close register in two-color printing.
    2. To produce outline letters

Unit 59

39. True
40. Receiver
41. False
42. They are used directly in the paste-up along with the line copy.

Unit 60

43. (C) Yellow
44. White
45. True
46. Reflection and Transmission
47. (B) Green
48. True
49. Electronic Color Scanning
50. False

Unit 61

51. To determine their quality and to correct the problems directly the film. Also, if there are observed problems, determine the causes so they can be corrected.
52. (C) Fog
53. False

Unit 62

54. True
55. False
56. (A) Once per week

SECTION 8: LETTERPRESS IMAGE CARRIERS

Unit 64

1. First generation, second generation
2. First generation
3. True
4. (A) Photoengraving
5. Plastic, rubber
6. (D) Flat

Unit 65

No questions appear in the *Student Manual* for this unit. Refer to Safety Test 3, "Letterpress Printing Safety" in Section 3 of the *Student Manual*. Answers to the questions for Safety Test 3 are found on the back pages of the *Instructor's Guide*.

Unit 66

7. (B) 1880
8. Zinc, copper, magnesium
9. True
10. The nonimage area is washed away, leaving the desired image to stand out in relief.
11. Blocking or mounting

Unit 67

12. False
13. Ultraviolet
14. The image would be distorted if the plate was curved after the image was formed.
15. Carbon dioxide
16. (C) Sodium hydroxide
17. False

Unit 68

18. True
19. Polyester film, aluminum, steel, special polymer composite material
20. False
21. (B) Dampening rollers

Unit 69

22. True
23. False
24. True
25. Copper
26. Silver, graphite

Unit 70

27. Relief
28. (C) 1974
29. False
30. True
31. Rubber design
32. Speed and accuracy are excellent plus artwork can be perfectly joined around the circumference of the printing roller.

Unit 71

33. (A) Platens
34. False

35. To protect the platens from the material sticking and to add needed thickness.
36. Positive, line-positive,
    Negative, line-negative
37. True
38. .918

SECTION 9: LETTERPRESS IMPOSITION

Unit 74
1. (B)   In the proper position and order.
2. True

Unit 75
3. (D)   Imposing table
4. False
5. (A)   Pica units
6. (B)   Reglets
7. False
8. Quoin

Unit 76
9. True
10. True
11. True
12. Planer
13. The typefaces and plates can be easily damaged if hit against a hard surface. Also, the entire lock-up may fall from the chase if there is a sudden jolt of the chase.

Unit 77
14. Dust and dirt can cause severe problems and type wear by making the type characters stand too high.
15. (C)   Next to the solid furniture.
16. False
17. (D)   After slightly tightening the quoins
18. (A)   Light tapping with a finger

Unit 78
19. This saves time and effort thus making each printing job less costly.
20. One

SECTION 10: LETTERPRESS IMAGE TRANSFER

Unit 80
1. (D)   Platen
2. True
3. True
4. Two
5. Gutenberg

Unit 81
6. True
7. Paper bags, books, packaging, business forms, plus several others.
8. (B)   Water
9. Stack-type, single-impression cylinder, inline design
10. (C)   1890
11. False

Unit 82
12. Complete books can be manufactured from beginning to end.
13. Belt
14. False
15. False
16. (A)   Number of pages
17. (C)   2 inches (5cm)

Unit 83
No questions appear in the *Student Manual* for this unit. Refer to Safety Test 3, "Letterpress Printing Safety" in Section 3 of the *Student Manual*. Answers to the questions for Safety Test 3 are found on the back pages of the *Instructor's Guide*.

Unit 84
18. (D)   Location of the unprinted sheets
19. (B)   Controls the printing impression
20. (A)   Ink distribution and transfer to rollers
21. (F)   Location of the printed sheets
22. (C)   The impression surface
23. (E)   Automatic ink supply for the rollers
24. True
25. (A)   Press board

Unit 85
26. Inspect the type, cuts, and plates for damage and check if they are type high.
27. True
28. (B)   Hanger sheet
29. False

Unit 86
30. There is little difference in the printing methods; generally the horizontal presses are larger in size.
31. Floating on air
32. True

Unit 87

33. False
34. (D) Daily
35. True

SECTION 11: LITHOGRAPHIC IMPOSITION

Unit 89

1. Stripper or litho artist
2. (1) To hold the negative(s) in the correct position.
   (2) To guard the plate from unwanted light during the plate exposure.
3. (D) Stripping
4. True

Unit 90

5. False
6. Stainless steel
7. Magnifying glass, scissors, knives, brushes
8. (A) Ultraviolet
9. False

Unit 91

10. It is very important to place registration marks on the copy during paste-up preparation.
11. (B) Plate bend
12. (C) ¼ to ⅜ inch (6.4 to 9.5 mm)
13. False

Unit 92

14. True
15. True
16. True
17. (D) ⅛ inch (3.175 mm)
18. False
19. False

Unit 93

20. It saves considerable time when making a plate. There is less handling and one plate exposure instead of two.
21. (A) Black or red
22. False
23. True

Unit 94

24. Register punch
25. Printing press
26. (C) Master flat
27. True

28. Two of the masking sheets serve as masks for selected areas of the negative(s) that is attached to the flat: One mask for plate one and the second mask for plate two.
29. Accuracy is extremely important as well as speed, thus computers are essential.
30. True

SECTION 12: LITHOGRAPHIC IMAGE CARRIERS

Unit 96

1. Paper, plastic, metal
2. False

Unit 97

3. Smooth, grained
4. Straight edge, Pinbar edge, and Slotted edge
5. True
6. Imagesetter
7. (C) Pre-sensitized
8. Flat
9. (B) Pre-sensitized
10. Long

Unit 98

11. Vacuum frame
12. The operator's eyes are protected from the bright light source.
13. (D) Metal Halide
14. It is a tool that is used to determine the correct length of exposure for litho plate.
15. False

Unit 99

16. True
17. They are used to hold the plate during hand processing.
18. Lacquer
19. (A) Desensitizing solution
20. (C) 6
21. False
22. True

Unit 100

23. True
24. (D) Direct-image
25. (B) Can produce a press-ready plate quickly.
26. (C) Plate processor
27. False

Unit 101

28. True
29. (C) Prevent the non-printing areas from oxidizing.
30. Hang

SECTION 13: LITHOGRAPHIC IMAGE TRANSFER

Unit 103

1. False
2. Feeding, cylinder, dampening, inking, delivery
3. (C) Three
4. Plate, impression
5. True

Unit 104

6. (A) Good register control
7. (D) 1927
8. Dampen the plate, engage the impression, ink the plate, feed the paper
9. False
10. True

Unit 105

No questions appear in the *Student Manual* for this unit. Refer to Safety Test 4, "Lithographic Printing Safety" in Section 3 of the *Student Manual*. Answers to the questions for Safety Test 4 are found on the back pages of the *Instructor's Guide*.

Unit 106

11. (C) Sets the suction delivered to the suction feet.
12. (I) Sets the amount of air delivered to the paper separators.
13. (D) Used to turn the duplicator manually through its full cycle.
14. (B) Helps to regulate the amount of fountain solution reaching the plate.
15. (G) Helps to regulate the amount of ink reaching the plate.
16. (J) Paper is jogged against this device.
17. (E) Used to lower and raise the paper pile.
18. (H) A three-position lever used to position the dampener form roller.
19. (A) Used when raising or lowering the image on the paper.
20. (F) Electrical power control for starting and stopping the press.

Unit 107

21. They should be centered over the front guides directly above the sheet separators.
22. (B) Feeding
23. (D) ⅛ inch (3.17mm)
24. False
25. True

Unit 108

26. (A) Apply dampening fountain solution.
27. True
28. False
29. 00000

Unit 109

30. (D) Pile Height Adjustment
31. (B) If the ink rollers have the correct plate pressure.
32. False

Unit 110

33. True
34. (B) The lack of moisture on the plate
35. Balanced

Unit 111

36. Ductor, oscillator, form
37. False
38. True
39. (D) Special ink solvent
40. Impression

SECTION 14: GRAVURE PRINTING PROCESS

Unit 113

1. Sunken
2. True
3. Newspaper supplements, trading stamps, packaging, catalogs, plus many others.
4. (C) 12 to 15 percent
5. (B) Long image life of the printing cylinder
6. (C) Karl Kleitsch
7. 1914

Unit 114

8. (D) Rigid plastic cylinder
9. Reflection, transparency
10. False
11. True
12. Chrome is much harder than the copper or plastic, thus it wears better giving longer runs.

Unit 115

13. (A) Doctor
14. False
15. False
16. To determine if corrections are needed and to save time in the total production process.
17. True

Unit 116

No questions appear in the *Student Manual* for this unit. Refer to Safety Test 5, "Gravure Printing Safety" in Section 3 of the *Student Manual*. Answers to the questions for Safety Test 5 are found on the back pages of the *Instructor's Guide*.

Unit 117

18. It is the material that serves to make the metal surface light sensitive.
19. (B) Low
20. This unit helps to distribute the photoresist evenly over the surface of the plate.
21. False

Unit 118

22. True
23. False
24. (A) Steel
25. Gravers
26. Stationery, business cards, announcements, invitations
27. Dampened

Unit 119

28. (B) Embossing
29. Heat writing
30. A heating unit that will melt and fuse the resin powder to the paper.
31. Letterpress, offset lithography, screen
32. False
33. True

SECTION 15: SCREEN PRINTING

Unit 121

1. True
2. (D) 1906
3. True
4. False
5. Knife-cut, photographic, washout (tusche)

Unit 122

6. (A) Flatbed-type
7. (C) Cylindrical objects
8. False
9. (D) Conveyor-belt dryer

Unit 123

10. Frame, fabric, squeegee, film cutting tools, drying equipment. Plus film, chemicals, ink solvent, and wiping cloths.
11. (B) 8xx
12. False
13. False
14. A razor-sharp blade can be placed in the pencil-lead holder so circles can be cut
15. (D) Textile printing with heavy ink deposits
16. (B) Ceramic products
17. (F) Flat objects and all general use
18. (A) Glass and nameplates
19. (C) Any products needing extra-heavy ink deposits.
20. (E) Products with uneven surfaces

Unit 124

No questions appear in the *Student Manual* for this unit. Refer to Safety Test 6, "Screen Printing Safety" in Section 3 of the *Student Manual*. Answers to the questions for Safety Test 6 are found on the back pages of the *Instructor's Guide*.

Unit 125

21. 2 by 3
22. (C) Kick leg
23. False
24. True

Unit 126

25. (A) Photographic
26. True
27. Black, dry transfer letters can be attached to transparent acetate sheets.
28. True

Unit 127

29. (B) Cut only the thin lacquer film
30. Mechanical treatment and degreasing
31. False
32. False

Unit 128

33. True
34. False
35. The build-up, which is about ⅛ inch thick, helps to insure that there will be pressure between the film and the screen fabric.
36. Hot water

Unit 129

37. False
38. Yellow
39. The thickness of the emulsion, method one produces a thin emulsion, method two produces an average thickness, and method three produces a thick emulsion for long printing runs.
40. True
41. False
42. (C)   59° to 104°

Unit 130

43. Support sheet, Cement, and Light-sensitive emulsion
44. 50
45. True
46. False
47. False

Unit 131

48. (A)   100
49. Lacquer
50. True
51. False

Unit 132

52. (D)   Oil-base ink
53. (A)   60°
54. (1)   It keeps the image area from drying and plugging between printings.
    (2)   It keeps a ready supply of ink in the image area for the next print.

Unit 133

55. False
56. (C)   Wipe both sides of the screen at the same time.
57. True

Unit 134

58. 200
59. This method is most often used to reproduce fine-art compositions.

Unit 135

60. Four, center register marks should be used and positioned no closer than one (1) inch to any of the copy.

SECTION 16: PHOTOGRAPHY

Unit 137

1. False
2. (1)   Expose the film with a camera
   (2)   Process the film to make negatives
   (3)   Make visible photographic prints from the negatives

Unit 138

3. (D)   Shutter
4. True
5. (B)   Single lens reflex
6. (A)   Still subjects

Unit 139

7. Panchromatic
8. Exposure of the film to light that has passed through a lens.
9. (C)   Film speed selected

Unit 140

10. Highlight
11. True
12. False
13. The camera shutter will open and close in $\frac{1}{125}$ of a second.

Unit 141

14. False
15. Fixer
16. 68° fahrenheit, 20° celsius

Unit 142

17. Fiber and resin-coated
18. (C)   Resin-coated
19. (B)   Red and yellow
20. False
21. True

Unit 143

22. Contact, projection
23. True
24. (D)   Projection
25. (A)   Easel
26. (1)   Developer,
    (2)   Stop bath,
    (3)   Fixer, and
    (4)   Water

Unit 144

27. True
28. False
29. Ferrotype
30. Dry mounting tissue

SECTION 17: DUPLICATING AND SPECIAL PRINTING PROCESSES

Unit 146

1. False
2. True
3. Duplicating and Copying

Unit 147

4. True
5. (A)   Alcohol
6. (C)   Stencil process
7. Electronic stencil maker
8. False

Unit 148

9. Plain
10. True
11. (B)   Zinc-oxide
12. False

Unit 149

13. False
14. (D)   Character generator
15. (A)   Mailing addresses
16. True
17. False
18. True

SECTION 18: FINISHING AND BINDING

Unit 151

1. To prepare the work of design and layout personnel, typesetters, camera operators, platemakers, and press operators as finished products to be used by the general public.
2. Clay tablet, scroll
3. True

Unit 152

No questions appear in the *Student Manual* for this unit. Refer to Safety Test 7, "Finishing and Binding Safety" in Section 3 of the *Student Manual*. Answers to the questions for Safety Test 7 are found on the back pages of the *Instructor's Guide*.

Unit 153

4. (C)   To collect single sheets of paper in proper order.
5. (H)   An image-transfer process for illustrating book covers.
6. (A)   Creating holes of different sizes in several hundred sheets of paper at one time.
7. (J)   Weakening paper fibers for ease in folding.
8. (D)   Assembling signatures in the correct order.
9. (F)   Removing a small amount of paper from the edges of books to improve their appearance.
10. (B)   Cutting paper into special shapes.
11. (I)   Doubling a sheet over to create a signature.
12. (E)   Protecting printed sheets with transparent film.
13. (G)   Cutting slits or punching holes to make it easy to tear sheets of paper.

Unit 154

14. False
15. (B)   16
16. (C)   4,350
17. False
18. (C)   Bottom, top, right side

Unit 155

19. False
20. (A)   Plastic cylinder
21. (D)   Single sheets may be included
22. True
23. (A)   Durable but costly

Unit 156

24. The plastic-cylinder contains many individual "tongues" and it is difficult to impossible to position them in the punched holes by hand.
25. (D)   Library
26. Signatures
27. (B)   Water

Unit 157

28. (D)   Body
29. False
30. Saddle, signature-to-signature, flat, cleat
31. (B)   Casing-in
32. They help to protect the book cover and give space for promotional material.

Unit 158

33. False
34. True
35. The saw cuts make openings in the fold of the signatures for the sewing operation.
36. Sewing tape
37. Nipping, rounding, smashing, backing

Unit 159

38. To preserve information in as little space as possible.
39. Roll film, film magazine, aperture card, microfiche
40. True
41. 19th
42. True

SECTION 19: PULP AND PAPER MANUFACTURING

Unit 161

1. (C)   1,000,000
2. Paper bags, gun cartridges, diapers, drinking cups, filters, polishing cloths, plus several others listed in the textbook.
3. Papyrus
4. 105 A.D.
5. (D)   Nicholas-Louis Robert
6. (A)   75,000

Unit 162

7. 95
8. True
9. False
10. (C)   Chipping
11. False
12. Mechanical
13. Screening and centricleaner

Unit 163

14. (B)   99
15. It is so named because the Fourdrinier Brothers of England developed the continuous-wire into a practical papermaking machine.
16. True
17. 80
18. The sizing liquid hardens the paper surface giving a good writing surface. Also, it helps to resist the effects of handling and helps to hold the paper fibers together.

19. (B)   Fourdrinier
20. (D)   Calender stack
21. Atlanta, Georgia

Unit 164

22. 500
23. False
24. (C)   File folders, record cards, time cards.
25. (A)   Reports, proposals, advertising & promotional materials.
26. (G)   Stationery, letterhead, invoices.
27. (D)   Bookkeeping records, statements, legal documents.
28. (F)   Newspapers, handbills, telephone directories.
29. (H)   Books, pamphlets, brochures.
30. (B)   Booklet covers, program covers, self-mailers.
31. (E)   Portfolios, quality booklets, announcements.
32. (B)   17×22 inches (43.2×55.9cm)

Unit 165

33. Sheet or roll
34. (C)   16 carton
35. False
36. (D) $3.04

Unit 166

37. Facial tissue, non-wet strength
38. Use a rolling pin to squeeze out excess water and then a regular hand-held clothing iron to press the sheet dry.

SECTION 20: PRINTING INK MANUFACTURING

Unit 168

1. Paper, Wood, Glass, Metal, plus Plastic, Textiles, and a variety of synthetics.
2. True
3. (A)   Chinese

Unit 169

4. False
5. (D)   Pigment carrier
6. False
7. True

Unit 170

8. (B)   Wetting down
9. True

10. False

11. True

Unit 171

12. True

13. These inks must pass through the screen, not damage the stencil, not dry on the screen, and adhere to a wide variety of substrates.

14. Absorption

15. False

Unit 172

16. False

17. (D)   Draw-down

18. (B)   Setoff

19. False

Unit 173

20. Glass

21. Scale

22. True

SECTION 21: LEGAL CONSIDERATIONS FOR THE PRINTER

Unit 175

1. 1790

2. False

3. True

Unit 176

4. (B)   To revise and sell another copyrighted work.

5. False

6. Library of Congress

7. It should appear on the title page or on the page immediately following.

Unit 177

8. False

9. Photocopier

10. True

11. False

Unit 178

12. At two times (1) in accepting the copy, and (2) on delivery of the printed product.

13. True

Unit 179

14. False

15. Red and blue

16. (A)   The size is less than ¾ the original

17. True

Unit 180

18. It is a written or unwritten set of guidelines by which a people or companies conduct themselves or their business.

SECTION 22: DESKTOP COMPOSITION

Unit 182

1. Text and Graphics

2. True

3. False

4. Hardware and Software

5. Central Processing Unit

6. (D)   Hard Disk

7. (A)   Scanner

8. (C)   Laser

9. (C)   DOS

10. False

11. (B)   Vector

12. True

13. These permit easy access to existing files, opening new files, and saving files.

14. False

15. True

16. (B)   Proofreader

Unit 184

17. False

18. Base

19. Template

20. Ready-made style sheets and templates permit a novice to simply add text and graphics to the pre-prepared pages.

21. (B)   Two

22. True

23. False

24. (D)   Dot Matrix

25. (A)   Downloading

SECTION 23: GRAPHIC ARTS CAREER OPPORTUNITIES

Unit 186

1. False

2. Supervision and management

3. True

4. There are many opportunities ranging from printing production, equipment installation, sales, service, and management.

5. True

Unit 187

6. True

7. Design and layout

8. False

9. True

10. Many chemicals and different kinds of light sensitive coatings are used to make image carriers for the different printing methods, thus a knowledge of chemistry can be helpful in analyzing new products and platemaking problems.

Unit 188

11. False

12. Handling paper and working with a variety of equipment is characteristic of this area, thus skillful hands are most beneficial.

Unit 189

13. Change

14. False

Unit 190

15. (A)   4,000

16. False

17. True

Unit 191

18. Industrial, civil, mechanical

19. Skilled people in law are needed to handle corporate documents and handle such business activities as patents, taxes, and real estate.

20. True

Unit 192

21. True

22. Education

23. (B)   Grocery store bulletin boards and windows.

24. Resumé

25. False

26. False

27. College/university courses, Workshops, Seminars, Industry expositions, Trade publications, etc.

28. True

29. Becoming involved in student organizations, working part-time in a graphic arts business, and observing other business and community leaders.

Unit 193

30. (D)   Strong motivation

31. (C)   Waits for things to happen

32. False

33. (C)   Six months

34. Venture

35. (B)   Partnership

36. Franchise

37. False

38. True

39. (D)   80%

40. (A)   Job description

APPENDIX L

ANSWERS TO DISCUSSION TOPICS IN TEXT

SECTION 1

1. **In what ways does civilization depend on the graphic arts industry?**
First, people need and demand printed products that are specifically designed to communicate information. Second, civilized people need printed products for their everyday living and business operations. Third, printed products serve as decorative objects in homes, offices, and public establishments.

2. **What trends have been seen in the graphic arts industry in recent years?**
There is now more sophistication through the utilization of computer technology in every phase of the graphic arts technology model. Also, some areas have been combined. For example, copy preparation equipment can be used to create visual images and then image printing plates, which are ready for use on the printing press.

3. **Describe the part that each of its divisions plays in the overall graphic arts industry.**
Divisions such as commercial printing, newspapers, form printers, and specialty shops are integral parts of the total industry. Each division serves separate markets. Basically, each division cannot function without the others.

4. **What are some of the major events in graphic arts that have contributed to our cultural development?**
Some of the major events are: the development of the alphabet, the invention of paper, the use of wood blocks for producing printed images, the first book, and the invention of movable metal type by Johann Gutenberg in about 1450.

5. **Why is the graphic arts industry a growth industry?**
The graphic arts industry is considered a "growth industry" because business economic experts believe there will be a continued rise in the production and use of printed products. The graphic arts industry is considered one of the few recession-resistant industries because people will continue to need printed products.

SECTION 2

1. **Why is it important to learn to recognize and understand typefaces?**
Typefaces serve as an important communication link between the author and reader. Typefaces in themselves are communicators of information. Some typefaces are easy to read, while others are difficult to read. Some demand attention; some designate age; and others suggest a bold, confident feeling. People who select and use typefaces, such as graphic designers and image setting personnel, need to know the communication value of the many typefaces.

2. **What were some forms of nonverbal communication used before the development of the alphabet?**
The three most common forms of nonverbal pre-alphabet communication were pictograms, ideograms, and phonograms. Pictograms are crude drawings or writings found on the walls of caves. Ideograms are picture drawings that represent an ideal or a happening. Phonograms are symbols that represent full words.

3. **Why was there a need for a written form of visual communications?**
A written form of visual communication was needed because the energetic civilized peoples of the world needed a method of accurately recording their daily business transactions. Also, people such as the Phoenicians, Greeks, and Romans desired to record their history. The pre-alphabet forms were not sufficiently sophisticated.

4. **Why is there a need for new typefaces to be designed?**
New typefaces need to be designed to meet the requirements of typesetting, imagesetting, and desktop composition equipment. New printing technology requires specific typeface designs. Also, graphic designers and advertising agency personnel demand new typefaces that can be used to better communicate their thoughts, ideas, and information.

5. **What is the difference between a type font, a type series, and a type family?**
Type fonts, series, and families all relate to the understanding and use of the hundreds of

specific typefaces. A type font refers to a specific kind and style of type containing upper case (capital) letters, lower case (small) letters, punctuation marks, and numbers. A type series refers to the many sizes of type that are available for a specific font. A type family includes several different styles of type under the same basic name (such as the "Times" type group).

SECTION 3

1. **Why is a layout for a printed product valuable?**
Layouts are valuable for many reasons. Among them are: the designer can review and revise the original layout before imagesetting is begun; accurate spelling, spacing, sizing, and placement of the image elements can be assured; and the customer and production personnel can provide input before it is too late to make improvements in the final printed product.

2. **What is the value of using the metric system instead of the linear-inch system?**
The metric system contains units in multiples of ten, which conforms to the standard numbering (decimal) system. Decimal points can be moved to change measurements quickly and accurately. Also, the decimal system is used in most countries of the world. This gives a standard measurement system for world trade and economic activity.

3. **How does color affect us? How is this put to use in the graphic arts?**
Color affects people through their emotions. For example, warm colors (yellow and red) tend to excite, while cool colors (green and blue) tend to be quieting. This is utilized in graphic arts by correctly selecting colors from the standard color wheel and using them appropriately in printed products.

4. **What is the purpose of preparing thumbnail sketches?**
Thumbnail sketches are used to place a number of printed product ideas on paper in graphic form. This then makes it possible for the graphic designer, and sometimes the customer, to select the best idea and develop it further. Thumbnail sketches should be prepared for detailed printed products prior to creating rough and comprehensive layouts.

5. **Why must the margins be chosen carefully when preparing layouts for a book, magazine, newspaper, or other printed matter?**
Margins should be chosen carefully because they are the "white" space that surrounds printed material. Margins have a strong effect on the beauty and readability of a printed page.

SECTION 4

1. **Briefly describe the two general classifications of type composition.**
The two general classifications of type composition are identified as hot and cold. Hot composition methods are those in which molten metal either has or is directly used to prepare the usable type character(s). Cold composition methods are the opposite of hot composition in that electronic, photographic, and hand mechanical methods are used to produce the usable typeface characters.

2. **Why do you think that foundry type composition is still taught in many schools offering graphic arts courses?**
Foundry type composition is still taught in many schools because of its historical significance. At one time, from the middle 1400's to the late 1800's, foundry type was the only available technology to creating typeset printed materials. Even today there are some printed jobs that can be economically produced by using foundry type composition. Finally, some schools still have type cases full of foundry type. Educators believe there is merit in using it for teaching measurement, word and letter spacing, typesetting terminology, and finger-hand dexterity.

3. **Briefly describe the four generations of phototypesetting machines.**
The four generations of phototypesetting machines are classified according to the technology utilized in producing the imaged type. For the first generation, the mechanical principles of hot-typesetting machines were used. Electromechanical principles were used for the second generation machines. Imaged type characters for the third generation machines were created electronically and transferred to photographic paper or film. Laser technology is being used to create type, illustrations, and photographs in fourth generation equipment.

4. **What makes a laser imagesetting machine valuable to the graphic arts industry?**
Laser imagesetting equipment is valuable in the graphic arts industry because it is very versatile. Computer software programs permit an almost endless number of choices for creating graphic images for type, line art (illustrations) and photographs (halftones).

5. **Briefly describe the concept of electronic publishing.**

Electronic publishing implies that the manufacture of printed products involves a complete, well-defined, system from beginning to end. Electronics (computer hardware and software) are used in designing, preparing, producing, and finishing the multitude of printed products that are prepared.

SECTION 5

1. **Why are proofing and proofreading important in preparing type composition?**

Proofing and proofreading are very important in preparing type and image composition because misspelled words greatly reduce the quality of a printed and published products. Misspelled words are annoying at best and can easily lead to providing incorrect information to readers.

2. **What is meant by the statement, "Many unsung heroes are involved in proofreading"?**

The statement "Many unsung heroes are involved in proofreading," simply means that proofreaders receive very little attention for their valuable work in identifying and correcting errors in typeset and image-set material.

3. **Explain the difference between reading proofs and reproduction proofs.**

Reading proofs are often "rough" in that the typeset material does not have to be in final form for the printed product. These proofs are primarily used to identify errors in spelling and grammar. Reproduction proofs are fully corrected for grammar and spelling. They are used for checking the spacing, positioning, and sizing of all image elements. These proofs are sometimes used for pasteups. More frequently, they are made from full-image or full-page pasteups. They serve as the final check before the job is taken into the photoconversion phase of the production process.

4. **Briefly describe the value and caution of using spell-check software when keyboarding copy for typesetting.**

Spell-check computer software is very valuable and time-saving. Most incorrectly spelled words are quickly detected and suggested correct spellings are identified. Caution must be exercised, however. "Spell-check" software cannot make the needed human decisions. The writer and keyboard operator still have major responsibilities to review and correct prepared desktop and typeset material.

5. **What is the primary purpose of proofreader's marks?**

Proofreader's marks are used to save time and accurately communicate information to keyboard operation personnel. Proofreader's marks give type and imagesetting personnel a system of communicating that reduces and frequently eliminates the need for elaborate oral or written exchange between themselves and production workers.

SECTION 6

1. **What are some factors to think about when choosing the base material for copy?**

Color—Some papers have dyes.
Weight—Use the heaviest possible material.
Surface—Use a base material to obtain the desired results.

2. **What is the difference between line copy and continuous tone copy?**

Line copy contains only solid black and whites. Continuous tone copy contains shades of gray like photographs.

3. **Why should copy be prepared the same size as or larger than the desired printed size?**

The copy will be photographed before reproduction. Defects will not be as visible because they will be the same size or smaller after they have been photographed.

4. **Explain how register marks are used.**

Register marks are placed on copy so the artist can align two or more elements in the copy. They assist the printer in causing multiple colors to be printed in the correct position.

5. **Name two kinds of process color copy and explain the difference between them.**

Reflection copy and transmission copy. Light is reflected from the surface of reflection copy and light passes through transmission copy.

SECTION 7

1. **What are the advantages and disadvantages of horizontal and vertical cameras?**

The advantage of a horizontal camera is that larger ones can produce large negatives from large copy. They also use less darkroom space if the copyboard is placed in the lightroom and exposures can be made in the darkroom. Exposures can be made in the darkroom without exposing photographic materials being processed. The disadvantage is that horizontal cameras require large amounts of floor space.

Vertical cameras do not use as much floor space as horizontal cameras. The disadvantages are that only smaller negatives can be made and light-sensitive materials cannot be used in the darkroom while exposures are being made.

2. **What is the major advantage of orthochromatic film over panchromatic film?**
Orthochromatic film can be used in the darkroom with red light, while panchromatic film must be used in total darkness.

3. **Name three methods of hand developing film and state their advantages and disadvantages.**
Time-temperature, inspection, and gray scale are the three methods of hand development.
The disadvantage of the time-temperature method is that it is difficult to control the temperature. The advantage is that when the temperature is controlled, the method is very accurate.
The inspection method can be used by experienced photographers, but beginners have some difficulty determining when both sides of the film are the same darkness.
The gray scale method is probably the most satisfactory method because uniform results can be obtained when the temperature and other variables change. The disadvantage is that the gray scale must be placed on each piece of copy when it is photographed.

4. **Explain how the dot formation should look in a good halftone negative.**
There should be dots in all parts of the halftone negative with small clear dots in the highlight areas and small black dots in the shadow areas. The dots should be black, rather than gray.

5. **Explain what happens when color copy is photographed through a filter.**
When light passes through a filter, only the wavelengths that are the same as the filter will pass through. If a red filter is used, only light with red wavelengths will pass through the filter.

SECTION 8

1. **Identify the several materials, metallic and nonmetallic, that are used to produce letterpress image carriers.**
Several of the materials used to make letterpress image carriers are metallic: copper, zinc, and magnesium. Lead, tin, and antimony are also used for other metallic image carriers. Nonmetallic materials such as plastics and rubber are being used very successfully.

2. **According to research, when do most accidents occur in the school laboratory?**
Based upon data from the National Safety Council, most school accidents occur around 10:00 A.M. and on Wednesdays. Also, days immediately before and after vacation periods are high accident days.

3. **Why are printing presses equipped with magnetic cylinders?**
Printing presses are equipped with magnetic cylinders so plates, large and small, can be easily positioned and held in place while the printing takes place. For magnetic cylinders to work, the printing plates must contain a conductive metal backing.

4. **How is the laser used in preparing flexographic printing rollers?**
Lasers are being used on flexographic platemaking machines to prepare the relief images. Nonimage material is selectively removed with great accuracy with high-power carbon dioxide lasers.

5. **Why should a special heat-resistant type be used in the rubber stamp press?**
Heat-resistant type should be used when making rubber stamps so the shape and height of the relief type will remain constant when the matrix (mold) is being formed with heat and pressure.

SECTION 9

1. **Why is it important to know the size of the typeform before making a chaser lockup?**
Because the first pieces of furniture around the typeform must be longer than the edges of the typeform.

2. **Why must care be taken when planing a letterpress typeform?**
Planing must be done carefully to be sure all of the type is flat and that the type faces are not damaged.

3. **Why is it important that all lines of a typeform be exactly the same length?**
If all lines of type are not the same length, the furniture cannot press against the type to be sure it is tight in the chase. It is possible that type characters could fall out of the typeform.

4. **What is meant by imposition of signatures?**
Imposition of signatures is the process of placing pages of a booklet, pamphlet, etc., in the correct position so they can be printed in the correct location after the sheet (signature) has been folded.

5. **What are the major advantages of using the work-and-turn and work-and-tumble methods of imposition?**

The work-and-turn method is used when it is important that the lead edge of a printed sheet remain the same when both sides of a sheet are printed. The advantage of the work-and-tumble method is to keep the side edge of the sheet the same. These are of most concern when precise detail must be maintained.

SECTION 10

1. **How are the sizes of the presses generally measured?**

Printing presses are generally measured according to the maximum size of paper that can run through the machines. With letterpress platen presses, the typical size designation is based upon the inside dimensions of the chase. Web presses are most commonly measured by the maximum width of the roll of paper or other substrate.

2. **How is flexography different from the standard method of letterpress image transfer?**

Flexography is a subdivision of the relief or letterpress printing method, but there are some differences. First, the printing plates are made of flexible rubber or synthetic (photopolymer) material as compared to rigid plates made of metallic or synthetic materials. Also, fast-drying solvent-based fluid inks are used instead of the paste-type inks used for the standard letterpress plates.

3. **What is different about the image carrier in the Cameron Book Production System?**

The Cameron Book Production System is unique in that several machines have been combined to make it possible to produce a book in one pass through the system. The printing plate (image carrier) is a long belt containing the relief images of all pages (current maximum is 320) in a book. The roll (web) of paper is fed into the system. All pages are printed. The paper is cut and folded, and a completely bound book including covers emerges—ready to be shipped to the customer.

4. **When should press adjustments be made?**

Press adjustments, as with all machinery, should be made when the press is stopped and the electrical switch is in the "lock" position.

5. **Why is it important to clean the platen and cylinder presses soon after use?**

Both platen and cylinder letterpress machines should be cleaned of ink soon after use because the ink dries and becomes difficult to remove from the ink rollers. Removing dried ink can be very damaging to ink rollers and sometimes ink fountains.

SECTION 11

1. **How is the flat used in the lithographic printing process?**

The flat is placed over a plate to expose the plate. Negatives are attached to the masking sheet in the correct location so they will be in the exact place on the plate.

2. **Why is it important for the stripper to mark the gripper margin on a masking sheet?**

Sheets of paper are pulled through a printing press with grippers on the printing cylinders of the press. Because of this, no image will print where the sheets are held by the grippers.

3. **Why are line and halftone negatives combined on a single flat?**

Line negatives must be made separate from halftone negatives because of the differences in the kind of copy. By placing them on a single flat, they can be printed at the same time.

4. **Why should register marks be used on paste ups, flats, and printing plates?**

Register marks serve as guides for locating parts of a printing job so they will be printed in the proper location on the printed sheet.

5. **Why are register punches valuable for both single- and multiple-color printing?**

For single-color printing, a register punch helps the printer align the flat with plates and sometimes on presses. Register punches help the printer align the flats and plates so colors will be in register when printed.

SECTION 12

1. **Describe image and non-image areas on a lithographic plate.**

The image area on a plate is an ink-receptive area and is what will be printed on the sheet. The non-image area is a water-receptive surface that will reject ink and not print on the sheet.

2. **Describe the difference between surface plates and deep-etch lithographic plates.**

Surface plates have the image placed on the surface of the plate. On deep-etch plates, the image is placed slightly below the surface of the plate. Deep-etch plates last much longer than surface plates.

3. **Describe the difference between additive and subtractive plates.**

Additive plates are developed to remove the unexposed emulsion and a lacquer-type solution is applied to the plate to make the image visible. The subtractive plate has the color as part of the emulsion before the plate is exposed. When the plate is developed, the emulsion, including the color, is removed except for the image areas.

4. **How is the sensitivity guide used in making a plate?**
The sensitivity guide is exposed on the plate at the same time the plate is exposed to a flat. It is used to determine whether the plate has been exposed for the proper amount of time.

5. **Describe the procedure for making a diffusion-transfer plate.**
The diffusion-transfer plate is exposed directly in the camera without making a flat. The plate material is processed to place the ink-receptive areas on the plate.

SECTION 13

1. **Compare the lithography duplicator and the lithography press.**
Litho duplicators are generally smaller than litho presses in that they have been designed to print smaller sheets or rolls of paper or other substrate. Also, duplicators contain fewer ink and dampening rollers than presses, thus limiting the amount of ink that can be printed. A third major difference is that sheet or web register is less sophisticated on litho duplicators than on litho presses.

2. **What are the advantages in using a central control station on a large lithography press?**
A central control station on a large litho press gives the operator(s) nearly complete printing control in one location. Consistent high quality and production can be maintained on litho sheet or web presses equipped with central control stations because computers are used to assist in many of the monitoring functions. This gives the press operator(s) more time to watch and make judgments in other critical areas of operating litho printing presses.

3. **What should be done to the inking system of the press before placing ink in the fountain?**
The ink rollers and ink fountain should be inspected before placing ink in the fountain. If paper lint, dust, or roller glaze are observed, it is necessary to clean the entire system thoroughly. It is very difficult to produce quality printed products when litho presses and duplicators are not properly cleaned and maintained.

4. **How can the surface and body of the lithographic blanket be preserved?**
A litho duplicator/press blanket must be handled and used with care. Ink should never be allowed to dry on the blanket surface. Excess amounts of solvent should not be used. Excess blanket wash (solvent) tends to swell the edges, causing an uneven image surface. When the press is not in use, the blanket should be loosened or removed to relax the tension placed on the material. Blankets should also be protected from sunlight and dust.

5. **When the non-image area of the lithographic plate accepts ink during a press run, what are the possible causes?**
Possible causes of ink adhering to non-image areas of a litho plate include: a poor or old plate, a plate fogged with room light while it was being exposed and processed, poor plate processing, too much ink on the rollers, not enough moisture on the plate, or dirty dampener roller covers.

SECTION 14

1. **How does the image-transfer principle of gravure differ from the principles of letterpress, lithography, and screen printing?**
The gravure image transfer principle is unique in that the image is recessed into the printing plate or cylinder. This differs from the raised image surface of letterpress, the smooth image surface of lithography, and the stencil-type image of screen printing.

2. **How does the electromechanical engraving machine form ink cells in the copper surface of the gravure cylinder?**
The electromechanical engraving machine is used to form ink cells in the copper surface of gravure cylinders by using a highly sophisticated computer-controlled cutting system. The photo-optical system on the copy cylinder reads the original copy and transmits electrical signals to the diamond cutting stylus, which removes individual cells that make up the image.

3. **What have electrostatic assist and computers done for the gravure method of image transfer?**
Electrostatic assist and computers have greatly improved the image transfer quality within the gravure printing method. With gravure ink containing polarity in the solvent, the ink is easily "pulled" from the ink cells and transferred to the substrate. Computers are being used on gravure presses to help control many of the operating functions just as in the other printing processes.

4. **Why should there always be a safety shower in an area where caustic chemicals or solutions are used?**

Nearby safety showers are a *must* when caustic chemicals and solutions are used. Water dilutes injurious liquids rapidly. Thus the shower head or stall must be very near the chemical work area.

5. **Compare engraving and etching.**

Engraving means to cut an object with a hand or mechanical tool. Etching means to remove material by chemical-acid. These terms are often used interchangeably, but definitely should not be. Both techniques are used to produce printing plates (image carriers), but by different methods.

SECTION 15

1. **How does screen printing differ from letterpress, lithography, and gravure image-transfer methods?**

Screen printing is a method whereby the ink passes through the image carrier rather than being transferred, as in letterpress, lithography, and gravure. The screen printing method can be used to place a thicker and denser ink on substrates than the other three common image-transfer methods.

2. **Name and briefly describe the principal press designs in common use today.**

The principal screen printing press designs are flatbed, cylinder, and rotary. The flatbed is most common for both hand and power-operated screen printing presses. With the flatbed or platen design, the screen and substrate are in total contact while the ink is being transferred. With the cylinder design, the screen is in a flat format, but the substrate is wrapped around a cylinder that turns under the screen stencil frame. The rotary press design contains cylinders for both the stencil frame and the impression surface.

3. **Why is it important to prepare artwork in full color for screen printing?**

Artwork is critical for all methods of printing. For screen printing, full-color artwork is critical to the success and quality of the finished product. With full-color artwork, the copy preparation personnel are completely communicating with the photoconversion and stencil-making personnel.

4. **Why should screen fabric, new or used, always be degreased before attaching a screen stencil?**

Degreasing is a critical screen fabric preparation step. This procedure helps to ensure that a well-prepared stencil can be attached to or integrated into the fabric. Degreasing is a cleaning function in which ink, stencil, and solvent residue are completely removed from the fabric strands so the new stencil material can be attached without any obstructions.

5. **Why is it important to select the correct screen printing ink for the material being printed?**

Many different substrates can and are printed with the screen printing method. Inks must be matched with the substrates so they will adhere and cover as expected. When in doubt, the screen printer should request assistance from the ink supplier as to which ink should be used on a particular substrate.

SECTION 16

1. **What are three advantages of a single-lens reflex camera?**

The photographer can see the exact image to be photographed through the rangefinder. Many different lenses can be used on a single-lens reflex camera. Light can be measured more accurately because only the light which passes through the lens is measured.

2. **How are film speed and grain found in negatives related?**

The grain is larger in faster film with a higher ISO (ASA) number.

3. **How do aperture numbers relate to the size of the aperture?**

The smaller the aperture number the larger the size of the aperture opening. When the aperture is set on f/2.8 the aperture has a larger opening than when the aperture is set on f/8. Each time the aperture is opened one stop (smaller number) the aperture area is doubled and twice as much light will enter the camera as entered with the previous stop.

4. **What is the purpose of each solution used in processing film?**

Developer turns exposed silver salt to black metallic silver. Stop bath stops the developing action of the developer. Fixer removes the unexposed silver salts and hardens the emulsion of the film.

5. **How do you determine the correct exposure for an enlargement?**
The correct exposure for an enlargement is found by making a series of test exposures of different times from the negative on a piece of photographic paper. The test is developed and the time is determined by finding the best test area.

SECTION 17

1. **What is the difference between duplicating and copying?**
Duplicating includes processes that require that an image carrier, like a plate or stencil, be prepared to make the printed material. Copying includes those processes that produce a copy from an original.

2. **In addition to its primary purpose of making mimeograph stencils, what value is there in using an electronic stencil maker?**
The electronic stencil maker is an example of a scanner that uses the same principles of scanners used for making other kinds of image carriers.

3. **Explain the difference between transfer and direct electrostatic copiers.**
The transfer electrostatic copier places the image on a plate and it is then transferred to plain paper. The direct electrostatic copier places the image directly on specially treated paper. The indirect electrostatic copier is most frequently used because of the cost of the paper.

4. **What is inkjet printing?**
Inkjet printing is a method that sprays a very fine spray of ink onto the surface of a material. It is controlled by a computer and actually sprays many tiny dots to create an image.

5. **What are some ways to print heat transfer patterns on the transfer paper?**
Common methods used to print heat transfer patterns on paper are gravure, screen process, offset, letterpress, and flexography.

SECTION 18

1. **Why have binding improvements followed developments in book production?**
It has been necessary that binding improvements be made as the developments in book production have increased. Faster printing presses required faster binding methods. Thus designers and engineers have designed equipment that can handle the high volume of printed material for bound publications.

2. **Why should a planning sheet be made before cutting a large amount of paper?**
A cutting-planning sheet is critical for accuracy when cutting and trimming large amounts of paper. When paper is cut, there usually is only one chance to "do-it-right." Knowing in advance the correct settings and positions will lead to successful cutting and trimming jobs.

3. **In producing saddle-wire and side-wire bound books, what is the main advantage of a wire stitching machine over a stapling machine?**
A wire stitching machine is generally more flexible than a wire stapling machine. With wire stitchers, the length of the staple can be readily adjusted for each product being bound. With wire staplers, the staples are of fixed sizes. Thus there is less flexibility when stapling different sizes (thicknesses) of saddle-wire and side-wire bound books and booklets.

4. **What would happen if a book body did not receive either of the two operations called nipping and smashing?**
Nipping and smashing operations are critical to quality bookbinding. If these two operations were not completed, the book body would be excessively thick and uneven. Both operations are designed to make book bodies of consistent thickness and shape.

5. **How is information located that has been stored by one of the microform methods?**
Stored microform information can be located by either hand (sight) or computer search methods. Using specially designed viewing machines aids in locating specific information.

SECTION 19

1. **Why is fresh water essential in the production of paper?**
A tremendous amount of water is used in the papermaking process. Thus a fresh water supply is critical to a successful operation. When paper pulp for several paper kinds is delivered to the Fourdrinier wire, it is 99% water.

2. **Why is a combination of the two wood categories generally used in paper production?**
A combination of the two wood categories (deciduous and coniferous) help to make

higher quality paper. Short wood fibers from hardwood (deciduous) trees give paper smoothness and opacity, while long wood fibers from softwood (coniferous) trees help to give paper strength and folding qualities.

3. **Why must the paper pulp contain much water when it enters the papermaking machine?**
The large quality of water serves as the carrier of the paper pulp and helps to evenly distribute the wood fibers during the initial paper-forming stage. Without a high percentage of water, the paper pulp would be much less manageable.

4. **What are the different ways of finishing paper after it has been delivered from the papermaking machines?**
There are several methods of finishing paper that include inspecting, sheeting, special finishing, and packaging. Some papers are supercalendered to give a smooth writing surface, while other papers are given a repeating pattern called embossing. Sheet slitters and cutters are also used to make the paper useful to printers and general customers.

5. **What is the advantage in purchasing large amounts of paper at one time?**
There is reduced cost when paper is purchased in large quantities. This is because there is less packaging and handling. Also, the convenience of moving larger amounts of paper appeals to paper manufacturers and suppliers.

SECTION 20

1. **What must printing ink withstand once it has been printed?**
Inks must withstand the effects of heat, abrasion, acids, alkalines, and other chemicals.

2. **What is the difference between opaque and transparent white ink?**
Opaque white ink will not permit the viewer to see the color behind the ink (paper or other ink). Transparent white ink permits the color to show through the ink.

3. **What is the purpose of grinding printing inks?**
The purpose of grinding inks is to make the pigment particles very small and to mix the pigment thoroughly with the vehicle and other additives.

4. **Describe two special features of gravure ink.**
Gravure inks must have enough body to be pulled from the gravure plate. Also, they must be able to dry very rapidly by absorption and evaporation.

5. **What is the best test for a printing ink?**
The best test of an ink is to actually print the ink on the material that will be used to produce the product.

SECTION 21

1. **How does the United States Constitution protect authors and writers?**
Article 1, Section 8 of the United States Constitution was written to secure for authors and writers protection for writings and discoveries. The protection refers to copyright and discoveries refers to patents.

2. **Why must a commercial printer be careful not to print a document protected by copyright?**
Printing a document that is copyrighted, either knowingly or unknowingly, can make a commercial printer an "infringer of the original copyright" of the document. This could lead to a major fine if the situation is pressed by the original copyright owner.

3. **Why is a publisher more vulnerable to the laws of obscenity than the printer?**
Publishers are more vulnerable to the laws of obscenity than are printers because they knowingly distribute the actual material. Printers are vulnerable only when accepting the original copy and when they deliver it to the publisher.

4. **Explain how counterfeiting can hurt the economy of a country.**
Counterfeiting dilutes the actual currency of a country because there are more pieces of currency (money) than have been authorized by the government. Innocent people who are left with counterfeit money lose in actual money because they often must assume the loss. This is discouraging to business people. They become reluctant to handle either cash or coin.

5. **What could happen to the printer who printed an untruth about an individual or a group?**
Printers who print untruths about individuals or groups could be charged with unlawful acts and given a fine or possibly a jail sentence. The printer could also lose considerable business because his or her reputation has been damaged.

SECTION 22

1. What guidelines should be observed in designing a page?

The same guidelines of page design should be observed with desktop composition as with standard imagesetting methods. These design principles are: page proportion, balance, contrast, unity, and rhythm.

2. What is the base page?

The base page is the space where all image content will be located on the computer screen. The base page size and shape are part of the desktop composition software.

3. What is a style sheet?

A style sheet is something created by the person using the desktop system. The style sheet is part of the software program. It greatly assists in producing an acceptably designed product.

4. What guidelines should be followed in choosing typefaces?

When selecting typefaces, it is important to remember that less is actually more. No more than two typefaces should be chosen and used for a specific one-page document. Too many typefaces on a page make it look gaudy.

5. What is the least expensive printer for printing a document?

The dot matrix printer is the least expensive printer for imaging a desktop composition file. It does, though, produce an acceptable image for some uses.

6. What is a service bureau?

A service bureau is a specialty company that will accept input from desktop composition software and provide quality output using sophisticated imagesetting equipment. This type of service greatly extends the flexibility and quality of desktop composition systems.

SECTION 23

1. Why will there continue to be a need for graphic arts products?

Graphic arts products will always be needed so long as there are people. The expansion of education, business, and industry all lead to a greater need for products with printed images.

2. How can a formal education help to train quality people to enter the graphic arts industry?

Formal education is the path to quick and quality preparation for a career in the graphic arts industry. Educational programs are available in high schools, vocational-technical schools, and colleges/universities for graphic arts careers. Industry training is also available for those people already employed.

3. Why will it be necessary for people in type composition to take part constantly in training programs?

As in all areas of graphic arts, the technology in typesetting and imagesetting is changing rapidly. New developments are announced frequently. This makes it imperative that people be constantly involved in retraining.

4. Why must a manager be good at the art of communication?

Managers are in contact with people each and every day. They must effectively communicate with those people serving within their group. Thus, managerial personnel must know the art of effective communication.

5. What are the opportunities in the paper industry for people who have an interest and competence in chemistry or law?

Considerable basic research is done in the paper industry and people knowledgeable in chemistry are involved in this area. Lawyers are needed for service in corporate, patent, tax, and real estate laws. Labor relations is also an area where those skilled in law can be very helpful.

APPENDIX M

VISUAL MASTERS

THE SIX PRODUCTION PHASES OF GRAPHIC ARTS

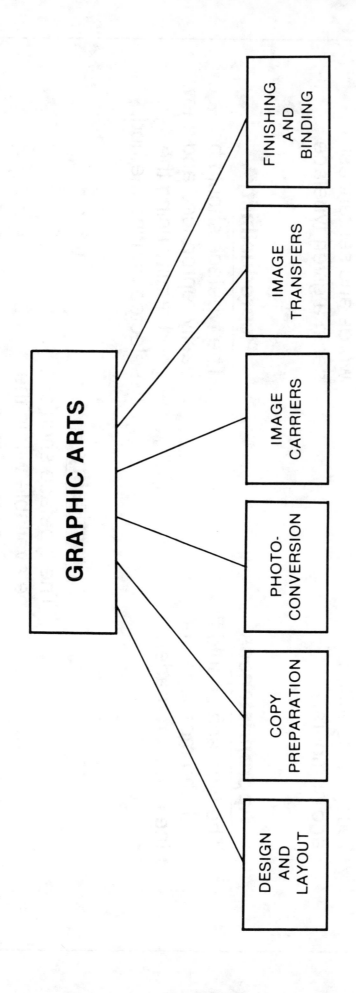

CHOOSING A TYPEFACE: FEATURES TO CONSIDER

Legibility

Ease of seeing and
recognizing letters
and numbers.

Appropriateness

The typeface should fit
both the message and
the intended reader.

Readability

Ease of reading
words and sentences
set in a given typeface.

Reproducibility

The typeface should be
easily reproduced and show
good quality using the
selected printing method.

Practicality

The typeface should
be available within the
graphic arts company
or be easily obtainable.

Two-dimensional Space is Valuable and Expensive.
It must be filled carefully with visual content.

Visual Master – 03

LAYOUT OF CALIFORNIA JOB CASE

ffi	fl	5-EM	4-EM	'	k			1	2	3	4	5	6	7	8		$						

| j | b | c | d | e | | i | s | f | g | ff | 9 | A | B | C | D | E | F | G |

| ? | | | | | | | | | | fi | 0 | | | | | | | |

| ! | l | m | n | h | o | y | p | w | , | EN QUADS | EM QUADS | H | I | K | L | M | N | O |

| z | | | | | | | | | | | | | | | | | | |

| x | v | u | t | 3-EM SPACES | a | r | ; : . - | 2-EM AND 3-EM QUADS | P | Q | R | S | T | V | W |

| q | | | | | | | | | X | Y | Z | J | U | & | ffl |

CHARACTERS DIFFICULT TO DISTINGUISH

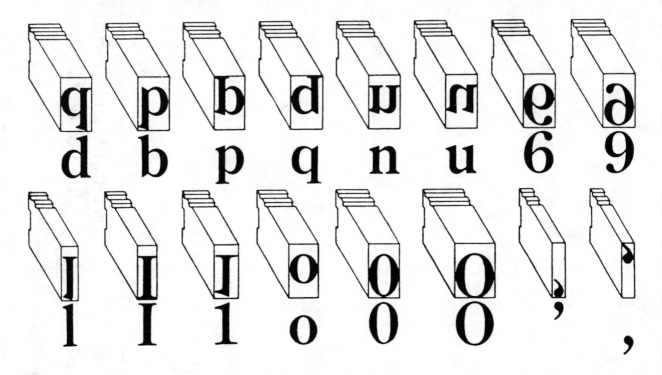

d   b   p   q   n   u   6   9

l   I   1   o   0   O   '   ,

PROOFREADING SYMBOLS (Part 1)

Meaning	Margin	Text
Dele, or delete, take out	ℰ	People ma~~r~~ke things happen.
Insert space	#	People makethings happen.
Close up, no space	⌒	People make things hap⌒pen
Insert apostrophe	∨	People make childrens things.
Character of wrong size or style, wrong font	wf	People make thi_ngs_ happen.
Put in lower case	lc	PEOPLE make things happen.
Reset in bold face	bf	People make things happen.
Reset in italic type	ital	People make things happen.
Let it stand; ignore marks above dots	stet	People make thing̶s̶ happen.
Make paragraph.	¶	People make ¶ Things happen.
No paragraph	no ¶	happen. ⌒ People make things happen.
Insert period	⊙	People make things happen⌃
Carry to the left	⌞	⌞ People make things happen.
Carry to the right	⌟	⌟ People make things happen.
Center the line (quad center)	QC	] People make things happen.[
Even left margin (quad left)	QL	[People make things happen.
Even right margin (quad right)	QR	] People make things happen.

Visual Master – 05

PROOFREADING SYMBOLS (Part 2)

	Symbol	Example
Lower as indicated	⌐⌐	People make things happen.
Raise as indicated	⌐⌐	People make things happen. / People make things happen.
Transpose	tr	People make things hip hop.
Insert hyphen	= /	People make things happen.
Reset in small capitals	sc	Yes, people make things happen.
Insert comma	⌄	People things happen.
Query to author	(make)?	People make ④ things happen.
Spell out circled matter	sp	People make things happen.
Space evenly	eq #	People make things happen.
Indent 1 em	□	People make things happen.
Indent 2 ems	□□	People make things happen.
1-em dash	|em|	People make things happen.
2-em dash	|2em|	People make things happen.
En dash	|n|	People make things 9-5.
Align	‖	People make things happen.
Insert quotation marks	" "	People make things happen.
Reset in Roman type	rom	People *make* things happen.
Words omitted	out see copy	People happen.
Reset in capitals	caps	people make things happen.

People make things happen.

LITHOGRAPHIC IMAGE TRANSFER

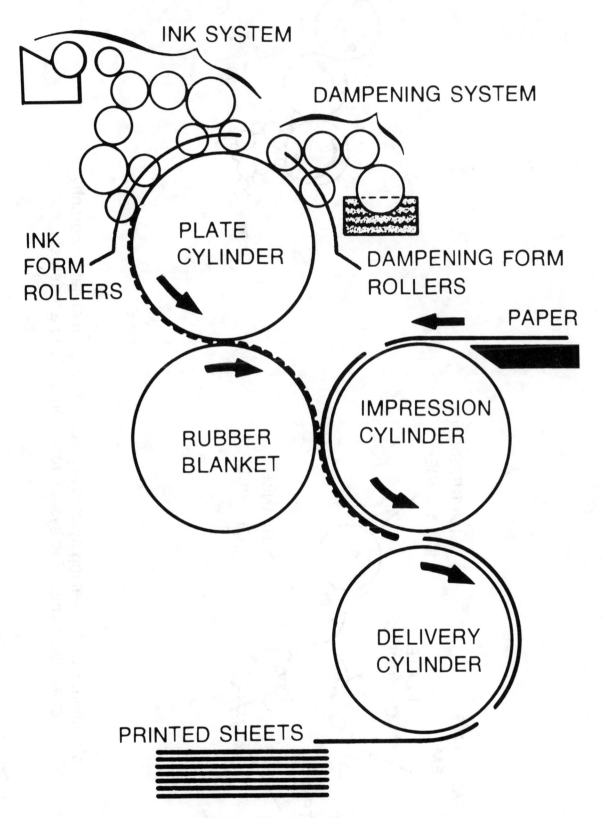

INK SYSTEM

DAMPENING SYSTEM

INK FORM ROLLERS

PLATE CYLINDER

DAMPENING FORM ROLLERS

PAPER

RUBBER BLANKET

IMPRESSION CYLINDER

DELIVERY CYLINDER

PRINTED SHEETS

The ink, dampening, and cylinder systems typical of a heavy-duty offset lithography press.

SCHEMATICS OF OFFSET-LITHOGRAPHY AND LETTERSET PRESSES

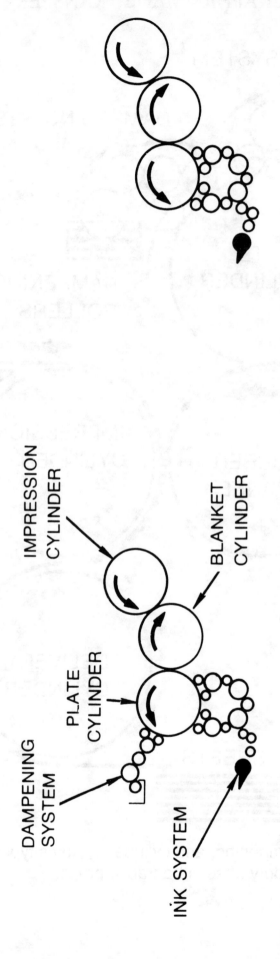

IMPRESSION CYLINDER

BLANKET CYLINDER

PLATE CYLINDER

DAMPENING SYSTEM

INK SYSTEM

Left schematic: dampening system in place, making an offset lithography press.
Right schematic: dampening system removed, making a letterset press.

LITHO DUPLICATOR INTEGRATED DAMPENING AND INKING SYSTEM

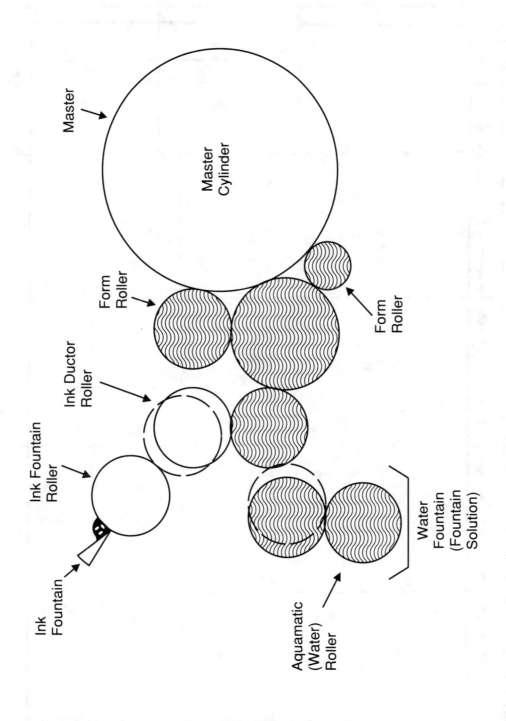

Master

Master Cylinder

Form Roller

Form Roller

Ink Ductor Roller

Ink Fountain Roller

Ink Fountain

Aquamatic (Water) Roller

Water Fountain (Fountain Solution)

PRESS SHEET CALCULATION

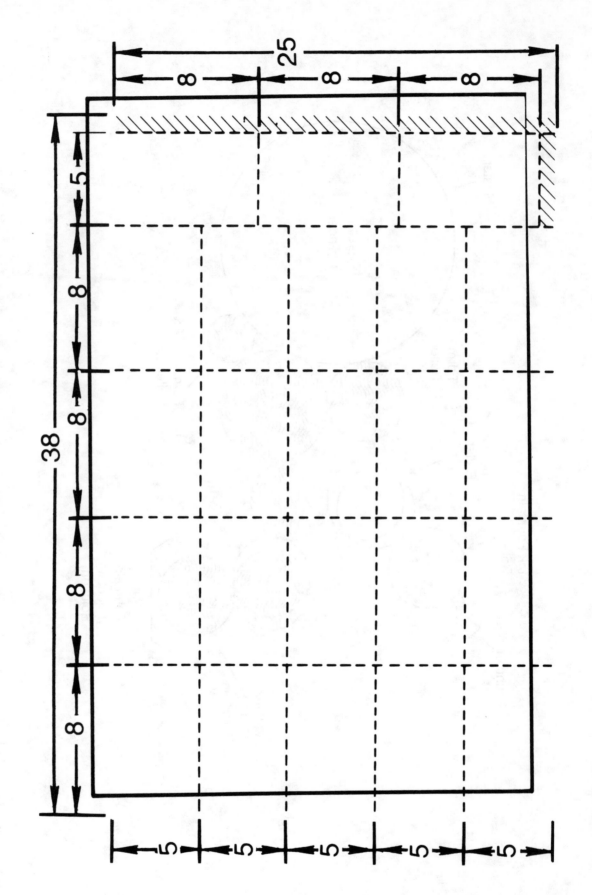

CUTTING ORDER LAYOUT

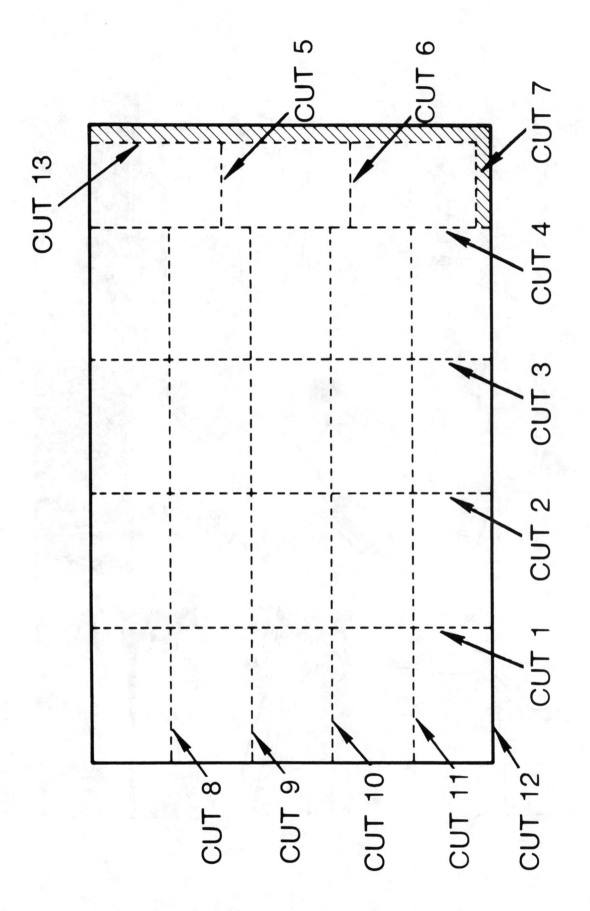

Visual Master – 11

MATERIALS NEEDED TO MAKE ONE TON OF PAPER

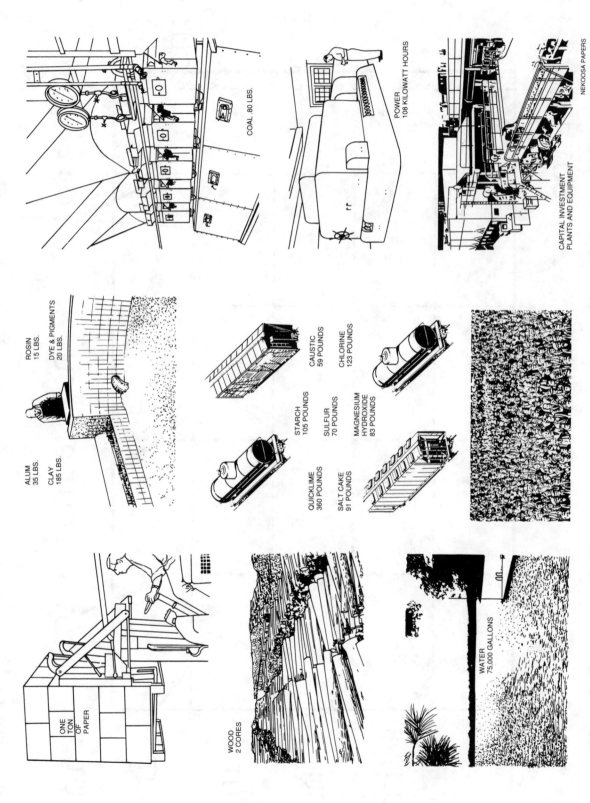

COAL 80 LBS.

POWER
108 KILOWATT HOURS

CAPITAL INVESTMENT
PLANTS AND EQUIPMENT

NEKOOSA PAPERS

ROSIN
15 LBS.

DYE & PIGMENTS
20 LBS.

ALUM
35 LBS.

CLAY
185 LBS.

STARCH
105 POUNDS

CAUSTIC
59 POUNDS

SULFUR
70 POUNDS

CHLORINE
123 POUNDS

MAGNESIUM
HYDROXIDE
83 POUNDS

QUICKLIME
360 POUNDS

SALT CAKE
91 POUNDS

ONE
TON
OF
PAPER

WOOD
2 CORES

WATER
75,000 GALLONS

Visual Master – 12

TABLE OF CALIPERS AND WEIGHTS

The calipers listed are approximate averages. Variations will be found from one mill run to another, either to the light or heavy side of the basis weight, within trade custom tolerances. One point equals 1 1000 of an inch.

BOND, MIMEO, DUPLICATOR
bs. 17 x 22

	13#	16#	20#	24#
Sulphite Bond	.003	.0035	.004	.0045
Cotton Fiber Bond				
Cockle Finish	.003	.0035	.004	.0045
Smooth Finish	.0025	.003	.0035	.004
Mimeo		.004	.005	.0055
Duplicator		.0025	.003	.0035

LEDGER
bs. 17 x 22

	24#	28#	32#	36#
Smooth Finish	.0045	.005	.0055	.006
Posting Finish	.005	.0055	.006	.0065

BOOK PAPERS
bs. 25 x 38

Offset	45#	50#	60#	70#
Regular	.0035	.004	.0045	.005
Antique	.004	.0045	.005	.006
Bulking		.0055	.0066	.0077
English Finish	.0032	.0035	.004	.0045
Supercalendered	.0022	.0025	.003	.0035
Gloss Coated		.0025	.003	.0035
Dull Coated		.003	.0035	.004
Coated 1 Side			.0032	.0037

bs. 25 x 38

Offset	80#	100#	120#	150#
Regular	.006	.0075	.009	.011
Antique	.007	.009	.011	.013
Bulking	.0088	.011	.0135	
Gloss Coated	.004	.0055		
Dull Coated	.0045	.006		
Coated 1 Side	.004			

COVER PAPERS
bs. 20 x 26

	50#	60#	65#	80#	90#	100#	130#
Uncoated							
Smooth	.007		.0065		.011		.013
Antique	.005		.010				.020
Coated		.0055	.006	.008	.009	.010	

bs. 20 x 26

	50#	65#	80#	94#	110#
Lusterkote	.0055	.0065	.008	.010	.012

INDEX BRISTOL
bs. 25½ x 30½

	90#	110#	140#	170#
Smooth Finish	.007 / .0075	.008 / .009	.0105 / .0115	.013 / .014

Visual Master – 13

CONSTANT FACTOR PAPER SCHEDULE

BOOK PAPER

Basis wt. 25x38/500	1000 Sheet Factor
25	.0526
30	.0632
35	.0737
40	.0842
45	.0947
50	.1053
60	.1263
70	.1474
80	.1684
100	.2105
120	.2526
140	.2947
150	.3158

NEWSPRINT, TAG AND CRAFT

Basis wt. 25x36/500	1000 Sheet Factor
32	.0741
34	.0787
35	.0810
40	.0926
50	.1157
60	.1389
100	.2315
125	.2894
150	.3472
175	.4051
200	.4630
250	.5787

BRISTOL

Basis wt. 22½ x 28½/500	1000 Sheet Factor
67	.2090
80	.2489
82½	.2573
90	.2807
100	.3119
120	.3743
140	.4366
160	.4990
180	.5614
200	.6238

BRISTOL

Basis wt. 23x35/500	1000 Sheet Factor
100	.2484
125	.3106
150	.3727
175	.4348
200	.4969
250	.6211

COVER PAPER

Basis wt. 20x26/500	1000 Sheet Factor
50	.1923
60	.2308
65	.2500
80	.3077
90	.3462
100	.3846
130	.5000

BONDS, WRITINGS AND LEDGER

Basis wt. 17x22/500	1000 Sheet Factor
8	.0428
9	.0481
11	.0588
12	.0642
13	.0695
16	.0856
20	.1070
24	.1283
28	.1497
32	.1711
36	.1925

INDEX BRISTOL

Basis wt. 25½ x 30½/500	1000 Sheet Factor
90	.2314
110	.2829
140	.3600
170	.4372
220	.5657

Leslie Paper Company